T0181262

Lecture Notes in Computer Science 13840

Founding Editors

Gerhard Goos
Juris Hartmanis

The series Lecture Notes in Computer Science (LNCS), including its subseries Lecture Notes in Artificial Intelligence (LNAI) and Lecture Notes in Bioinformatics (LNBI), has established itself as a medium for the publication of new developments in computer science and information technology research, teaching, and education.

LNCS enjoys close cooperation with the computer science R & D community, the series counts many renowned academics among its volume editors and paper authors, and collaborates with prestigious societies. Its mission is to serve this international community by providing an invaluable service, mainly focused on the publication of conference and workshop proceedings and postproceedings. LNCS commenced publication in 1973.

Abdelkader Hameurlain · A Min Tjoa
Editors

Transactions on Large-Scale Data- and Knowledge- Centered Systems LIII

Springer

Editors-in-Chief

Abdelkader Hameurlain
IRIT, Paul Sabatier University
Toulouse, France

A Min Tjoa
IFS, Technical University of Vienna
Vienna, Austria

ISSN 0302-9743   ISSN 1611-3349 (electronic)
Lecture Notes in Computer Science
ISSN 1869-1994   ISSN 2510-4942 (electronic)
Transactions on Large-Scale Data- and Knowledge-Centered Systems
ISBN 978-3-662-66862-7   ISBN 978-3-662-66863-4 (eBook)
https://doi.org/10.1007/978-3-662-66863-4

This Springer imprint is published by the registered company Springer-Verlag GmbH, DE,
part of Springer Nature
The registered company address is: Heidelberger Platz 3, 14197 Berlin, Germany

Preface

This volume contains six fully revised regular papers, covering a wide range of very hot topics in the fields of time series management from edge to cloud, segmentation for time series representation, similarity research, semantic similarity in a taxonomy, linked data semantic distance, linguistics-informed natural language processing, graph neural networks, protected features, imbalanced data, causal consistency in distributed databases, actor models, and elastic horizontal scalability.

We would like to sincerely thank the editorial board for thoroughly refereeing the submitted papers and ensuring the high quality of this volume. Furthermore, we would like to wholeheartedly thank the Springer team for their ready availability, management efficiency, and very pleasant collaboration in the realization of the TLDKS journal volumes.

December 2022

Abdelkader Hameurlain
A Min Tjoa

Organization

Editors-in-Chief

Abdelkader Hameurlain   Paul Sabatier University, IRIT, France
A Min Tjoa   Technical University of Vienna, IFS, Austria

Editorial Board

Contents

ModelarDB: Integrated Model-Based Management of Time Series from Edge to Cloud

Søren Kejser Jensen$^{(\boxtimes)}$ ⓘ, Christian Thomsen ⓘ, and Torben Bach Pedersen ⓘ

Department of Computer Science, Aalborg University, Aalborg, Denmark
{skj,chr,tbp}@cs.aau.dk

Abstract. To ensure critical infrastructure is operating as expected, high-quality sensors are increasingly installed. However, due to the enormous amounts of high-frequency time series they produce, it is impossible or infeasible to transfer or even store these time series in the cloud when using state-of-the-practice compression methods. Thus, simple aggregates, e.g., 1–10-minutes averages, are stored instead of the raw time series. However, by only storing these simple aggregates, informative outliers and fluctuations are lost. Many Time Series Management System (TSMS) have been proposed to efficiently manage time series, but they are generally designed for either the edge or the cloud. In this paper, we describe a new version of the open-source model-based TSMS ModelarDB. The system is designed to be modular and the same binary can be efficiently deployed on the edge and in the cloud. It also supports continuously transferring high-frequency time series compressed using models from the edge to the cloud. We first provide an overview of ModelarDB, analyze the requirements and limitations of the edge, and evaluate existing query engines and data stores for use on the edge. Then, we describe how ModelarDB has been extended to efficiently manage time series on the edge, a novel file-based data store, how ModelarDB's compression has been improved by not storing time series that can be derived from base time series, and how ModelarDB transfers high-frequency time series from the edge to the cloud. As the work that led to ModelarDB began in 2015, we also reflect on the lessons learned while developing it.

1 Introduction

High-quality sensors are increasingly used for monitoring and to facilitate automation and error detection, e.g., for Renewable Energy Sources (RES) installations like wind turbines and solar panels. However, the limited amount of bandwidth available for transferring data between the edge and the cloud generally makes transferring high-frequency time series impossible. In addition, it is often either infeasible or prohibitively expensive to store the high-frequency time series in the cloud. Thus, simple aggregates, e.g., 1–10-minutes averages, are generally stored in the cloud instead of the high-frequency time series. However, this removes informative outliers and fluctuations. To remedy this problem, many Time Series Management System (TSMS) have been proposed to

ⓒ The Author(s) 2023
A. Hameurlain and A. M. Tjoa (Eds.): TLDKS LIII, LNCS 13840, pp. 1–33, 2023.
https://doi.org/10.1007/978-3-662-66863-4_1

efficiently ingest, query, and store time series [4,10,11]. However, most TSMSs are designed to be deployed on either the edge (e.g., in a wind turbine) or the cloud. Thus, these TSMSs cannot optimize ingestion, query processing, storage, and data transfer across the edge and cloud. Users must also often add additional systems, e.g., Apache Kafka, to continuously transfer data points from the edge to the cloud.

ModelarDB is a state-of-the-art modular model-based TSMS that was originally designed specifically for deployment on a cluster of cloud nodes [12–14]. In the context of ModelarDB, a model is any representation that can reconstruct the values of a group of time series within a user-defined error bound (possibly 0%). For example, a linear function is a model that can approximately represent increasing, decreasing, or constant values from a group of time series efficiently. In general, model-based compression of time series provides much better compression than general-purpose compression methods like DEFLATE, LZ4, and Snappy, especially if a small amount of error is allowed [9,12–14,26]. This paper provides an overview of the current version of ModelarDB and describes how it has been extended so it can be deployed on individual edge nodes, be deployed on a cluster of cloud nodes, and continuously transfer data points efficiently compressed using models from the edge nodes to the cloud nodes. ModelarDB is an open-source project and the source code for the version of ModelarDB described in this paper is available at https://github.com/skejserjensen/ModelarDB. To differentiate between the different versions of ModelarDB referenced in this paper, we use *the previous version of ModelarDB* to refer to the version of ModelarDB documented in our previous papers [12–14], while we use *the current version of ModelarDB* to refer to the version of ModelarDB with the extensions described in this paper. In this paper we make the following contributions:

1. Provide an overview of the open-source model-based TSMS ModelarDB.
2. Analyze the requirements and limitations of the edge for RES installations.
3. Analyze existing query engines and data stores and evaluate which of them are most suitable for use by ModelarDB when deployed on the edge.
4. Extend ModelarDB to efficiently ingest, query, and store groups of similar time series using multiple different types of models on the edge.
5. Extend ModelarDB with a novel file-based data store for the edge and cloud.
6. Extend ModelarDB to reduce the number of time series that are physically stored by efficiently recomputing the time series that can be derived from a base time series using user-defined functions and dynamic code generation.
7. Extend ModelarDB with a data transfer component that continuously transfers data points compressed using models from the edge to the cloud.
8. Reflect on the lesson learned while designing and developing ModelarDB.

The paper is structured as follows. Definitions are provided in Sect. 2. Section 3 describes the architecture of ModelarDB. The extensions added to ModelarDB so it can be efficiently deployed on the edge are described in Sect. 4. Then each part of ModelarDB is described in detail with ingestion described in Sect. 5, query processing described in Sect. 6, storage described in Sect. 7, and data transfer described in Sect. 8. The lessons learned while designing and developing ModelarDB are documented in Sect. 9. Related work is described in Sect. 10, while our conclusion and future work are presented in Sect. 11.

2 Preliminaries

The definitions and the values used in the examples in this section are reused from [14] as the work in this paper builds upon our previous work [12–14].

Definition 1. *Time Series: A* time series *TS is a sequence of* data points, *in the form of timestamp and value pairs, ordered by time in increasing order* $TS = \langle (t_1, v_1), (t_2, v_2), \ldots \rangle$. *For each pair* (t_i, v_i), $1 \leq i$, *the timestamp* t_i *represents when the value* $v_i \in \mathbb{R}$ *was recorded. A time series* $TS = \langle (t_1, v_1), \ldots, (t_n, v_n) \rangle$ *with a fixed number of n data points is a* bounded time series.

Definition 2. *Regular Time Series: A time series* $TS = \langle (t_1, v_1), (t_2, v_2), \ldots \rangle$ *is* regular *if the time elapsed between each pair of consecutive data points is always the same, i.e.,* $t_{i+1} - t_i = t_{i+2} - t_{i+1}$ *for* $1 \leq i$ *and* irregular *otherwise.*

Definition 3. *Sampling Interval: The* sampling interval *SI of a regular time series* $TS = \langle (t_1, v_1), (t_2, v_2), \ldots \rangle$ *is the time elapsed between each pair of consecutive data points in the time series:* $SI = t_{i+1} - t_i$ *for* $1 \leq i$.

For example, the time series $TS_e = \langle (100, 9.43), (200, 9.09), (300, 8.96), (400, 8.62), (500, 8.50), \ldots \rangle$ is a regular unbounded time series with a 100-milliseconds sampling interval. A bounded time series can be constructed from TS_e by extracting the data points with the timestamps $100 \leq t \leq 500$.

Definition 4. *Gap: A* gap *between a regular bounded time series* $TS_1 = \langle (t_1, v_1), \ldots, (t_s, v_s) \rangle$ *and a regular time series* $TS_2 = \langle (t_e, v_e), (t_{e+1}, v_{e+1}), \ldots \rangle$ *with the same sampling interval SI and recorded from the same source, is a pair of timestamps* $G = (t_s, t_e)$ *with* $t_e = t_s + m \times SI$, $m \in \mathbb{N}_{\geq 2}$, *and where no data points exist between* t_s *and* t_e.

No gaps exist in TS_e as there is a data point for all timestamps matching the sampling interval. However, for $TS_g = \langle (100, 9.43), (200, 9.09), (300, 8.96), (400, 8.62), (500, 8.50), (1100, 7.08), \ldots \rangle$ there is a gap $G = (500, 1100)$ which separates two regular time series. For simplicity, we say that multiple time series recorded from the same source but separated by gaps is one time series containing gaps. As the sampling interval is undefined for a time series with gaps, a regular time series with gaps is defined as a time series where all data points in a gap have the special value $\perp$ indicating that no real values were collected.

Definition 5. *Regular Time Series with Gaps: A regular time series with gaps is a regular time series,* $TS = \langle (t_1, v_1), (t_2, v_2), \ldots \rangle$ *where* $v_i \in \mathbb{R} \cup \{\perp\}$ *for* $1 \leq i$. *All sub-sequences in TS of the form* $\langle (t_s, v_s), (t_{s+1}, \perp), \ldots, (t_{e-1}, \perp), (t_e, v_e) \rangle$ *where* $v_s, v_e \in \mathbb{R}$, *are denoted as gaps* $G = (t_s, t_e)$.

As an example, $TS_{rg} = \langle(100, 9.43), (200, 9.09), (300, 8.96), (400, 8.62), (500, 8.50), (600, \perp), (700, \perp), (800, \perp), (900, \perp), (1000, \perp), (1100, 7.08), \ldots\rangle$ is a regular time series with gaps and has a sampling interval of 100 milliseconds.

The values of time series can be represented by *models* which are functions mapping from timestamps to estimates of values such that each estimate is within a given error bound from the actual value. A model-based representation enables efficient compression of time series.

Definition 6. *Model: A model of a time series $TS = \langle(t_1, v_1), (t_2, v_2), \ldots\rangle$ is a function m. For each t_i, $1 \leq i$, m is a real-valued mapping from t_i to an estimate of the value v_i for the corresponding data point in TS.*

Definition 7. *Model Type: A model type is pair of functions $M_T = (m_t, e_t)$. $m_t(TS, \epsilon)$ is a partial function, which, when defined for a bounded time series TS and a non-negative real number ϵ, returns a model m of TS such that $e_t(TS, m) \leq \epsilon$. e_t is a mapping from TS and m to a non-negative real number representing the error of the values estimated by m. We call ϵ the error bound.*

A model type (e.g., linear regression) determines the set of parameters required to create a specific model of that type for approximating the values of a time series. Models represent the values of a time series as the function m with the error of the representation within the error bound ϵ as computed by the model type's function e_t. We say that a model is fitted to a bounded regular time series, e.g., $TS_b = \langle(100, 9.43), (200, 9.09), (300, 8.96), (400, 8.62), (500, 8.50)\rangle$, when determining the parameters of a model using a model type. A single model may also be able to efficiently represent the values from a group of time series within a given error bound if the time series in the group have similar values.

Definition 8. *Time Series Group: A time series group is a set of regular time series, possibly with gaps, $TSG = \{TS_1, \ldots, TS_n\}$, where for $TS_i, TS_j \in TSG$ it holds that they have the same sampling interval SI and that $t_{1i} \bmod SI = t_{1j} \bmod SI$ where t_{1i} and t_{1j} are the first timestamp of TS_i and TS_j, respectively.*

A time series group can only contain time series with the same sampling interval and aligned timestamps. This ensures that a data point is received from all time series in a group at each sampling interval unless gaps occur. If the time series in a group do not have approximately the same values, scaling can be applied to allow a single stream of models to represent the values of all time series in the group. By representing the values from a time series group using one stream of models, the compression ratio can be significantly increased compared to a model-based representation of each individual time series in the group.

Definition 9. *Segment: A segment is a 5-tuple $S = (t_s, t_e, SI, G_{ts} : TSG \rightarrow 2^{\{t_s, t_s+SI, \ldots, t_e\}}, m)$ representing the data points for a bounded time interval of a time series group TSG. The 5-tuple consists of start time t_s, end time t_e, sampling interval SI, a function G_{ts} which for the $TS \in TSG$ returns the set of timestamps for which $v = \perp$ in TS, and where the values for all other timestamps are defined by the model m multiplied by a scaling constant $C_{TS} \in \mathbb{R}$.*

To provide an example of a segment, we use the following three time series:

$$TS_1 = \langle(100, 9.43), (200, 9.09), (300, 8.96), (400, 8.62), (500, 8.50)\rangle$$
$$TS_2 = \langle(100, 8.78), (200, 8.55), (300, 8.32), (400, 8.09), (500, 8.96)\rangle$$
$$TS_3 = \langle(100, 9.49), (200, 9.20), (300, 8.92), (400, 8.73), (500, 8.65)\rangle$$

These three time series are grouped together in a time series group. The values in this time series group can be efficiently compressed as the linear function $m = -0.003 \times t_i + 9.40$. Using the uniform norm this model has an error of $|8.96 - (-0.003 \times 500 + 9.40)| = 1.06$. If we assume that the error bound is 1, a segment like $S = (100, 400, 100, G_{ts} = \emptyset, m = -0.003 \times t_i + 9.40), 1 \leq i \leq 4$, must be created for the model-based representation to be within the error bound.

We also informally define edge nodes based on discussions with owners of RES installations. Thus, an *edge node* is a low-end commodity PC, e.g., 4 CPU Cores, 4 GiB RAM, and an HDD, that collects data points from a set of sensors. It is deployed very close to the sensors it collects data from and has a connection with limited bandwidth to the cloud, e.g., 500 Kbits/s to 5 Mbits/s. Each edge node continuously transfers data points to the cloud. Thus, edge nodes provide limited processing power but can access the latest data points with low latency.

Likewise, we informally define a *cloud node* as a VM, e.g., 8 Virtual CPU Cores, 32 GiB RAM, and an SSD, running on a high-end server that processes data points collected from sensors by a set of edge nodes. It is deployed in a data center far from the sensors the data points are collected from. Multiple cloud nodes are connected to form a cluster using connections with ample bandwidth. Thus, cloud nodes provide almost unlimited processing power but the latency from a data point is collected until it can be processed by a cloud node is high.

3   ModelarDB Architecture

ModelarDB was designed to be modular and consists of a Java library named ModelarDB Core which can be interfaced with different query engines and data stores depending on the use case [12]. Switching between different query engines and data stores does not require ModelarDB to be recompiled, instead, users can simply specify which query engine and data store to use in a configuration file. Thus, the same ModelarDB binary can be efficiently deployed on both the edge and in the cloud. The indented configuration for an efficient deployment on the edge is using H2 as the query engine (see Sect. 4) and a JDBC-compatible RDBMS, Apache Parquet files written to the local file system, or Apache ORC files written to the local file system as the data store as shown in Fig. 1. To use ModelarDB with this configuration, the ModelarDB binary and its configuration file simply have to be copied to an edge node, and the binary executed on the edge node using a JVM. The indented configuration for a scalable deployment on a cluster of nodes in the cloud is using Apache Spark as the query engine and Apache Cassandra, Apache Parquet files written to HDFS, or Apache ORC files written to HDFS as the data store as shown in Fig. 2. To use ModelarDB with this configuration, a cluster with stock versions of Apache Spark and Apache

Cassandra or HDFS must be available. Then ModelarDB's configuration file must be copied to the Apache Spark Master and the ModelarDB binary deployed using the `spark-submit` script included with Apache Spark. While ModelarDB was designed to use these specific combinations of query engines and data stores, the system does support arbitrary combinations of query engines and data stores.

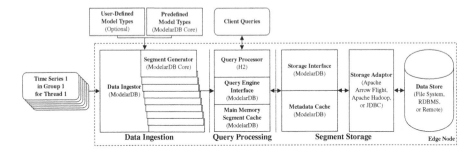

Fig. 1. Architecture of ModelarDB with the primary implementors of the components that are used when ModelarDB is deployed on the edge nodes. Segments are continuously transferred to the cloud nodes by writing them to the remote data store.

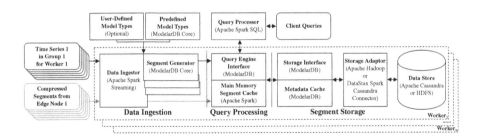

Fig. 2. Architecture of ModelarDB with the primary implementors of the components that are used when ModelarrDB is deployed on the cloud nodes. Segments received from the edge nodes are shown in gray and bypass the Segment Generators.

ModelarDB's architecture consists of three sets of components as shown in Fig. 1 and Fig. 2. The *Data Ingestion* components ingest data points and compress them to segments containing metadata and models (see Sect. 5) or receive such compressed segments from another ModelarDB instance, the *Query Processing* components cache segments and execute queries on the segments that are stored locally (see Sect. 6), and the *Segment Storage* components provide a uniform interface for reading from and writing to local data stores (see Sect. 7) and for transferring segments to another ModelarDB instance represented by a remote data store (see Sect. 8). The remote data store uses Apache Arrow Flight for communicating with the other instance of ModelarDB. By transferring segments instead of data points, ModelarDB significantly reduces the amount of bandwidth required. Data transfer was implemented as a data store so only minor changes had to be made to the remainder of the system. This remote data store also maintains a reference to the local data store the system is configured to use for reading and writing data locally. While ModelarDB is designed to transfer segments from an instance on the edge that uses H2 as the query engine to an instance in the cloud that uses Apache Spark as the query engine, the system is not limited to this configuration. For example, segments can be transferred between instances that are both configured to use H2 as the query engine.

4   Supporting Query Processing and Storage on the Edge

ModelarDB was originally designed to run distributed in the cloud using Apache Spark for query processing and Apache Cassandra for storage [12]. The current version of ModelarDB has been extended to be efficiently deployed on both the edge and in the cloud. This was done by analyzing the requirements for ModelarDB to be deployed on the edge nodes, analyzing the limitations caused by the hardware currently used on the edge nodes, evaluating existing query engines and data stores to determine which are appropriate for deployment on the edge nodes, integrating the RDBMS H2, and developing a new data store that operates directly on files and supports Apache Parquet and Apache ORC.

4.1   Analysis of Requirements and Limitations on the Edge

To efficiently deploy ModelarDB on the edge, the hardware currently used by practitioners for their edge nodes must be taken into account. The hardware being used is a key concern as the hardware used for edge nodes differs significantly depending on the domain, and a system that is designed to run on a commodity PC will be very different compared to a system designed to run on a microcontroller. From conversations with owners of RES installations we learned that the hardware they deploy on their edge nodes is similar to low-end commodity PCs, e.g., 4 CPU Cores, 4 GiB RAM, 250 GiB HDD, and a 1 Gbit/s Network Card. Due to the high number of CPU cores compared to the amount of memory and the use of an HDD, a high compression ratio should be prioritized higher than CPU usage. A high compression ratio ensures that high-frequency time series can be ingested and written to the HDD despite its low write speed and that a large number of data points can be cached in memory for faster query performance without consuming a large fraction of the available memory. Also, to ensure that alerts can be provided on time through real-time analytics, support for executing queries on the time series during ingestion must be provided.

  A key benefit of compressing time series using models is that many models represent the values of data points using functions where the number of coefficients required for each function is constant and thus unrelated to the number of values represented by the model. For example, a linear function can approximately represent an unlimited number of increasing, decreasing, or constant values using only two coefficients. This significantly reduces the amount of storage required. Of course, the used functions must match the structure of the time series, e.g., approximately representing increasing values with constant functions requires multiple functions, while approximately representing constant values using a linear function requires an unnecessary coefficient. ModelarDB already compensates for this by using multiple different model types per time series.

In addition to allowing high-frequency time series to be stored for long periods of time on the edge nodes, a high compression ratio is also required for the time series to be transferred to the cloud nodes. From conversations with owners of RES installations, we learned that the available bandwidth from the edge nodes to the cloud nodes can be as low as 500 Kbits/s to 5 Mbits/s depending on the installation. So, high-frequency time series must be highly compressed on the edge nodes before it becomes feasible to transfer them to the cloud nodes instead of transferring simple aggregates. Also, ingestion, compression, and transfer of the time series must be performed automatically and continuously. Finally, until the compressed time series have been successfully transferred to the cloud nodes and can be queried there, it must be possible to execute queries against them on the edge nodes. As the instances of ModelarDB deployed on the edge nodes and the cloud nodes will be an integrated system, ModelarDB must also support executing the exact same queries on both the edge nodes and the cloud nodes.

In summary, for ModelarDB to be used on the edge nodes it must provide a high compression ratio to reduce the amounts of storage and bandwidth required, allow queries to be executed during ingestion, and support executing the exact same queries on the edge nodes and on the cloud nodes. While the previous version of ModelarDB's model-based compression already provides state-of-the-art compression for time series groups, its use of Apache Spark and Apache Cassandra makes it unsuitable for deployment on the edge nodes due to their limited hardware. Also, it does not provide support for automatically transferring compressed time series and metadata between multiple instances of the system.

4.2   Evaluation of Query Engines and Data Stores for the Edge

The hardware requirement of Apache Spark and Apache Cassandra significantly exceeds the hardware available on the edge nodes and their ability to run distributed across multiple nodes is not beneficial when deploying ModelarDB on the edge nodes. Thus, a query engine and data store optimized for the edge nodes are required. However, while ModelarDB was designed to be modular, the only query engine integrated with ModelarDB Core was Apache Spark. Thus, all queries had to be executed by Apache Spark and it was also required to ingest multiple time series groups in parallel. Thus, a query engine that can execute the same queries as Apache Spark must be integrated with ModelarDB Core to efficiently execute queries while ingesting time series groups in parallel on the edge nodes. ModelarDB supports using RDBMSs through JDBC for the data store, so a lightweight RDBMS can be used instead of Apache Cassandra when running on the edge nodes. The set of requirements for an edge-optimized query engine and data store to be integrated with ModelarDB Core is shown in Table 1.

Table 1. Requirements for a query engine and data store to be used on the edge.

Requirement	Argument
The system's license must be compatible with version 2.0 of the Apache License.	ModelarDB is open-source and licensed under version 2.0 of the Apache License.
The system must be designed for running on a single node instead of multiple nodes.	A distributed system is not needed on the edge nodes as each queries its own data.
A relational query interface with support for SQL.	Ensures the same queries can be executed on the edge nodes and the cloud nodes.
Extensible using a JVM-based language.	Allows integration with ModelarDB Core.
A stable version 1.0 has been released.	Indicates the system is mature enough.
Quality documentation must be available.	Significantly reduces development time.
The code must have been updated recently.	Indicates the system is being maintained.

Based on these requirements a large set of candidate systems were collected from db-engines.com and dbdb.io. Small-scale experiments were then used to reduce the set of candidate systems, e.g., by testing if their APIs were expressive enough for their query engines to be efficiently integrated with ModelarDB Core and if they were fast enough to process high-frequency time series. As shown in Table 2, most query engines were discarded due to a lack of functionality or documentation, while PostgreSQL was discarded due to poor query performance when queries were executed through PL/Java (22.51x to 47.28x slower than H2).

After the small-scale experiments were performed, only Apache Derby, H2, and HyperSQL remained. A proof-of-concept implementation was created using each of these three systems and their performance was evaluated. During the development of these proofs-of-concept, HyperSQL was also discarded due to its apparent lack of predicate push-down and support for user-defined aggregates with multiple arguments. To compare the query performance of Apache Derby and H2 the following experimental setup and query workloads were used:

Hardware: i7–2620M, 8 GiB 1333 MHz DDR3, 7,200 RPM HDD.

Software: Ubuntu Linux 16.04 on ext4, Apache Derby v10.15.2.0, H2 v1.4.200, and InfluxDB 1.4.2 (Baseline and current top TSMS on db-engines.com).

Data Sets: *EP* which consists of 45,353 short regular time series with gaps and uses 339 GiB when stored as CSV, and *EF* which consists of 197 long regular time series with gaps and uses 372 GiB when stored as CSV.

Query Workloads: Three types of queries are used to determine the strengths and weaknesses of each system's query engine. The types of queries used are shown with examples in Listing 1. The aggregate queries are included as we learned from owners and manufacturers of wind turbines that aggregate queries are their most common query type. Thus, the aggregate queries are representative of the real-life use cases ModelarDB was designed for. For ModelarDB, the aggregate queries are manually rewritten so they are executed much faster directly on the segments. The point/range queries are mainly included to get a more complete evaluation of the query engines.

Table 2. Systems evaluated for use by ModelarDB as the query engine and data store on the edge nodes. Systems marked ✓ are selected, O are fallback, and ✗ are discarded.

Query Engine and Data Store		Argument
H2 v1.4.200	✓	Is highly extensible, provides adequate performance, and allows the same queries to be executed on the edge nodes and the cloud nodes
Apache Calcite v1.26.0	O	The large amount of implementation required to efficiently execute arbitrary SQL queries. Could replace H2 if control over execution becomes more important than development time or if H2's performance becomes a limitation.
Apache Arrow DataFusion v5.0.0	O	Performs well and is highly extensible, but it must be integrated with the JVM through the JNI. Considered an alternative to Apache Calcite if H2's performance becomes a limitation.
Apache Spark SQL v3.1.1	O	The high overhead and hardware requirement. Could be used to compile SQL queries to Java code on the cloud nodes and then execute the resulting Java code on the edge nodes if H2's performance becomes a limitation.
Apache Derby v10.15.2.0	✗	Lack of predicate push-down for all `WHERE`-clauses containing `OR` or `IN`. Segment View and Data Point View must be wrapped in `TABLE()`. UDAFs requiring multiple inputs require user-defined types. H2 provides better performance.
Cubrid v10.2.2.8874	✗	`CUBRIDResultSet` is only useable with JDBC.
Firebird v3.0.1 FB/Java v1.0.0-beta-1	✗	No stable releases exist for FB/Java v1.0.0 and it could not connect to the Firebird RDBMS.
HyperSQL v2.5.1	✗	Lack of predicate push-down, the result set from table expressions are fully materialized, and UDAFs only support one input parameter.
MonetDBLite-Java Commit: fe4c165	✗	No support for JVM-based UDFs and UDAFs.
PostgreSQL v13 PL/Java 1.6.0	✗	Large performance overhead when transferring small rows between the JVM and PostgreSQL.
VanillaDB VanillaCore v0.4.1	✗	End user documentation is very limited.
Virtuoso OSE v7.2.5.1	✗	The latest stable release was from 2018, the documentation was very limited, and the development branch did not compile successfully.

```
1   -- Large Aggregates, e.g.,
2   SELECT Tid, MIN(Value) FROM DataPoint GROUP BY Tid
3
4   -- Small Aggregates, e.g.,
5   SELECT Tid, MAX(Value) FROM DataPoint
6   WHERE Tid IN (113, 131, 70, 97, 68) GROUP BY Tid
7
8   -- Point/Range, e.g.,
9   SELECT * FROM DataPoint
10  WHERE Timestamp >= '2010-11-23 10:28:46'
11  AND Timestamp <= '2010-11-23 10:28:47'
```

Listing 1. Query workloads used to evaluate query engines for use on the edge.

Setup: ModelarDB uses H2 as the data store in all experiments so only the query engine differs between Apache Derby and H2. In addition, ModelarDB is configured to store the value of each data point within a 10% error bound.

Table 3. The query performance of both InfluxDB (error bound 0%), ModelarDB when executing queries using H2 (error bound 10%), and ModelarDB when executing queries using Apache Derby (error bound 10%) on the real-life EP and EF data sets.

Query Workload	InfluxDB	H2	Apache Derby
EP			
Large Aggregates	Out of Memory	17H 3M 43.025S	Out of Memory
Small Aggregates	19.064S	7.952S	15H 36M 31.207S
Point/Range	33.059S	1H 55M 11.539S	2H 26M 32.697S
EF			
Large Aggregates	7H 47M 42.408S	4H 59M 44.11S	8H 51M 26.944S
Small Aggregates	16M 12.846S	8M 28.77S	6H 8M 27.492S
Point/Range	8.802S	15M 5.377S	11M 37.056S

The results for Apache Derby, H2, and InfluxDB are shown in Table 3. In general, H2 was 1.27x to 7066x faster than Apache Derby, while Apache Derby was only 1.30x faster than H2 for a single set of queries on a single data set (point/range queries on a few long time series). The largest difference between Apache Derby and H2 was for small aggregate queries and is primarily due to

Apache Derby lacking predicate push-down for `WHERE Tid IN { ... }` statements where `Tid` is a time series identifier. In terms of accuracy, ModelarDB provides a per data point error guarantee. However, the actual average error is often significantly lower than the error bound as shown in [14]. For example, even when using a 10% error bound, the highest average actual error was only 0.34% for EP and only 1.72% for EF [14]. This was also reflected in the average actual error of the query results. Specifically, the average query result error was 0.024% for large aggregates, 0.033–0.28% for small aggregates, 0.012–2.01% for point/range, and 0.0027–0.17% for multidimensional aggregates [14]. Thus, the average actual error is typically very small in practice. Of course, if a 0% error bound is used ModelarDB is *guaranteed to produce exact query results*.

As it provided much better performance than Apache Derby, H2 was selected as the query engine ModelarDB should use when deployed on edge nodes. While the proof-of-concept implementation indicated that H2 provides the necessary functionality and performance, we also determined that it could be replaced with a new query engine built using Apache Calcite, Apache Arrow DataFusion, or pre-compiling queries to Java in the cloud using Apache Spark SQL if necessary. However, these solutions would require more time to develop than integrating H2 with ModelarDB Core. Thus, they were initially considered secondary options. H2 was also selected as the data store ModelarDB should use when deployed on edge nodes. However, as H2 required a significant amount of storage for indexes to efficiently retrieve the requested data, a file-based data store optimized for OLAP was later implemented as a replacement as described in Sect. 7.2.

4.3   Integrating H2 with ModelarDB

As ModelarDB was designed to be modular, adding an additional query engine to the system did not require significant changes to the architecture or the existing components. However, the original implementation was implicitly assuming that Apache Spark would be the sole query engine in multiple parts of the system. So, some components had to be refactored to accommodate the new query engine. For example, the default methods for reading and writing segments were removed from the storage interface as specialized storage interfaces had to be implemented for each query engine to efficiently support predicate push-down as described in Sect. 7.1. Methods that could be used by both Apache Spark and H2 were also moved to a shared component. However these changes were all internal, so users only need to configure ModelarDB to use H2 as the query engine and data store through ModelarDB's configuration file when deploying it on the edge nodes. Thus, as described in Sect. 3, the same ModelarDB binary can be deployed on both the edge nodes and the cloud nodes with different configurations.

ModelarDB's modular architecture made it much simpler to integrate H2 as an additional query engine and data store compared to a monolithic architecture. However, this modularity also significantly increased the complexity of the system and made some optimizations significantly harder to implement or required them to be implemented for each combination of query engine and data store. For example, as stated above, the new storage interfaces provide specialized read and write methods for each query engine to achieve higher performance compared to a shared set of read and write methods. However, this adds complexity to the implementation and increases development time. Another example is the query interface. The previous version of ModelarDB used JSON for query results and the current version uses JSON or Apache Arrow. These formats make it very easy for programs to consume data from ModelarDB, however, they require a conversion step compared to using Apache Spark's and H2's binary formats.

5   Ingestion

ModelarDB uses the *Group Online Lossy and lossless Extensible Multi-Model (GOLEMM)* compression method [14] for compressing time series groups within a user-defined error bound (possibly 0%). The method assumes that the time series in each group have the same regular sampling interval and that the timestamps of the time series in each group are aligned. GOLEMM is a window-based approach that dynamically splits time series groups into dynamically sized subsequences and then compresses the values of each sub-sequence using one of multiple different model types. By using a window-based approach, bounded time series (e.g., bulk-loaded from files) and unbounded time series (e.g., ingested online from sockets) can be compressed using the exact same compression method.

5.1   Model-Based Compression

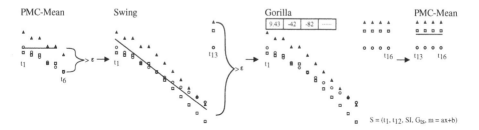

Fig. 3. Online compression of a time series group containing three time series using GOLEMM. The group is split into dynamically sized sub-sequences and the values of each sub-sequence are represented by the model providing the best compression ratio.

ModelarDB includes extended versions of three different model types [14]: PMC-Mean [17] fits a constant function to the data points' values, Swing [7] fits a linear function to the data points, and Gorilla [24] compresses the data points' values using XOR and a variable-length binary encoding. These three model types can all be incrementally updated as data points are received. Users can optionally add more model types through an API as described in Sect. 5.2. As both user-defined and predefined model types are dynamically loaded, ModelarDB does not need to be recompiled when additional model types are added.

An example of compressing a time series group containing three time series using GOLEMM is shown in Fig. 3. At t_1 a data point is received from each time series in the group and the first model type is used to fit a model to these data points. In this example, PMC-Mean is used. At t_6 a data point is received that PMC-Mean cannot represent using the current model within the error bound. Thus, GOLEMM switches to the next model type, which is Swing in this example. To initialize Swing, the data points from t_1 to t_6 are passed to it so an initial linear function can be fit to them. Then, at t_{13} a data point is received that Swing cannot represent using the current model within the error bound, so GOLEMM switches to Gorilla, which is the last model type in this example. To initialize Gorilla, the data points from t_1 to t_{13} are passed to it so their values can be compressed using XOR and a variable-length binary encoding. As Gorilla uses lossless compression, it will never exceed the error bound, so instead, it uses a user-configurable length bound. In this example, the length bound is exceeded at t_{16}. After all of the model types have tried to fit models to the time series group, GOLEMM emits the model that provides the best compression ratio as part of a segment containing metadata and the model. In this example, a model of type Swing is emitted as it could represent the data points from t_1 to t_{12}. Then, GOLEMM restarts compression of the group from t_{13} using PMC-Mean.

ModelarDB can only execute queries against models that have been emitted as part of a segment. Thus, the latency from a data point is received to it can be queried is theoretically unbounded as the error bound may never be exceeded. To remedy this, ModelarDB allows users to set an upper limit on the number of data points that cannot be queried. If this limit is reached, a temporary segment is emitted which contains a model that represents all of the values models are currently being fitted to for the time series group. This temporary segment is only stored in memory from where it can be queried, but it is never persisted to disk. Thus, ModelarDB provides efficient and extensible model-based compression of bounded and unbounded time series groups. It also ensures that the latency, i.e., the time from a data point is ingested until it is ready to be queried, is bounded.

5.2   User-Defined Model Types

As stated, ModelarDB supports dynamically loading user-defined model types. Thus, users can optimize ModelarDB by implementing specialized model types for their domain. For a model type to be used by ModelarDB it must derive from the abstract class `ModelType` whose overridable methods are shown in Table 4. Users must implement all of these methods with the exception of `withinErrorBound()` which only needs to be overridden if the model type does not provide a relative per data point error guarantee. To load user-defined model types, the classes' canonical names must be added to ModelarDB's configuration file and the corresponding class files must be added to the JVM's classpath.

For each model type, a corresponding segment must also be available to represent the metadata and models returned by the model type's `get()` method. Although, it is not a requirement that each model type has a unique corresponding segment, e.g., multiple model types that fit linear functions to data points

Table 4. The abstract class user-defined and predefined model types must derive from. Methods marked with ● must be overridden while those marked with ○ are optional.

ModelType	Functionality
new(MTid, ErrorBound, LengthBound): ModelType	● Construct an instance of the model type that fits models to time series within ErrorBound or LengthBound, and assign the model type identifier MTid to it.
append([DataPoint]): Bool	● Try to update the current model to also represent the next data points from the time series in the group. Return True if the model could be updated to also represent [DataPoint], otherwise False.
initialize([[DataPoint]])	● Discard the current model, create a new model, and fit the new model to as many data points in [[DataPoint]] as possible within the user-defined bounds.
getModel(StartTime, EndTime, SI, [[DataPoint]]): [Byte]	● Serialize and return the current model. The format is model type dependent.
get(Tid, StartTime, EndTime, SI, Model, Offsets): Segment	● Create a Segment that matches this ModelType and represents the data points from StartTime to and including EndTime for the time series with Tid using a Model returned by getModel().
length(): Int	● Return how many groups of data points from the time series group the current model represents. Thus, it is independent of the time series group's size.
size(StartTime, EndTime, SI, [[DataPoint]]): Float	● Return the size of the current model in bytes or NaN if a model could not be fitted to any of the provided data points.
withinErrorBound(ErrorBound, [DataPoint], [DataPoint]): Bool	○ Return True if the first sequence of data points are within the ErrorBound of the second sequence of data points. Can be overridden as each model type can interpret the error bound differently.

can share the same segment. For a segment to be used by ModelarDB it must derive from the abstract class **Segment** whose overridable methods are shown in Table 5. Of these methods, only **Segment**'s **new()** and **get()** methods must be implemented, while the remaining methods can optionally be overridden to compute aggregates directly from the segment. If these methods are not overridden the aggregates are computed by reconstructing the data points represented by the segment, using **get()** to compute all of the values, and then computing the aggregate. An example of how **sum()** is implemented for the type of segment created by Swing is shown in Listing 2 and described in detail in Sect. 6.

Table 5. The abstract class user-defined and predefined segments must derive from. Methods marked with ● must be overridden while those marked with ○ are optional.

Segment		Functionality
`new(Tid, StartTime, EndTime, SI, Model, Offsets): Segment`	●	Construct an instance of the segment which represents the data points from `StartTime` to `EndTime` for the time series with `Tid` using `Model`.
`get(Timestamp, Index): Float`	●	Return the value computed for the data point with `Timestamp` and which is the `Index`'th data point represented by the segment. The `Timestamp` and `Index` both specify the same data point, however, some types of segments are simpler to implement using one or the other.
`min(): Float`	○	Compute the minimum value represented by the segment directly from the model if overridden, otherwise it is computed from reconstructed data points.
`max(): Float`	○	Compute the maximum value represented by the segment directly from the model if overridden, otherwise it is computed from reconstructed data points.
`sum(): Double`	○	Compute the sum of the values represented by the segment directly from the model if overridden, otherwise it is computed from reconstructed data points. `sum()` is also used to compute averages.

6   Query Processing

ModelarDB uses SQL as its query language and is designed to support multiple different query interfaces. Originally, queries could only be submitted to ModelarDB through sockets or a text file and query results were returned as JSON to make it simple to use from other programming languages and command-line applications like Telnet [12]. Subsequent versions added support for HTTP and a REPL to the system. These interfaces also return query results as JSON. However, while the use of JSON makes it simple to query ModelarDB and view the result, converting to and from JSON adds a significant performance overhead.

Thus, the current version of ModelarDB has been extended to accept queries and return query results using Apache Arrow Flight. Apache Arrow provides a binary in-memory column-based data format that is designed to be programming language-independent and implementations exist in many different programming languages, such as C++, Go, Java, and Rust. Apache Arrow Flight provides functionality for sending and receiving data in Apache Arrow's data format. To reduce the overhead of converting Apache Spark's and H2's in-memory row-based data format to Apache Arrow's column-based data format, dynamic code generation is used. By dynamically generating the methods performing the conversion based on the schema of the query result, the conversion of each row can be performed without any branches. Static and dynamic code generation is also heavily used for projections to remove branches. However, as ModelarDB dynamically generates and compiles high-level Scala code, the use of dynamic code generation can increase the query processing time in some cases. This is a general problem when using high-level languages like C++ and Scala for dynamic code generation [22]. For example, ModelarDB does not use dynamic code generation when evaluating queries that only need to process a small amount of data and Apache Spark is used as the query engine. To determine how much data Apache Spark has to process, the number of partitions in the Apache Spark RDD to process is used as a heuristic [14]. For H2 dynamic code generation is always used as the compiled code is easy to cache when running on a single node.

Regardless of the query interface and query engine used, ModelarDB exposes the ingested time series at the data point and segment level. This is implemented as two views with the following schemas where `<Dimensions>` are user-defined denormalized dimensions, i.e., metadata that describes the ingested time series:

Data Point View: `Tid int, Timestamp timestamp, Value float,`
   `<Dimensions>`.
Segment View: `Tid int, StartTime timestamp, EndTime timestamp,`
   `MTid int, Model blob, Offsets blob, <Dimensions>`.

The Data Point View allows users to query the ingested time series as data points and thus supports arbitrary SQL queries. This is enabled by the requirement that every model can reconstruct the values it represents within a user-defined error bound (possibly 0%). However, while the Data Point View supports arbitrary queries, as stated, many aggregates can be executed more efficiently directly from the metadata and models contained in each segment than reconstructed data points. ModelarDB supports this through the Segment View using a set of UDFs and UDAFs. To simplify using these functions, ModelarDB implements one extension to SQL in the form of `#`. This is a specialized version of `*` which is replaced with the columns required to compute aggregates using the UDAFs. An example of how `SUM()` is computed by the type of segment created by Swing using the Data Point View and the Segment View is shown in Fig. 4.

This example shows that when `SUM()` is computed using the Data Point View, all of the ingested data points are reconstructed within the error bound and the aggregate is computed by iterating over these data points. The values are

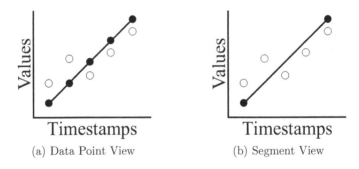

(a) Data Point View   (b) Segment View

Fig. 4. How ModelarDB evaluates queries that compute SUM() for a model of type Swing using the Data Point View (a) or the Segment View (b). The ingested data points are shown in white, while the reconstructed data points are black.

computed using the Segment.get() method shown in Table 5. In contrast, when the query is computed using the Segment View, the Segment.sum() method shown in Table 5 is used to compute SUM(). Thus, a specialized method can be used for each type of segment. The implementation of Segment.sum() for the type of segment created by Swing is shown in Listing 2. This method only needs to compute the value for the first and last data point, compute the average for the segment, and then multiply it with the length. Thus, for the type of segment created by Swing, using the Segment View instead of the Data Point View reduces the complexity from linear time to constant time for each segment.

```
1   @Override
2   public double sum() {
3       double first = this.a * this.getStartTime() + this.b;
4       double last = this.a * this.getEndTime() + this.b;
5       double average = (first + last) / 2;
6       return average * this.length();
7   }
```

Listing 2. Implementation of Segment.sum() for the type of segment created by Swing.

In summary, when a query is received from a client, all instances of # are replaced with the required columns and the query is forwarded to the query engine ModelarDB is configured to use. The query engine then parses the query and executes it using the view specified in the FROM-clause. The view retrieves the relevant segments from the data store ModelarDB is configured to use, computes the complete query result, and returns it to the client as JSON or Apache Arrow.

7   Storage

7.1   Data Store Overview

As described in Sect. 3, ModelarDB supports storing time series groups as segments containing metadata and models using three different data stores: JDBC-compatible RDBMSs, files read from and written to a local file system or HDFS, and Apache Cassandra. The file-based data store currently supports reading and writing both Apache Parquet and Apache ORC files. The data stores ModelarDB currently supports and their recommended usage are shown in Table 6.

Table 6. The data stores ModelarDB currently supports and their recommended usage.

Data Store	Storage Format	Recommended Usage
RDBMS (JDBC)	RDBMS Dependent	Edge Nodes
File-Based Data Store (Local File System)	Apache Parquet Apache ORC	Edge Nodes
Apache Cassandra	SSTable	Cloud Nodes
File-Based Data Store (HDFS)	Apache Parquet Apache ORC	Cloud Nodes

From a user's perspective, the data stores all provide the same functionality. However, the RDBMSs and the file-based data store (when reading and writing to the local file system) are designed for use with H2 on the edge nodes, while Apache Cassandra and the file-based data store (when reading and writing to HDFS) are designed for use with Apache Spark on the cloud nodes. To ensure that each query engine can efficiently read and write segments from the data stores, ModelarDB defines an interface for each query engine that the data stores must implement. Thus, H2 interfaces with the data stores through the `H2Storage` interface which is shown in Table 7, and Apache Spark interfaces with the data stores through the `SparkStorage` interface shown in Table 8. By implementing separate methods for each query engine they can perform predicate push-down without converting their encoding of the predicates to a shared representation. The native representation used by each query engine for segments can also be passed and returned, thus removing the expensive step of converting all segments to and from a shared representation for both query engines. Of course, this comes at the cost of development time as separate methods must be implemented for reading and writing for each combination of data store and query engine.

`open()` performs the necessary setup before the data store can be used, e.g., creating tables for the RDBMSs and Apache Cassandra. `H2Storage` does not contain an H2 specific `open()` method as it isn't necessary to pass any H2 specific information to the data stores. Thus, the general `open()` method required by the abstract class `Storage`, that all data stores must derive from, can be

Table 7. The interface data stores must implement to be used by H2.

H2Storage	Functionality
storeSegmentGroups([SegmentGroup])	Write the segment groups in the parameter [SegmentGroup] to the data store.
getSegmentGroups(TableFilter): [SegmentGroup]	Read at least the segment groups that match the predicates provided by H2 as TableFilter from the data store.

Table 8. The interface data stores must implement to be used by Apache Spark. The DataFrames can contain multiple SegmentGroups like [SegmentGroup] in Table 7.

SparkStorage	Functionality
open(SparkSessionBuilder, Dimensions): SparkSession	Open a connection to the data store, perform the required setup, and get or create an instance of SparkSession from the parameter SparkSessionBuilder.
storeSegmentGroups(SparkSession, DataFrame)	Write the segment groups in DataFrame to the data store using SparkSession.
getSegmentGroups(SparkSession, [Filter]): DataFrame	Read at least the segment groups that match the predicates provided by Apache Spark as [Filter] from the data store.

used. The method storeSegmentGroups() writes batches of segment groups to the data store, while getSegmentGroups() retrieves segment groups from the data store. SegmentGroup is the type used by ModelarDB to represent a dynamically sized sub-sequence of data points from a time series group and it can be converted to one Segment per time series it represents data points for. The segment groups are batched in memory before each batch is passed to storeSegmentGroups(). To reduce the amount of data retrieved from the data store by getSegmentGroups(), predicate push-down is performed by passing query engine-specific representations of the predicates to getSegmentGroups(). ModelarDB only requires that the data stores return at least the requested segment groups. Thus, the returned data is also filtered by the query engine ModelarDB is configured to use.

As the file-based data store has been added to the current version of ModelarDB, its implementation is documented in detail in Sect. 7.2. The other data stores are described in the papers documenting the previous version [12–14].

7.2   File-Based Data Store

The file-based data store is designed to durably store metadata and segment groups directly as files instead of using a DBMS. It was primarily added as H2 required a significant amount of storage for indexes to efficiently retrieve the requested data as described in Sect. 4. Also, the use of RDBMSs and Apache Cassandra limits the optimizations that can be implemented in ModelarDB. For example, both the start time and the end time of the time interval each segment group stores data points for, are stored as part of each segment group. Thus, if a data store partitions the segment groups by their time series group id and sorts them by their start time, they will generally also be sorted by their end time and vice versa. However, to our knowledge, no RDBMSs nor Apache Cassandra can be configured to exploit such a relationship between attributes.

The file-based data store stores metadata about time series, metadata about model types, and the segment group batches passed to `storeSegmentGroups()` as separate immutable files. To make reading more efficient, the many small files created during ingestion are regularly merged into fewer larger immutable files. It is also designed to make adding support for different file formats (existing and new) simple by splitting the implementation into a super-class that contains shared functionality and sub-classes that contain functionality for each file format. Specifically, `FileStorage` implements shared functionality such as determining which files to read for a query, periodic merging without deleting files currently used by a query, and durable writes. `ParquetStorage` and `ORCStorage` are sub-classes of `FileStorage` which implement functionality for reading, writing, and merging Apache ORC and Apache Parquet files, respectively. Support for other file types can be added by creating a new class that derives from `FileStorage` and implements the abstract methods shown in Table 9.

As stated, `FileStorage` is designed to provide durability for metadata and segment groups that have been successfully written completely to files. Thus, if ModelarDB is terminated while writing a batch of segment groups, the entire batch is lost. Durability is implemented by never modifying existing files, writing new files to a temporary location before renaming them, and using logging when merging multiple files containing segment groups. The log is required when merging to support recovering from abnormal termination while deleting the input files after the new merged file has been written to a temporary location. Merging is currently performed synchronically by the thread writing the tenth batch of segment groups. This very simple merge strategy provides an acceptable trade-off between read and write performance. However, when to merge is determined by the method `FileStorage.shouldMerge()`, so a more complex strategy can easily be used by changing this method. For example, an alternative strategy could dynamically decide when to merge based on a trade-off between the available resources (CPU, RAM, disk) and the required query performance.

The files that are currently used by a query cannot be deleted and are thus purposely not included in merge operations as their data points otherwise would be duplicated. `FileStorage` tracks which files are currently used by a query using an approach similar to two-phase locking. In addition to retrieving the relevant segment groups, `getSegmentGroups()` also increments a counter for *all of the files being read* and creates a Java `PhantomReference` to the iterator before returning it. Files with a non-zero counter are skipped when a merge is performed. After the query is complete the iterator is no longer phantom reachable [23], thus the `PhantomReference` is automatically added to a `ReferenceQueue`. Before performing a merge operation, the writing thread

Table 9. The abstract class format-specific file-based data stores must derive from.

FileStorage	Functionality
getFileSuffix: String	Return the file suffix used by data store.
getMaxID(ColumnName, Path): Int	Get the current maximum time series id or time series group id used by the data store.
mergeFiles(Path, [Path])	Merge the content of all files in [Path] and write it to the file passed as Path.
writeTimeSeriesFile([[Metadata]], Path)	Write the time series group metadata passed as the parameter [[Metadata]] to the file passed as Path.
readTimeSeriesFile(Path): [Tid, [Metadata]]	Read the time series group metadata stored in the file passed as Path.
writeModelTypeFile([Name, MTid], Path)	Write the model type metadata passed as the parameter [Name, Mtid] to the file passed as Path.
readModelTypeFile(Path): [Name, MTid]	Read the model type metadata stored in the file passed as Path.
writeSegmentGroupsFile([SegmentGroup], Path)	Write the segment groups from H2 in [SegmentGroup] to the file passed as Path.
readSegmentGroupsFiles(TableFilter, [Path]): [SegmentGroup]	Read at least the segment groups from the files passed as [Path] that match the predicates provided by H2 as TableFilter.
writeSegmentGroupsFolder(SparkSession, DataFrame, Path)	Write the segment groups from Apache Spark in DataFrame to files in the folder passed as Path using SparkSession.
readSegmentGroupsFolders(SparkSession, [Filter], [Path]): DataFrame	Read at least the segment groups from the files in the folders passed as [Path] using SparkSession that match the predicates provided by Apace Spark as [Filter].

retrieves the PhantomReferences in the ReferenceQueue and decrements the counters for the corresponding files. Thus, the counter for each file used by a query is incremented when the query starts and only decremented when the query is complete. This could also be implemented by requiring the iterators returned by readSegmentGroupsFiles() and readSegmentGroupsFolders() to increment and decrement the counters. However, this would require duplicating code as these iterators are returned by methods implemented by the format-specific sub-classes of FileStorage. It would also require code that is guaranteed to execute no matter how the query was terminated as the file counters must always be decremented. In contrast, by using PhantomReferences the current implementation of FileStorage only requires that sub-classes implement how to read, write and merge files.

7.3   Supporting Derived Time Series

As stated, ModelarDB can group time series with similar values and compress them as one stream of models [14]. This significantly reduces the amount of storage required compared to compressing each time series separately. However, it requires that the same model can represent the values from all of the time series in a group for every data point. Thus, for the sub-sequences where the values from each time series in a group are very similar, PMC-Mean and Swing can generally be used to provide excellent compression. However, sub-sequences, where the values differ more than allowed by the error bound, can only be represented by Gorilla due to its use of lossless compression. As a result, the compression ratio for a time series group is highly dependent on the actual values of each time series in the group in addition to their structure. Thus, while ModelarDB tries to mitigate this problem by dynamically splitting and merging time series groups when a significant drop in compression ratio is detected [14], compressing n time series together rarely provides a n-times reduction in the amount of storage required. However, for some time series, the relationship between their values is static, meaning that the values of one time series can be computed exactly from the values of another time series by a function. In that case, only a single base time series needs to be physically stored as the values of all the other time series can be derived from it (i.e., calculated using a function) during query processing.

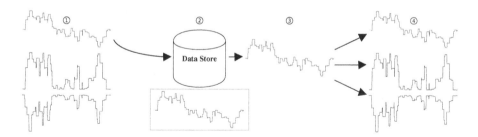

Fig. 5. Example of how ModelarDB can compress time series by not storing them and instead compute their values by applying functions to a base time series's values. To do so, only the base time series is ingested ① and physically stored in the data store ②. During query processing, the base time series is read ③ and functions dynamically compiled to Java bytecode are applied to create the derived time series ④. (Color figure online)

Support for these *derived time series* has been added to the current version of ModelarDB. This is implemented by allowing users to specify which time series can be derived from another time series, thus allowing the system to not store the derived time series. This is shown in Fig. 5. At ① the direction of an object which turns over time, e.g., a wind turbine nacelle, is measured. This produces the time series shown in red. Two other time series with the cosine and sine, respectively, of the angels in the first time series are also needed for later analysis. These time series are shown in blue and green, respectively. However, as these two time series can be computed directly from the base time series, ModelarDB only stores the base time series (red) at ② and not the two derived time series (blue and green). When ModelarDB receives a query that includes the derived time series, it reads the base time series at ③ and applies the user-defined functions $\cos(value \times \pi/180)$ and $\sin(value \times \pi/180)$ where $value$ is measured in degrees, to create the cosine (blue) and sine (green) time series at ④.

ModelarDB cannot automatically detect that a time series can be derived from another as the time series are being ingested as streams. So, users must explicitly specify all derived time series in ModelarDB's configuration file by stating the source from which the base time series is ingested from, the source which the derived time series will be associated with, and the user-defined function that must be applied to transform the values in the base time series to the values in the derived time series. The source the derived time series will be associated with is required so different dimension members can be assigned to the base time series and the derived time series as described in Sect. 6. The function must be specified as the Scala code to be executed for each value in the base time series. The Scala code is dynamically compiled to Java bytecode at startup to significantly reduce its execution time compared to interpreting the code. The specification of derived time series is purposely only stored in ModelarDB's configuration file, and not in the data store, to make it easy for users to add, modify, and remove derived time series. Also, as a derived time series is a *mapping of values* in the base time series to values in the derived time series, the function cannot be used to aggregate values (e.g., to change the sampling interval) or generate more values (e.g., for forecasting). However, these restrictions are only limitations of the current implementation and not the method.

8   Data Transfer

As stated in Sect. 3, the current version of ModelarDB was extended with support for continuously transferring segment groups from the edge nodes to the cloud nodes using Apache Arrow Flight. An example that shows m edge nodes transferring segment groups to n cloud nodes, where $m \gg n$, is shown in Fig. 6. Usually, each cloud node can receive segments from many edge nodes as the cloud nodes generally have more powerful hardware than the edge nodes. During ingestion, the data points can be queried on each edge node using H2. When an edge node has created a user-defined number of segment groups, they are transferred in a batch to the cloud nodes. After the segment groups have been transferred, the data points they represent can be queried on the cloud nodes using Apache Spark. Even though ModelarDB was designed to transfer segment groups from low-powered edge nodes running H2 to powerful cloud nodes running Apache Spark, it is not limited to this configuration. For example, segment groups can be transferred between two instances configured to use H2 as the query engine and data store. ModelarDB only requires that users specify which instance is the client and which is the server in their configuration files.

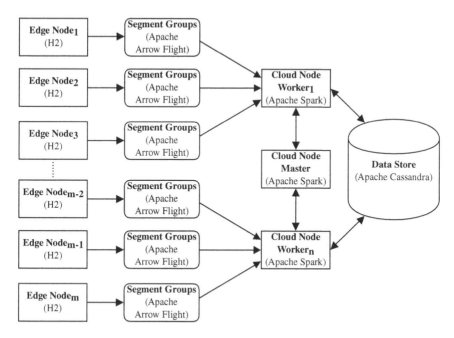

Fig. 6. Segment groups continuously being transferred from m edge nodes (where H2 is both the query engine and data store) to n cloud nodes (where Apache Spark is the query engine and Apache Cassandra is the data store) using Apache Arrow Flight.

The steps required to start transferring segment groups from an edge node to a cluster of cloud nodes are shown in Fig. 7. First ModelarDB must be deployed on the cloud nodes with at least one Apache Spark Master and at least one Apache Spark Worker. Then, at ① each Apache Spark Streaming Receiver registers its address with the Apache Spark Master. When a new edge node is deployed, it communicates with the Apache Spark Master to determine where to transfer its segment groups to. At ② the edge node requests the time series ids and time series group ids to use from the Apache Spark Master. Then, at ③ the edge node requests an endpoint to transfer its segment groups to from the Apache Spark Master. The Apache Spark Master selects the endpoint that currently is receiving the lowest number of data points per minute compressed as segment groups containing metadata and models and returns its address to the edge node. The ModelarDB instance deployed on the edge node then ensures that it and the ModelarDB instance deployed on the cloud nodes use the same model types and refers to them using the same model type ids at ④. The setup process is completed at ⑤ as the edge node transfers the time series metadata to the Apache Spark Master. With the setup process complete, the edge node starts ingesting data points from time series groups, compresses them as described in Sect. 5, and transfers the segment groups to the cloud nodes in batches at ⑥.

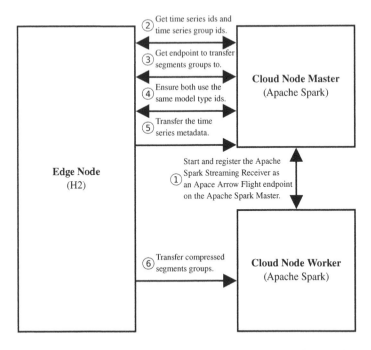

Fig. 7. Setup data transfer from each edge node using H2 to a cluster of cloud nodes using Apache Spark (one Apache Spark Master and multiple Apache Spark Workers).

9   Lessons Learned

The work that led to ModelarDB began in 2015. Since then existing TSMSs have been analyzed [10,11], the system has been designed and implemented [12], and later extended in multiple directions [13,14]. In this section, we present the lessons we learned while developing ModelarDB and from the feedback we have received from collaborators and potential users. While some of these lessons are already described in the literature, they are reiterated for completeness.

Systems Research is Time Intensive and Reusing Components Limits Optimizations: While creating a proof-of-concept implementation using existing components can be done in relatively little time, making a usable and competitive novel system requires a significant time investment. In addition, removing quick workarounds from ModelarDB generally took significantly more time than anticipated as other components in the system inevitably, and sometimes very quickly, started depending on small differences between the workarounds and the proper implementation. Also, while the time required to implement a system can be significantly reduced by reusing existing components, these components are rarely a perfect fit and generally cannot provide the same level of performance as a bespoke component. For example, the observation that segment groups are sorted on both their start time and end time when sorted on one of them could not be exploited when RDBMSs and Apache Cassandra were used for storage as described in Sect. 7. As another example, the use of Apache Spark meant that even the initial version of ModelarDB [12] was scalable as it could process queries in parallel across multiple distributed nodes. However, as Apache Spark Executors by design are black boxes, it is not possible to optimize how they process queries, e.g., a local mutable cache or index cannot be created directly in the Apache Spark Executor. Also while implementing the Data Point View as an Apache Spark Data Source significantly reduced development time, Apache Spark's stable APIs only provided required columns and the predicates for each query. Thus, it was not possible to automatically rewrite queries to efficiently compute aggregates directly from the segments containing metadata and models. As a result, the Segment View was added as a workaround despite the increase in complexity for users of the system. The use of Apache Spark also meant that ModelarDB would be implemented on top of the JVM, thus reducing both development time and performance compared to native code. For example, the authors of the Java-based data analytics engine MacroBase found that its throughput was on average 12.76x lower than hand-optimized C++ [1]. IBM also replaced Apache Spark with the Db2 BLU column-based query engine [25] in Db2 Event Store as Apache Spark could not handle low latency queries [8].

Modularity Adds Complexity and Limits Optimizations: Early it was decided that ModelarDB should use an highly extensible and modular architecture to facilitate experimentation with different model types, query engines, and data stores. While this provided a lot of flexibility, it also significantly increased the complexity and development time of the system. For example, to integrate two types of components, either specialized methods had to be implemented for each combination or a shared intermediate format had to be created. To integrate the query engines and data stores we chose the first option by implementing both `H2Storage` and `SparkStorage` for all data stores, as described in Sect. 7, due to the additional overhead converting to and from an intermediate representation would add. The use of a modular architecture also meant that significantly more testing was required to ensure all combinations of the different components worked as intended. In addition to increasing complexity and development time, ModelarDB's extensibility also limited which optimizations could be implemented. For example, ModelarDB's API for adding user-defined model types is designed to be as flexible as possible such that users can implement the compression methods and use the definition of error that is most suitable for their domain. Thus, ModelarDB cannot make any assumptions about these model types. However, the flexibility, unfortunately, proved to not be beneficial for users. From the feedback we received it is very clear that users generally prefer systems that work well enough "out of the box" instead of systems they can fine-tune specifically for their use case. Surprisingly, this was even the case for users with a strong background in computer science, e.g., users with a master's or PhD degree. So while ModelarDB's flexibility made it easy to add support for multiple model types, query engines, and data stores, it was not only a benefit as it also added a significant amount of complexity, significantly increased development time, and made some optimizations impossible to implement. Failing to dynamically load dependencies at run-time also caused run-time errors that were incomprehensible for most users, e.g., when deploying ModelarDB to an unsupported version of Apache Spark or when a JDBC driver was missing.

Code Generation Enables Optimizations but Generally Trades Latency for Throughput and Adds Complexity: To improve the performance of ModelarDB, specialized Scala code was generated through both static [12] and dynamic [14] code generation. This enabled additional optimizations, e.g., removal of branches from projections by generating a specialized method for each permutation of columns in a schema. However, while improving performance, the use of code generation also had multiple downsides. For static code generation, some of the generated methods had to be arbitrarily split into multiple methods as the Java Virtual Machine Specification requires each method to be less than 64 KiB [18]. In addition, due to the amount of code initially generated through static code generation, e.g., we initially generated a specialized method for each permutation of columns in the Segment View, the time required to compile ModelarDB significantly increased. This significantly discouraged experimentation. To remedy this problem, a specialized projection method was only generated for the most commonly used permutations of columns in the Segment View, e.g., those required for the UDFs and UDAFs described in Sect. 6. If another permutation of columns is received, a fallback method implemented using branches or dynamic code generation is used. For dynamic code generation, the main drawback was the significant amount of time required at runtime to compile the Scala code as described in Sect. 6. Thus, it proved more efficient to not use dynamic code generation in some cases, e.g., when evaluating queries that only need to process a small amount of data when using Apache Spark. To determine when to use dynamic code generation in this situation, ModelarDB uses the number of partitions in the Apache Spark RDD representing the data to be processed as a heuristic. Other techniques have been proposed for solving this problem, such as using multiple query execution methods and then only compiling the query if it would improve query execution time based on the estimated time remaining and directly generating x86_64 machine code to reduce compilation time [22].

Dynamic code generation is always used for H2, as the compiled code can be cached much more easily when ModelarDB is running on a single node. Dynamic code generation and compilation also significantly increased the amount of testing required as we had to ensure that the correct code was generated.

Pull-Based Data Ingestion Improves Performance but Increases Complexity: ModelarDB uses pull-based ingestion to read data points from sources such as files or sockets. While this removes the need for an external process that converts from the source representation to a representation ModelarDB supports, thus improving performance and theoretically reducing complexity, it has a number of downsides. For example, it limits the number of data formats ModelarDB can support as support for a new data format has to be implemented in the system itself. Also, pull-based data ingestion requires a mechanism for adding new sources to pull data points from to ModelarDB or for ModelarDB to automatically detect new sources to pull data points from. This significantly increases the complexity of the system compared to push-based data ingestion as it only requires that ModelarDB provides an endpoint that clients can push a single data format to. As a result, the current version of ModelarDB requires that the sources to ingest data points from are added to its configuration file, and the system must be restarted whenever a new source is added. Similarly, Google changed Monarch's data ingestion from pull-based to push-based as the infrastructure needed for Monarch to discover the entities to pull data points from made the system's architecture more complex and limited its scalability [2].

10   Related Work

As the amount of time series data increases, many TSMSs have been proposed. Surveys of TSMSs developed through academic and industrial research can be found in [10,11] and a survey of open-source TSMSs can be found in [4].

10.1   Querying Compressed Time Series

Several TSMSs have been proposed that can execute different types of queries directly on compressed time series. FunctionDB [27] supports fitting polynomial functions to data points and evaluating queries directly on the polynomial functions. Plato [15] supports fitting different types of models to data points and supports user-defined model types. Plato evaluates queries directly on the models if the necessary functions are implemented, otherwise, queries are evaluated on data points reconstructed from the models. Plato was extended to provide deterministic error guarantees for some types of queries [19]. Tristan [21] is a TSMS based on the MiSTRAL architecture [20]. It compresses time series using dictionary compression and can execute queries on this compressed representation. Tristan's compression method was later extended to take correlation into account [16]. SummaryStore [3] splits time series into segments, compresses each segment using different compression methods, and then uses the most appropriate representation when answering queries. Over time the segments are combined, this reduces the amount of storage required but can increase the error of the representations. Compared to FunctionDB [27] and Tristan [16,20,21], ModelarDB compresses each time series group using multiple different model types. Also, ModelarDB can run distributed unlike Plato [15,19] and SummaryStore [3].

10.2 Data Transfer

Unlike ModelarDB, most TSMSs are designed for deployment on either the edge or in the cloud and do not support transferring ingested data points to the cloud. However, a few exceptions do exist. Respawn [5] is designed to be deployed on both edge nodes and cloud nodes. Queries are submitted to a Dispatcher that redirects the clients to the appropriate nodes. To reduce latency, Respawn continuously migrates data points from the edge nodes to the cloud nodes. Storacle [6] was designed for monitoring smart grids and it periodically transfers data points to the cloud. The most recent data points are not immediately deleted after being transferred so they can still be accessed on the edge nodes with low latency. Apache IoTDB [28] is designed to be used as an embedded TSMS, a standalone TSMS, or a distributed TSMS depending on the available hardware. Apache IoTDB uses the novel column-based TsFile file format for storage, which is similar to Apache Parquet. It also supports transferring TsFiles using a File Sync component. Compared to Respawn [5], Storacle [6], and Apache IoTDB [28], ModelarDB supports both lossless and lossy compression of time series groups, automatic selection of the type of model that provides the best compression ratio for each dynamically sized sub-sequence, and it exploits that the time series are stored as models to much more efficiently answer aggregate queries.

11 Conclusion and Future Work

Motivated by the need to efficiently manage high-frequency time series from sensors across the edge and the cloud, we presented the following: (i) an overview of the open-source model-based TSMS ModelarDB, (ii) an analysis of the requirements and limitations of the edge, (iii) an evaluation of existing query engines and data stores for use on the edge, (iv) extensions for ModelarDB to efficiently manage time series on the edge, (v) a file-based data store, (vi) a method for not storing time series that can be derived from base time series, (vii) extensions for ModelarDB to transfer high-frequency time series from the edge to the cloud, and (viii) reflections on the lessons learned while developing ModelarDB.

In future work, we plan to simplify the use of ModelarDB and increase its performance by: (i) replacing pull-based data ingestion with push-based data ingestion; (ii) dynamically combining similar models within the error bound instead of statically grouping time series; (iii) support ingestion and querying of irregular multivariate time series; (iv) replace the Segment View with a query optimizer; (v) develop novel pruning techniques that exploit that the time series are stored as models; (vi) perform high-level analytics, e.g., similarity search, directly on the models. These items are already under active development as we are rewriting ModelarDB in Rust using Apache Arrow, Apache Arrow Data-Fusion, Apache Arrow Flight, and Apache Parquet. The rewrite is being done as an open-source project at https://github.com/ModelarData/ModelarDB-RS and the source code is licensed under version 2.0 of the Apache License.

Acknowledgements. This research was supported by the MORE project funded by Horizon 2020 grant number 957345. We also thank our industry partners for providing detailed information about their domain and access to real-life data.

References

1. Abuzaid, F., et al.: MacroBase: prioritizing attention in fast data. ACM Trans. Database Syst. **43**(4), 1–45 (2018). https://doi.org/10.1145/3276463
2. Adams, C., et al.: Monarch: Google's planet-scale in-memory time series database. Proc. VLDB Endow. **13**(12), 3181–3194 (2020). https://doi.org/10.14778/3181-3194
3. Agrawal, N., Vulimiri, A.: Low-latency analytics on colossal data streams with SummaryStore. In: Proceedings 26th ACM Symposium on Operating System Principles, pp. 647–664. ACM (2017). https://doi.org/10.1145/3132747.3132758
4. Bader, A., Kopp, O., Michael, F.: Survey and comparison of open source time series databases. In: Datenbanksysteme für Business, Technologie und Web - Workshopband, pp. 249–268. GI (2017)
5. Buevich, M., Wright, A., Sargent, R., Rowe, A.: Respawn: a distributed multi-resolution time-series datastore. In: Proceedings of IEEE 34th Real-Time Systems Symposium, pp. 288–297. IEEE (2013). https://doi.org/10.1109/RTSS.2013.36
6. Cejka, S., Mosshammer, R., Einfalt, A.: Java embedded storage for time series and meta data in smart grids. In: 2015 IEEE International Conference on Smart Grid Communications, pp. 434–439. IEEE (2015). https://doi.org/10.1109/SmartGridComm.2015.7436339
7. Elmeleegy, H., Elmagarmid, A.K., Cecchet, E., Aref, W.G., Zwaenepoel, W.: Online piece-wise linear approximation of numerical streams with precision guarantees. Proc. VLDB Endow. **2**(1), 145–156 (2009). https://doi.org/10.14778/1687627.1687645
8. Garcia-Arellano, C., et al.: DB2 event store: a purpose-built IoT database engine. Proc. VLDB Endow. **13**(12), 3299–3312 (2020). https://doi.org/10.14778/3415478.3415552
9. Hung, N.Q.V., Jeung, H., Aberer, K.: An evaluation of model-based approaches to sensor data compression. IEEE Trans. Knowl. Data Eng. **25**(11), 2434–2447 (2013). https://doi.org/10.1109/TKDE.2012.237
10. Jensen, S.K., Pedersen, T.B., Thomsen, C.: Time series management systems: a 2022 survey. In: Palpanas, T., Zoumpatianos, K. (eds.) Data Series Management and Analytics. ACM (forthcoming)

11. Jensen, S.K., Pedersen, T.B., Thomsen, C.: Time series management systems: a survey. IEEE Trans. Knowl. Data Eng. **29**(11), 2581–2600 (2017). https://doi.org/10.1109/TKDE.2017.2740932

12. Jensen, S.K., Pedersen, T.B., Thomsen, C.: ModelarDB: modular model-based time series management with spark and cassandra. Proc. VLDB Endow. **11**(11), 1688–1701 (2018). https://doi.org/10.14778/3236187.3236215

13. Jensen, S.K., Pedersen, T.B., Thomsen, C.: Demonstration of ModelarDB: model-based management of dimensional time series. In: Proceedings of ACM SIGMOD International Conference on Management of Data, pp. 1933–1936. ACM (2019). https://doi.org/10.1145/3299869.3320216

14. Jensen, S.K., Pedersen, T.B., Thomsen, C.: Scalable model-based management of correlated dimensional time series in ModelarDB$_+$. In: Proceedings of 37th International Conference on Data Engineering, pp. 1380–1391. IEEE (2021). https://doi.org/10.1109/ICDE51399.2021.00123

15. Katsis, Y., Freund, Y., Papakonstantinou, Y.: Combining databases and signal processing in Plato. In: Proceedings of 7th Biennial Conference on Innovative Data Systems Research, pp. 1–9 (2015)

16. Khelifati, A., Khayati, M., Cudré-Mauroux, P.: CORAD: correlation-aware compression of massive time series using sparse dictionary coding. In: Proceedings of 2019 IEEE International Conference on Big Data, pp. 2289–2298. IEEE (2019). https://doi.org/10.1109/BigData47090.2019.9005580

17. Lazaridis, I., Mehrotra, S.: Capturing sensor-generated time series with quality guarantees. In: Proceedings of 19th International Conference on Data Engineering, pp. 429–440. IEEE (2003). https://doi.org/10.1109/ICDE.2003.1260811

18. Limitations of the Java Virtual Machine. https://docs.oracle.com/javase/specs/jvms/se11/html/jvms-4.html#jvms-4.11

19. Lin, C., Boursier, E., Papakonstantinou, Y.: Plato: approximate analytics system over compressed time series with tight deterministic error guarantees. Proc. VLDB Endow. **13**(7), 1105–1118 (2020). https://doi.org/10.14778/3384345.3384357

20. Marascu, A., et al.: MiSTRAL: an architecture for low-latency analytics on massive time series. In: Proceedings of 2013 IEEE International Conference on Big Data, pp. 15–21. IEEE (2013). https://doi.org/10.1109/BigData.2013.6691772

21. Marascu, A., et al.: TRISTAN: real-time analytics on massive time series using sparse dictionary compression. In: Proceedings of 2014 IEEE International Conference on Big Data, pp. 291–300. IEEE (2014). https://doi.org/10.1109/BigData.2014.7004244

22. Neumann, T.: Evolution of a compiling query engine. Proc. VLDB Endow. **14**(12), 3207–3210 (2021). https://doi.org/10.14778/3476311.3476410

23. Package java.lang.ref. https://docs.oracle.com/en/java/javase/11/docs/api/java.base/java/lang/ref/package-summary.html

24. Pelkonen, T., et al.: Gorilla: a fast, scalable, in-memory time series database. Proc. VLDB Endow. **8**(12), 1816–1827 (2015). https://doi.org/10.14778/2824032.2824078

25. Raman, V., et al.: DB2 with BLU acceleration: so much more than just a column store. Proc. VLDB Endow. **6**(11), 1080–1091 (2013). https://doi.org/10.14778/2536222.2536233

26. Sathe, S., Papaioannou, T.G., Jeung, H., Aberer, K.: A survey of model-based sensor data acquisition and management. In: Aggarwal, C.C. (ed.) Managing and Mining Sensor Data, pp. 9–50. Springer, Boston (2013). https://doi.org/10.1007/978-1-4614-6309-2_2

27. Thiagarajan, A., Madden, S.: Querying continuous functions in a database system. In: Proceedings of ACM SIGMOD International Conference on Management of Data, pp. 791–804 (2008). https://doi.org/10.1145/1376616.1376696

28. Wang, C., et al.: Apache IoTDB: time-series database for internet of things. Proc. VLDB Endow. **13**(12), 2901–2904 (2020). https://doi.org/10.14778/3415478.3415504

Variable-Size Segmentation for Time Series Representation

Lamia Djebour[(✉)], Reza Akbarinia, and Florent Masseglia

Inria, University of Montpellier, CNRS, LIRMM, Montpellier, France
{lamia.djebour,reza.akbarinia,florent.masseglia}@inria.fr

Abstract. Given the high data volumes in time series applications, or simply the need for fast response times, it is usually necessary to rely on alternative, shorter representations of time series, usually with information loss. This incurs approximate comparisons of time series where precision is a major issue. We propose a new representation approach called ASAX, coming with two techniques ASAX_EN and ASAX_SAE, for segmenting time series before their transformation into symbolic representations. Our solution can reduce significantly the error incurred by possible splittings at different steps of the representation calculation, by taking into account the entropy of the representations (ASAX_EN) or the sum of absolute errors (ASAX_SAE), particularly for datasets with unbalanced (non-uniform) distributions. This is particularly useful for time series similarity search, which is the core of many data analytics tasks. We provide theoretical guarantees on the lower bound of similarity measures, and our experiments illustrate that our approach can improve significantly the time series representation quality.

Keywords: Time series · SAX · Representation · Segmentation · Similarity search · Information retrieval

1 Introduction

Many applications in different domains generate time series data at an increasing rate. That continuous flow of emitted data may concern personal activities (*e.g.*, through smart-meters or smart-plugs for electricity or water consumption) or professional activities (*e.g.*, for monitoring heart activity or through the sensors installed on plants by farmers). This results in the production of large and complex data, usually in the form of time series that challenges knowledge discovery [10,11,15,17,19–22,24,27]. Data mining techniques on such massive sets of time series have drawn a lot of interest since their application may lead to improvements in a large number of these activities, relying on fast and accurate similarity search in time series for performing tasks like, *e.g.*, Classification, Clustering, and Motifs Discovery [16,20,30].

As a consequence of the high data volumes in such applications, similarity search can be slow on raw data. One of the issues that hinder the analysis

© Springer-Verlag GmbH Germany, part of Springer Nature 2023
A. Hameurlain and A. M. Tjoa (Eds.): TLDKS LIII, LNCS 13840, pp. 34–65, 2023.
https://doi.org/10.1007/978-3-662-66863-4_2

of such data is the dimensionality. This is why time series approximation is often used as a means to allow fast similarity search. SAX (Symbolic Aggregate ApproXimation) [13] is one of the most popular time series representations, allowing dimensionality reduction on the classic data mining tasks. SAX constructs symbolic representations by splitting the time domain into segments of equal size where the mean values of segments represent the time series intervals. This approximation technique is effective for time series having a uniform and balanced distribution over the time domain. However, we observe that, in the case of time series having high variation over given time intervals, this division into segments of fixed length is not efficient.

To illustrate the impact of a fixed length division of the series into segments, let us consider Fig. 1. It shows a set D of time series, taken from *ECGFiveDays* dataset of UCR Archive [6]. In this dataset, the time series length is 136 and the data distribution in the time domain is unbalanced. We can notice that there is almost no variation from time point 1 to 45 and from 95 to the end. On the other hand, the remaining part, from time point 45 to 95, shows an important variation in the data values. Figure 1b shows the SAX division on D, with a fixed-size segmentation on the time series. In this example, the segment size is 10, leading to 13 segments in total. If we take any time series X from D and convert it into its SAX representation, the first 4 segments are always represented by the same symbol, all the values of these 4 segments being close to each other. Actually, there is no need to consider these 4 distinct segments. And the same applies to the last 3 segments. Meanwhile, for segments 5–10, all the values of each segment are represented by a single symbol while the data values present great variations, causing a significant loss of information on these segments.

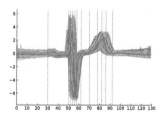 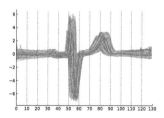

(a) ASAX_SAE segmentation on D, with 13 segments.

(b) SAX segmentation on D, with 13 segments

Fig. 1. ASAX_SAE segmentation vs. SAX segmentation

As one can observe, it is not necessary to split the parts that are constant or where the variation is low since they don't carry any relevant information and would therefore better form a single segment. It is more efficient to divide into several small segments the parts where variation is important in order to preserve potentially relevant information as shown in Fig. 1a. The splitting of Fig. 1a is the actual splitting obtained by our variable-size segmentation approach using our ASAX_SAE technique (based on the representations's sum of absolute errors) with a segment budget limited to 13. It would be rather counter-intuitive to merge segments 1–5 and 10–13, while it is the opposite for Fig. 1b. But, the time intervals where data values show important differences should be split to create more segments, *e.g.*, between time point 50 and 90. By proposing such a customized splitting, we aim at improving the performance of information retrieval algorithms that will rely on our data representation. As illustrated by our experiments, the precision gain of ASAX_SAE compared to SAX for kNN search is 38% over the dataset of Fig. 1 (*i.e.*, *ECGFiveDays* dataset).

Our main contribution is to provide an adaptive interval distribution, rather than an equal distribution in time. However, the number of possible segmentations of k segments with n can be very high. Furthermore, when searching for the best variable-size segmentation, a large number of computation may be repeated. Therefore, it is important to efficiently carry out the computations involved. We propose an new time series representation approach, called *ASAX*, that by smart selection of variable-size segments from the time domain allows to significantly reduce the information loss in the time series representation. To perform the variable-size segmentation in ASAX, we propose two different techniques *ASAX_EN* and *ASAX_SAE*. Briefly, we make the following contributions in this paper:

- We propose two new representation techniques, called ASAX_EN (based on the entropy) and ASAX_SAE (based on SAE the Sum of Absolute Errors), that allow obtaining a variable-size segmentation of time series with better precision in retrieval tasks thanks to the lower information loss.
- We propose a lower bounding method that allows approximating the distance between the original time series based on their representations in ASAX.
- We propose an efficient algorithm, called ASAX_DP, for improving the execution time of our segmentation approach, by means of dynamic programming.
- We implemented our solution and conducted empirical experiments using several real world datasets. The results illustrate that it can obtain significant performance gains in terms of precision for similarity search compared to SAX, particularly for datasets with non-uniform distributions. They suggest that the more the data distribution in the time domain is unbalanced (non-uniform), the greater is the precision gain of our approach. For example, for the *ECGFiveDays* dataset that has a non-uniform distribution in the time domain, the precision of ASAX_SAE is 93% and 82% for ASAX_EN compared to 55% for SAX. Furthermore, the results illustrate the effectiveness of our dynamic programming algorithm ASAX_DP, *e.g.*, up to ×40 faster than the basic algorithm over some datasets.

This article is an extension of [7], with at least 30% of added value. Particularly, in Sect. 5, we propose ASAX_SAE, that is a variable-size segmentation algorithm based on SAE measurement. The execution time of ASAX_SAE is lower than that of previously proposed ASAX_EN, and its precision is often better. Furthermore, in Sect. 6, we propose a dynamic programming solution, called ASAX_DP, which significantly improves the execution time of ASAX_SAE. In addition, in Sect. 8, we report new experimental results done for evaluating the performance of ASAX_SAE and ASAX_DP.

The rest of the paper is organized as follows. In Sect. 2, we define the problem we address. We discuss the related work in Sect. 3. In Sect. 4, we propose ASAX_EN for efficient segmentation of time seires, and in Sect. 5, we propose ASAX_SAE. In Section, 6 we propose ASAX_DP, the dynamic programming version of ASAX_SAE. In Sect. 7 we present a formula for approximating the Euclidean distance of time series based on their representation given by ASAX_EN or ASAX_SAE. In Sect. 8, we present the experimental evaluation of our approaches, and we conclude in Sect. 9.

2   Problem Definition and Background

In this section, we first present the background about SAX representation, and then define the problem we address.

Table 1. Some frequently used symbols

D	Time series database
X, Y, Q	Time series
$n = |X|$	The length of time series X
l	The segment size
w	The number of PAA segments
a	The cardinality (the alphabet size)
$\overline{X}$	The PAA representation of time series X
$\hat{X}$	The SAX representation of time series X
k	The k nearest neighbors

A time series X is a sequence of values $X = \{x_1, ..., x_n\}$. We assume that every time series has a value at every timestamp $t = 1, 2, ..., n$. Thus, all time series in a database have the same length. The length of X is denoted by $|X|$.

SAX allows a time series T of length n to be reduced to a string of arbitrary length w. Table 1 lists the notations used in this paper.

2.1   SAX Representation

Given two time series $X = \{x_1, ..., x_n\}$ and $Y = \{y_1, ..., y_n\}$, the Euclidean distance between X and Y is defined as [9]:

$$ED(X, Y) = \sqrt{\sum_{i=1}^{n} (x_i - y_i)^2}$$

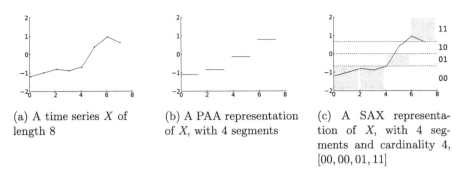

(a) A time series X of length 8

(b) A PAA representation of X, with 4 segments

(c) A SAX representation of X, with 4 segments and cardinality 4, $[00, 00, 01, 11]$

Fig. 2. A time series X is discretized by obtaining a PAA representation and then using predetermined break-points to map the PAA coefficients into SAX symbols. Here, the symbols are given in binary notation, where 00 is the first symbol, 01 is the second symbol, etc. The time series of Fig. 2a in the representation of Fig. 2c is [first, first, second, fourth] (which becomes $[00, 00, 01, 11]$ in binary).

The Euclidean distance is one of the most popular similarity measurement methods used in time series analysis.

The Symbolic Aggregate ApproXimation (SAX) is based on the Piecewise Aggregate Approximation (PAA) [13] which allows for dimensionality reduction while providing the important lower bounding property as we will show later. The idea of PAA is to have a fixed segment size, and minimize dimensionality by using the mean values on each segment. Example 1 gives an illustration of PAA.

Example 1. Figure 2b shows the PAA representation of X, the time series of Fig. 2a. The representation is composed of $w = |X|/l$ values, where l is the segment size. For each segment, the set of values is replaced with their mean represented in the figure with solid horizontal lines. The length of the final representation w is the number of segments (and, usually, $w << |X|$).

By transforming the original time series X and Y into PAA representations $\overline{X} = \{\overline{x}_1, ..., \overline{x}_w\}$ and $\overline{Y} = \{\overline{y}_1, ..., \overline{y}_w\}$, the lower bounding approximation of the Euclidean distance for these two representations can be obtained by:

$$DR_f(\overline{X}, \overline{Y}) = \sqrt{\frac{n}{w}} \sqrt{\sum_{i=1}^{w} (\overline{x}_i - \overline{y}_i)^2}$$

The SAX representation takes as input the reduced time series obtained using PAA. It discretizes this representation into a predefined set of symbols, with a given cardinality, where a symbol is a binary number. Example 2 gives an illustration of the SAX representation.

Example 2. In Fig. 2c, we have converted the time series X to SAX representation with size 4, and cardinality 4 using the PAA representation shown in Fig. 2b. The discretization is achieved by considering a series of breakpoints running parallel to the x-axis represented in the figure with dashed horizontal lines for each segment depending on the PAA coefficient an alphabet symbol is mapped to that segment based on the breakpoints interval it falls in. We denote $SAX(X) = [00, 00, 01, 11]$.

The lower bounding approximation of the Euclidean distance for SAX representation $\hat{X} = \{\hat{x}_1, ..., \hat{x}_w\}$ and $\hat{Y} = \{\hat{y}_1, ..., \hat{y}_w\}$ of two time series X and Y is defined as:

$$MINDIST_f(\hat{X}, \hat{Y}) = \sqrt{\frac{n}{w}} \sqrt{\sum_{i=1}^{w} (dist(\hat{x}_i, \hat{y}_i))^2}$$

where the function $dist(\hat{x}_i, \hat{y}_i)$ is the distance between two SAX symbols $\hat{x}_i$ and $\hat{x}_i$. The lower bounding condition is formulated as:

$$MINDIST_f(\hat{X}, \hat{Y}) \leq ED(X, Y)$$

2.2 Similarity Queries

The problem of similarity queries is one of the main problems in time series analysis and mining. In information retrieval, finding the k nearest neighbors (k-NN) of a query is a fundamental problem. Let us define *exact* and *approximate* k nearest neighbors.

Definition 1 (EXACT k NEAREST NEIGHBORS). *Given a query time series Q and a set of time series D, let $R = ExactkNN(Q, D)$ be the set of k nearest neighbors of Q from D. Let $ED(X, Y)$ be the Euclidean distance between two time series X and Y, then the set R is defined as follows:*
$$(R \subseteq D) \wedge (|R| = k) \wedge (\forall a \in R, \forall b \in (D - R), ED(a, Q) \leq ED(b, Q))$$

Definition 2 (APPROXIMATE k NEAREST NEIGHBORS). *Given a set of time series D, a query time series Q, and $\epsilon > 0$. We say that $R = AppkNN(Q, D)$ is the approximate k nearest neighbors of Q from D, if $ED(a, Q) \leq (1+\epsilon)ED(b, Q)$, where a is the kth nearest neighbor from R and b is the true k^{th} nearest neighbor.*

2.3 Time Series Approximation

The SAX representation proceeds to an approximation by minimizing the dimensionality: the original time series are divided into segments of equal size.

This representation does not depend on the time series values, but on their length. It allows SAX to perform the segmentation in $O(n)$ where n is the time series length. However, for a given reduction in dimensionality, the modeling error may not be minimal since the model does not adapt to the information carried by the series. Our claim is that, by taking into account the information carried by time series for choosing the segments, we may obtain significant increase in the precision of kNN queries. This issue motivated us for proposing an adaptive representation aiming at minimizing the information loss.

2.4   Problem Statement

Our goal is to propose a variable-size segmentation of the time domain that minimizes the loss of information in the time series representation.

The problem we address is stated as follows. Given a database of time series D and a number w, divide the time domain into w segments of variable size such that the representation of the times series based on that segmentation lowers the error of similarity queries.

3   Related Work

Several techniques have been yet proposed to reduce the dimensionality of time series. Examples of such techniques that can significantly decrease the time and space required for similarity search are: singular value decomposition (SVD) [9], the discrete Fourier transformation (DFT) [1], discrete wavelets transformation (DWT) [4], piecewise aggregate approximation (PAA) [12], random sketches [5], Adaptive Piecewise Constant Approximation (APCA) [3], and symbolic aggregate approXimation (SAX) [14].

SAX [14] is one of the most popular techniques for time series representation. It uses a symbolic representation that segments all time series into equi-length segments and symbolizes the mean value of each segment. Some extensions of SAX have been proposed for improving the similarity search performance via indexing [2,23]. For example, iSAX [23] is an indexable version of SAX designed for indexing large collections of time series. iSAX 2.0 [2] proposes a new mechanism and also algorithms for efficient bulk loading and node splitting policy, which is not supported by iSAX index. In [2], two extensions of iSAX 2.0, namely iSAX 2.0 Clustered and iSAX2+, have been proposed. These extensions focus on the efficient handling of the raw time series data during the bulk loading process, by using a technique that uses main memory buffers to group and route similar time series together down the tree, performing the insertion in a lazy manner.

There have been SAX extensions designed to improve the representation of each segment, while using the SAX fixed-size segmentation, e.g., [18,25,29]. For example, SAX_TD improves the representation of each segment by taking into account the trend of the time series. It uses the values at the starting and ending points of the segments to measure the trend. TFSA [28] and SAX_CP [26] are other trend-based SAX representation methods. TFSA proposes a representation method for long time series based on the trend, and SAX_CP considers abrupt change points while generating the symbols in order to capture time series' trends.

ABBA [8] is a symbolic representation of time series based on an adaptive polygonal chain approximation of the time series into a sequence of tuples, followed by a mean-based clustering to obtain the symbolic representation. However, the authors of ABBA have not proposed an approximate function for comparing the time series in their representation form, and this prevents ABBA from being used for kNN search over the representations.

To increase the quality of time series approximation, our ASAX approach is based on variable-length segmentation. ASAX is complementary to the existing SAX extensions, *e.g.*, indexing based techniques or those that use the trend for representing the segments. This makes our variable-size segmentation an advantageous alternative for segmenting the time domain in indexing solutions like iSAX.

4   Adaptive SAX Based on Entropy

In this section, we propose ASAX_EN, our first variable-size segmentation technique for the time series representation. To create a segmentation with minimum information loss, ASAX_EN divides the time domain based on the representation entropy.

In the rest of this section, we first describe the notion of entropy for the time series representation. Then, we describe our algorithm for creating the variable-size segments based on this measurement.

4.1   Entropy

Entropy is a mathematical function which intuitively corresponds to the amount of information contained or delivered by a source of information. This source of information can be of various types. The more the source emits different information the higher is the entropy. If the source always sends the same information, the entropy is minimal. Formally, entropy is defined as follows.

Definition 3. *Given a set X of elements, and each element $x \in X$ having a probability P_x of occurrence, the entropy H of the set X is defined as:* $H(X) = -\sum_{x \in X} P_x \times \log P_x$

In our context, we calculate the entropy on a set containing the different symbolic representations obtained from the transformation of the original time series of a dataset according to a given segmentation. The entropy computed on this set allows to measure the quantity of information contained in the time series representations. Let us illustrate this using an example.

Example 3. Consider the database $D=\{x,y,z\}$ in Fig. 3 where x, y and z are time series with $l=8$. Let us create a representation having two segments (e.g., 0–4, and 4–8) obtained by dividing the time domain into two segments of the same size (the split is represented with the red dashed line). Then we compute the entropy of the representation of the set D. To generate the representation of the time series x, y and z, they are discretized by obtaining their PAA representation and then using predetermined break-points to map the PAA coefficients into the corresponding symbols like the SAX representation proceeds. We have converted the 3 time series into symbolic representations with size 2, and cardinality 4. Thus, the symbolic representations of x, y and z are $\hat{x} = [00, 10]$, $\hat{y} = [00, 10]$ and $\hat{z} = [00, 10]$, respectively. We notice that the 3 time series have the same symbolic representation, thus, the set X consists of only this unique symbolic representation with an occurrence equal to 3., $i.e.$, $X = \{[00, 10]\}$. The entropy $H(X)$ of X is computed as follows:

$$H(X) = -(P(x = [00, 10]) \times \log_2 P(x = [00, 10]))$$

where the probability for the word x is $P(x = [00, 10]) = \frac{3}{3} = 1$. Therefore, we have $H(X) = -(1 \log 1) = 0$ meaning that in the representation X there is no information allowing to distinguish the three original time series from each other. This is explained by the fact that they have the same representation with a fixed-size segmentation.

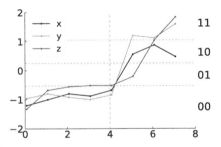

Fig. 3. ASAX_EN segmentation with 2 segments

In the next subsection, we describe our algorithm to create variable-size segments based on entropy.

4.2   Variable-Size Segmentation Based on Entropy Measurement

Given a database of time series D, and a number w, our goal is to find the k variable size segments that minimize the loss of information in time series representations.

Intuitively, our algorithm works as follows. First it splits the time domain into two segments of equal size. Then, it performs $w - 2$ iterations, and in each iteration it finds the segment s whose split makes the minimum loss in entropy, and it splits that segment. By doing this, in each iteration a new segment is added to the set of segments. This continues until having w segments.

Let us now describe ASAX_EN in more details. The pseudo-code is shown in Algorithm 1. It first splits the time domain into two equal parts and creates two segments that are included to the set *segments* (Line 1). Then, it sets the current number of segments, denoted as k, to 2 (Line 2).

Afterwards, in a loop, until the number of segments is less than w the algorithm proceeds as follows. For each segment i (from 1 to k), i is divided into two equal parts, if its size is greater than $minSize$, which is the minimum possible size of a segment, and it's default value is 1. Then, a temporary set of segments *tempSegments* is created including the two new segments and all previously created segments except i (i.e., expect the one that has been divided). Then, for each time series ts in the database D, the algorithm generates the symbolic representation of ts (denoted as *word*) using the segments included in *tempSegments* with the given cardinality a (Line 12), and inserts it to a hash table (Line 13). Note that for all time series, ASAX_EN uses the same cardinality to map the PAA coefficients into the corresponding symbols. After having inserted all the representations of the time series contained in D to the hash table, the entropy of the representations is calculated (Line 14). If the entropy is higher than the maximum entropy obtained until now, the algorithm sets i as the segment to be split, and keeps the entropy of the representation. This procedure continues by splitting one of the segments at each time, and computing the entropy. The algorithm selects the one whose entropy is the highest, and updates the set of the segments by removing the selected segment, and inserting its splits to the set *segments* (Lines 18–20). Then, the variable k, which shows the number of current segments, is incremented by one. The algorithm ends if the number of segments is equal to the required number, *i.e.*, w.

Example 4. Let us consider the dataset D in Fig. 3 which represents the initialization of the algorithm, i.e., the time domain is divided into two segments of the same size. The next step is to create the 3rd segment by splitting one of the two existing segments. Two different scenarios are possible.

Scenario 1: The first scenario is shown in Fig. 4a where the left segment is divided into two equal parts. We generate the symbolic representation of the time series x, y, and z by using the 3 segments. Let's assume the cardinality is 4. Then, $\hat{x} = [00, 00, 10]$, $\hat{y} = [00, 00, 10]$ and $\hat{z} = [00, 00, 10]$ are the symbolic representation of x, y and z, respectively. Thus, the set X_1 consists of only one representation *[00,00,10]* with an occurrence of 3, *i.e.*, $X_1 = [00, 00, 10]$. The entropy is then calculated as: $H(X_1) = -(P(x = [00, 00, 10]) \log P(x = [00, 00, 10]))$ where $P(x = [00, 00, 10]) = \frac{3}{3} = 1$ and we have $H(X_1) = -(1 \log 1) = 0$.

Scenario 2: This scenario is shown in Fig. 4b in which the right segment is split. As for Scenario 1 we generate the symbolic representation of time series x, y and z using the 3 segments, and cardinality of 4. $\hat{x} = [00, 01, 10]$, $\hat{y} = [00, 01, 11]$ and $\hat{z} = [00, 01, 11]$ are the symbolic representation of x, y and z, respectively. In this

---

Algorithm 1: ASAX_EN variable-size segmentation

Input: D: time series database; n: the length of time series; $minSize$: the minimum possible size of a segment; a: cardinality of symbols; w: the required number of segments

Output: w variable-size segments

1   $segments = \{[0, \frac{n}{2} - 1], [\frac{n}{2}, n - 1]\};$ // split time domain into two equal size segments

2   $k = 2$

3   **while** $k \neq w$ **do**

4      $segmentToSplit = 1$

5      $entropy = 0$

6   **for** $i=1$ to k **do**

7          $tempSegments = segments$

8   **if** $length(tempSegments[i]) > minSize$ **then**

9   split segment i into two equal parts, and replace the segment i by its corresponding parts in $tempSegments$

10            $hashtable = $ new HashTable

11   **foreach** $ts \in D$ **do**

12               $word = $ Symbolic-Representation(ts, $tempSegments$, a)

13               $hashTable$.put($word$)

14            $e = $ entropy($hashTable$)

15   **if** $e > entropy$ **then**

16               $segmentToSplit = i$

17               $entropy = e$

18   split $segmentToSplit$ into two equal size segments s_1 and s_2

19      $segments = segments$ - $\{segmentToSplit\}$

20      $segments = segments \bigcup \{s_1, s_2\}$

21      $k = k+1$

22 **return** $segments$

---

scenario the representation set X_2 consists of *[00,01,10]* with an occurrence of 1 and *[00,01,11]* with an occurrence of 2, *i.e.*, $X = [00, 01, 10], [00, 01, 10]$. The entropy is calculated as:

$$H(X_2) = -(P(x = [00, 01, 10]) \log P(x = [00, 01, 10])$$
$+P(x = [00, 01, 11]) \log P(x = [00, 01, 11]))$ where $P(x = [00, 01, 10]) = \frac{1}{3}$ and $P(x = [00, 01, 11]) = \frac{2}{3}$. Then, $H(X_2) = -(\frac{1}{3} \log \frac{1}{3} + \frac{2}{3} \log \frac{2}{3}) = 0.918$.

After having calculated the entropy for the two scenarios, we see that $H(X_1) < H(X_2)$. We aim to maximize the entropy, therefore we choose the segmentation generated in Scenario 2 for this iteration of our algorithm. We continue the next iterations, until the number of segment reaches w.

Let us now analyze the complexity of ASAX_EN algorithm. Let $|D|$ be the number of time series in the database, n the time series length, and w the desired

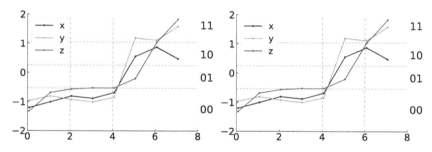

(a) Scenario 1 of ASAX_EN segmentation with 3 segments

(b) Scenario 2 of ASAX_EN segmentation with 3 segments

Fig. 4. The two different scenarios of ASAX_EN segmentation with 3 segments. Scenario 4b is the one chosen because it optimizes the entropy.

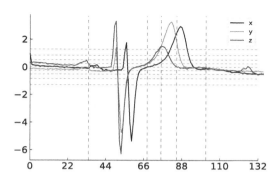

Fig. 5. The Gaussian based distribution of symbols in SAX are not suitable for ASAX_EN since they would favor minor information gain.

number of segments. In the *while* loop, the algorithm performs $w-2+1$ iterations, and in each iteration it tries the division of each segment and computes the entropy of the segmentation. Thus, in total the number of entropy computations is $O(w^2)$. For each entropy computation, the database should be scanned, and the representation of each time series created. This is done in $O(|D| \times n)$. Therefore, in total the time complexity of the algorithm is $O(|D| \times n \times w^2)$.

4.3 Uniform Distribution of Symbols

SAX breakpoints divide the value domain into regions of different size where small regions are concentrated on the middle of the value domain and regions at extreme values are larger. This is illustrated by Fig. 5, with three time series from our motivating example in Fig. 1 with 6 segments. The breakpoints of SAX with 10 symbols are represented by horizontal lines, and, logically, they appear close to the center of the distribution. If we keep such distribution of symbols, then we would have two issues. First, the extreme values of the series like those above 2 or below -4 would be assigned the same symbol (their PAA value on the segment would fall in the same symbol). Second, the adaptive segmentation would consider that the slight variations around zero are more important than the ones at extreme values, ending in irrelevant splits that favor minor information gain. For this reason, we propose to calculate the breakpoints differently. In ASAX_EN, the discretization is done based on breakpoints that produce uniform distributions of symbols. These breakpoints divide the value domain into regions of equal size. In the case of Fig. 5 the 10 symbol regions will be evenly distributed in the range of data values.

5   Adaptive SAX Based on SAE

In this section, we propose ASAX_SAE, our second variable-size segmentation approach for time series representation. Here, to create a segmentation with minimum information loss on time series approximation, ASAX_SAE divides the time domain by taking into account the *sum of absolute errors (SAE)* of the representation with a bottom-up strategy instead of a top-down strategy as used in the previous approach. Our experimental results have shown that this method is faster than ASAX_EN, and its precision is often better.

In the rest of this section, we first describe the notion of sum of absolute errors (SAE) for the time series representation, and then, we describe the algorithm that creates the variable-size segments based on SAE measurement.

5.1   Sum of Absolute Errors (SAE)

SAE (Sum of Absolute Errors) calculates the sum of the absolute difference between the actual and the estimated values. Formally, SAE is defined as follows.

Definition 4. *Given a vector X of n elements and a vector $\tilde{X}$ being the estimated values generated from X, SAE of the estimation is given by:*

$$SAE(X, \tilde{X}) = \sum_{i=1}^{n} |x_i - \tilde{x}_i|$$

In our context, we calculate the SAE on the PAA representation obtained from the transformation of the original time series of a dataset according to a given segmentation. The SAE computed on this representation allows to measure the approximation error on the time series by the PAA representation compared to the original time series. The lower the SAE, the closer is the PAA representation to the original data.

By transforming a time series $X = \{x_1, ..., x_n\}$ into a PAA representation $\overline{X} = \{\overline{x}_1, ..., \overline{x}_w\}$, X is reduced to the PAA representation composed of w segments. For each segment, the set of values is replaced with their mean. We can compute the SAE for each segment, that is in this case, the sum of the absolute differences between each value (original value) and its segment's mean (estimated value). In the following, we explain how to compute the SAE of a PAA representation for a given segmentation.

Let $\overline{X}$ be the PAA representation of X with w segments. The SAE of $\overline{X}$ for a particular segment is the sum of the absolute errors for the time series values in this segment. Formally, SAE of $\overline{X}$ for a segment s_i is computed as:

$$SAE(s_i, \overline{x}_i) = \sum_{j=LB(s_i)}^{UB(s_i)} |x_j - \overline{x}_i|$$

where s_i is the selected segment, $LB(s_i)$ and $UB(s_i)$ are the start and end time points of s_i respectively.

In the next subsection, we describe our algorithm that creates variable-size segments thereby providing an accurate representation of time series based on the SAE measurement.

5.2   Variable-Size Segmentation Based on SAE Measurement

Given a database of time series D, and a number w, our goal is to find the w variable size segments that minimize the loss of information in time series representations by minimizing the approximation error of these representations.

Intuitively, our algorithm works as follows. Based on a starting segment size value $size$, it firstly splits the time domain into segments of length $size$. The default value of $size$ is 2. Let k be the initial number of segments. The algorithm performs $k - w$ iterations, and in each iteration it finds the two adjacent segments s_i and s_{i+1} whose merging gives the minimum SAE (MSAE) on the representations, and merges them. By doing this, in each iteration the two selected segments are merged to form a single segment which replaces them in the set of segments, reducing the number of segments by one. This continues until having w segments.

Let us now describe our algorithm in more details. The pseudocode is shown in Algorithm 2. It first sets the current number of segments, denoted as k, to $\frac{n}{size}$ where n is the length of time series (Line 1). Then, it splits the time domain into k segments of length $size$ that are included to the set $segments$ (the set containing the current segmentation) (Line 2).

Afterwards, in a loop, until the number of segments is more than w the algorithm proceeds as follows. For each segment s_i (i from 1 to $k - 1$), s_i is merged with segment s_{i+1} to form a single segment denoted as s (Line 7). Then, for each time series ts in the database D, the algorithm generates its PAA representation on segment s and calculates the corresponding SAE and adds the result of the computed SAE to sae (Line 10).

After having calculated the sum of the SAE for the PAA representation of all the time series contained in D, if the SAE is less than the MSAE (minimum SAE) obtained so far, the algorithm sets i as the segment to be merged with the next one, and keeps the SAE of the representation (Lines 12, 13). This procedure

---

Algorithm 2: ASAX_SAE variable-size segmentation

Input: D: time series database; n: the length of time series; $size$: the starting size of segments; w: the required number of segments

Output: w variable-size segments

1 $k = \lceil \frac{n}{size} \rceil$

2 $segments = \{\bigcup_{i=0}^{k-1}[size \times i, size \times (i+1) - 1]\}$ // split time domain into k segments of size $size$

3 **while** $k \neq w$ **do**

4       $segmentsToMerge = null$

5       $msae = \infty$

6   **for** $i=1$ to $k-1$ **do**

7           $s = $ merge (s_i, s_{i+1})

8           $sae = 0$

9   **foreach** ts in D **do**

10              $sae = sae + SAE(ts, s)$

11   **if** $sae < msae$ **then**

12              $segmentsToMerge = i$

13              $msae = sae$

14      $s = $ merge $(s_{segmentsToMerge}, s_{segmentsToMerge+1})$

15      $segments = segments - \{s_{segmentsToMerge}, s_{segmentsToMerge+1}\}$

16      $segments = segments \bigcup s$

17      $k = k\text{-}1$

18 **return** $segments$

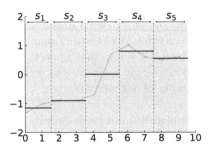

Fig. 6. The PAA representation of time series X contains 5 segments.

continues by trying the merging of every two adjacent segments of *segments* at each time, and computing the SAE. The algorithm selects the merging whose SAE is the lowest, and updates the set of the segments by removing the selected segments, and inserting its merging to *segments* (Lines 14–16). Then, the number of current segments (*i.e.*, k), is decremented by one (Line 17). The algorithm ends when k gets equal to the required number, *i.e.*, w.

    Let us illustrate the principle of our algorithm using an example. For simplicity, we consider a dataset containing only a single time series.

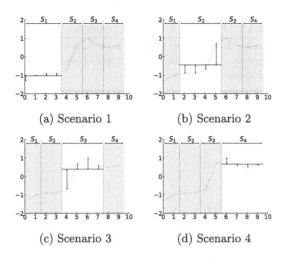

(a) Scenario 1   (b) Scenario 2

(c) Scenario 3   (d) Scenario 4

Fig. 7. The four different scenarios of ASAX_SAE segmentation with 4 segments. Scenario 1 is the one chosen because it provides the minimum SAE.

Example 5. Let us apply our algorithm on the time series X in Fig. 6 by taking the initial size of 2 for the starting segments. Notice that the PAA encoding is represented with black horizontal lines. The algorithm starts by dividing the time domain into 5 segments of size 2. The next step is to reduce the number of segments from 5 to 4. For this purpose, the algorithm tests the merging of every two adjacent segments of the 5 existing segments, in order to find the one that has the minimum SAE. Four different scenarios are possible:

Scenario 1: The first scenario is shown in Fig. 7a where s_1 and s_2 of the initial segmentation (shown in Fig. 6) are merged into one segment. We calculate the values's mean on the resulting segment (denoted $S1$ in Fig. 7a), and then compute the SAE of this approximation that is $SAE_1(X, \overline{X}) = 0.55$.

Scenario 2: This scenario is shown in Fig. 7b in which s_2 and s_3 of the initial segmentation are merged. As for Scenario 1, we compute the mean of X on the current segment S_2. Here, $SAE_2(X, \overline{X}) = 2.3$.

Scenario 3: This scenario is shown in Fig. 7c, where we merge s_3 and s_4. For this merging (S_3), $SAE_3(X, \overline{X}) = 2.2$.

Scenario 4: The last scenario is shown in Fig. 7d, where we merge s_4 and s_5. For this segment S_4, $SAE_4(X, \overline{X}) = 0.65$.

We have calculated the SAE for the 4 scenarios. Since we aim to minimize the SAE, we choose Scenario 1 that leads to the minimum SAE value (MSAE), that is $MSAE = 0.55$ (obtained by merging s_1 and s_2). After merging the segments s_1 and s_2, the algorithm continues the next iterations, until the number of segment reaches w.

Algorithm 3: ASAX_DP variable-size segmentation

Input: D: time series database; n: the length of time series; $size$: the starting
size of segments; w: the required number of segments
Output: w variable-size segments

1 $k = \lceil \frac{n}{size} \rceil$
2 $segments = \{\bigcup_{i=0}^{k-1}[size \times i, size \times (i+1) - 1]\}$ // split time domain into k
   segments of size $size$
3 $matrix$ = matrix of $k \times k$ values initialized to -1
4 **while** $k \neq w$ **do**
5     $segmentsToMerge = null$
6     $msae = \infty$
7   **for** $i=1$ to $k - 1$ **do**
8        $s = $ merge (s_i, s_{i+1})
9        $r, c =$Compute the position in $matrix$ corresponding to s
10       $sae = 0$
11   **if** $matrix[r,c] = $ -1 **then**
12   **foreach** ts in D **do**
13             $sae = sae + SAE(ts)$
14          $matrix[r,c]=sae$
15   **else**
16          $sae = matrix[r,c]$
17   **if** $sae < msae$ **then**
18          $segmentsToMerge = i$
19          $msae = sae$
20    $s = $ merge $(s_{segmentsToMerge}, s_{segmentsToMerge+1})$
21    $segments = segments - \{s_{segmentsToMerge}, s_{segmentsToMerge+1}\}$
22    $segments = segments \bigcup s$
23    $k = k$-1
24 **return** $segments$

Let us now analyze the complexity of ASAX_SAE algorithm. Let $|D|$ be the number of time series in the database, n the time series length, and w the desired number of segments. The initial number of segments is $\frac{n}{size}$, where $size$ is the initial size of the segments. In the *while* loop, the algorithm performs $\frac{n}{size} - w + 1$ iterations, and in each iteration it tries the merging of each segment with its next segment, and computes the SAE of the segmentation. The maximum value for $\frac{n}{size}$ is n, *i.e.*, with $size = 1$. Thus, the maximum number of SAE computations is $O(n - w)^2$. For each SAE computation, the database should be scanned, and the error of each time series representation computed. This is done in $O(|D| \times n)$. Therefore, in total the time complexity of the algorithm is $O((n-w)^2 \times |D| \times n)$.

6   ASAX_SAE Based on Dynamic Programming

The ASAX_SAE algorithm, which we presented in the previous section, can reduce significantly the information loss in time series representations and is much more efficient than ASAX_EN in terms of accuracy and calculation time, as illustrated by our experiments. However, its execution time may be high, particularly over large time series datasets as shown by our experiments (e.g., see Fig. 12 in Sect. 8). In this section, we present an efficient version of ASAX_SAE, called ASAX_DP, for improving the execution time of our segmentation technique using dynamic programming. In ASAX_DP, we use a data structure (matrix) to keep track of the result of the SAE computation for each iteration. In the matrix, if the value of a cell (i, j) is positive, then it corresponds to the SAE of merging all adjacent segments from segment s_i to segment s_j. In each iteration, after testing the merging of two adjacent segments, the computed SAE of the merging is kept in the matrix, in order to be used in the case where this merging needs to be evaluated again in the next steps.

Let us describe ASAX_DP algorithm in more details. Algorithm 3 presents the pseudocode of the improved approach. As for the ASAX_SAE algorithm (described in the previous section), ASAX_DP splits the time domain into k segments of length $size$ to create the set $segments$ (Lines 1, 2). A matrix of size $k \times k$ denoted as $matrix$ is allocated and all its values are initialized to -1 (Line 3). Then, in a loop, until the number of segments is more than w the algorithm proceeds as follows. For each segment s_i (i from 1 to $k - 1$), the algorithm tests the merging of s_i with segment s_{i+1}. For this, the algorithm computes the position in the matrix corresponding to the merging of these two segments by finding the row and column number (r, c) (Line 9). If it is the first time that these two segments merging is tested (*i.e.*, if the SAE value in the corresponding cell in the matrix is equal to -1), then the algorithm has to compute the SAE for each time series ts in the database D on the segment s made from merging s_i and s_{i+1} (Line 13). By summing up the SAE of PAA representation of all the time series contained in D, ASAX_DP adds the result of the computed SAE to sae and stores this value in the matrix by replacing the existing value (-1) by the calculated SAE (Line 14). In the case where the merging of s_i and s_{i+1} has already been tested (*i.e.*, if the SAE value in the matrix is not -1), the algorithm simply has to get the SAE value from the matrix which is already computed and sets sae to this value (Line 16). After having obtained the SAE value, if it is less than the MSAE (minimum SAE) obtained so far, the algorithm sets i as the segment to be merged with the next one, and keeps the SAE of the representation (Lines 18, 19). This procedure continues by testing the merging of every two adjacent segments of $segments$ at each time by making use of the matrix to avoid redundant SAE computations. The algorithm selects the merging whose SAE is the lowest, and updates the set of the segments (Lines 20–22). The procedure continues until k reaches the required number of segments w.

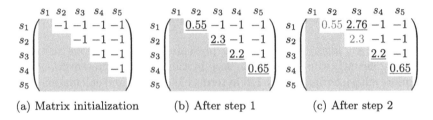

Fig. 8. State of the matrix at different steps of the algorithm. The updated values are in red and the possible scenarios are underlined in each step. (Color figure online)

Bellow, we illustrate our algorithm using an example.

Example 6. Let us apply ASAX_DP on the time series X shown in Fig. 6 by taking the initial size of 2 for the segments. Suppose the number of desired segments is $w = 3$. The algorithm starts by dividing the time domain into 5 segments of size 2 and initializes the matrix that will keep track of the SAE computation (Fig. 8a). This matrix's row (and column) size is 5 which is the initial number of segments, each value corresponds to a possible merging of the initial segments (two segments or more). The value of cell (i, j) in the matrix corresponds to the SAE of merging of all adjacent segments from s_i to s_j. The final number of segments is $w=3$, thus the algorithm consists of 2 steps:

Step 1: Reduce the Number of Segments from 5 to 4. The algorithm tests the merging of every two adjacent segments of the 5 existing segments, 4 different scenarios are possible (presented previously in Example 6). Each of these 4 merging possibilities are tested, the corresponding SAE for each possible merging is computed, and the results are stored in the matrix. Figure 8b shows the content of the matrix after the update (the updated values are in red). The possible scenarios are underlined. For this step, we choose the segmentation generated in Scenario 1 shown in Fig. 7a, resulting from merging s_1 and s_2, since it provides the minimum SAE value (MSAE), that is $MSAE = 0.55$.

Step 2: Reduce the Number of Segments from 4 to 3. In the previous step, the initial segments s_1 and s_2 have been merged into a single segment. Now, we have 4 segments as shown in Fig. 7a. To reduce the 4 segments to 3, three merging scenarios are possible:

Scenario 1: The first scenario is shown in Fig. 9a where the first segment S_1 of Fig. 7a (the segment resulting from merging s_1 and s_2) and S_2 are merged, i.e. s_1, s_2 and s_3 of the initial segmentation are merged into one segment. This merging is tested for the first time until now $(matrix[1, 3] = -1)$, then, we calculate the values's mean of X on the resulting segment, and then compute the SAE that is $SAE_1(X, \overline{X}) = 2.76$. The matrix cell that corresponds to this merging is updated (Fig. 8c).

Scenario 2: This scenario is shown in Fig. 9b in which s_3 and s_4 of the initial segmentation are merged. This merging has already been tested in the previous step $(matrix[3, 4] \neq -1)$, the SAE value is retrieved from our matrix from the cell $(3, 4)$. Here, $SAE_2(X, \overline{X}) = 2.2$.

Scenario 3: The last scenario is shown in Fig. 9c, where we merge s_4 and s_5. The SAE for this merging has been already computed in step 1, that is $SAE_3(X, \overline{X}) = 0.65$.

We have now the SAE for the three scenarios. We choose the minimum SAE value, that is $MSAE = 0.65$ corresponding to the segmentation generated in Scenario 3, which is chosen for this iteration.

After this step, we have 3 segments shown in Fig. 9c. Since, the number of segment reaches w, the algorithm ends.

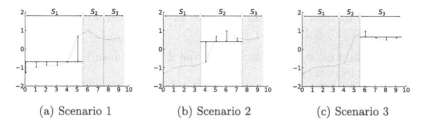

(a) Scenario 1   (b) Scenario 2   (c) Scenario 3

Fig. 9. The three different scenarios of ASAX_SAE segmentation with 3 segments. Scenario 9c is selected since it provides the minimum SAE.

7 Lower Bounding of the Similarity Measure

Having introduced the new representation of time series, we will now define a distance measure on it. SA [14] defines a distance measure on the representation of time series as described in Sect. 2.1. Given the representation of two time series, the $MINDIST_f$ function allows obtaining a lower bounding approximation of the Euclidean distance between the original time series. By the following theorem, we propose a lower bounding approximation formula for the case of variable size segmentation in ASAX (whether it is done by ASAX_EN or ASAX_SAE).

Theorem 1. *Let X and Y be two time series. Suppose that by using ASAX we create a variable size segmentation with w segments, such that the size of the ith segment is l_i.*

Let $\overline{X}$ and $\overline{Y}$ be the PAA representation of variable size of X and Y in ASAX, $DR_v(\overline{X}, \overline{Y})$ gives a lower bounding approximation of the Euclidean distance between X and Y:

$$DR_v(\overline{X}, \overline{Y}) = \sqrt{\sum_{i=1}^{w} ((\overline{x}_i - \overline{y}_i)^2 \times l_i)}$$

Let $\hat{X}$ and $\hat{Y}$ be the representations of X and Y in ASAX obtained by converting $\overline{X}$ and $\overline{Y}$ into symbolic representation. Then, $MINDIST_v(\hat{X},\hat{Y})$ gives a lower bounding approximation of the Euclidean distance between X and Y:

$$MINDIST_v(\hat{X},\hat{Y}) = \sqrt{\sum_{i=1}^{w}(dist(\hat{x}_i,\hat{y}_i)^2 \times l_i)}$$

Proof: To generate the ASAX representation of a time series, we need to first generate its PAA representation using the variable size segmentation (by taking the mean of the time series in each segment), and then we convert the PAA representation to ASAX by creating a symbol for each segment.

Our proof is done in two steps. In the first step, we show that the distance of X and Y in the PAA representation, denoted as $DR_v(\overline{X},\overline{Y})$, is lower than or equal to their Euclidean distance. In the second step, we show that $MINDIST_v(\hat{X},\hat{Y}) \leq DR_v(\overline{X},\overline{Y})$.

Step 1: In the first step, we show that the DR_v distance lower bounds the Euclidean distance, that is:

$$\sqrt{\sum_{i=1}^{n}(x_i - y_i)^2} \geq \sqrt{\sum_{j=1}^{w}((\overline{x}_j - \overline{y}_j)^2 \times l_j)} \tag{1}$$

To prove the above inequality, it is sufficient to prove that the PAA distance of two time series *in each segment* is lower than or equal to their Euclidean distance in the segment. Without loss of generality, let us take the first segment S_1, and suppose that its size is l_1. Thus, we need to prove the following inequality:

$$\sqrt{\sum_{i=1}^{l_1}(x_i - y_i)^2} \geq \sqrt{\sum_{i=1}^{l_1}((\overline{x}_i - \overline{y}_i)^2} \tag{2}$$

Let $\overline{X}$ and $\overline{Y}$ be the means of time series X and Y, respectively. We can rewrite the above inequality as:

$$\sqrt{\sum_{i=1}^{l_1}(x_i - y_i)^2} \geq \sqrt{(\overline{X} - \overline{Y})^2 \times l_1}$$
$$\text{Or: } \sqrt{\sum_{i=1}^{l_1}(x_i - y_i)^2} \geq \sqrt{l_1}\sqrt{(\overline{X} - \overline{Y})^2}$$

By squaring both sides, we have:

$$\sum_{i=1}^{l_1}(x_i - y_i)^2 \geq l_1(\overline{X} - \overline{Y})^2$$

For each point x_i in X, $x_i = \overline{X} - \Delta x_i$. The same applies to each point y in Y. Then, we substitute the rearrangement:

$$\sum_{i=1}^{l_1}((\overline{X} - \Delta x_i) - (\overline{Y} - \Delta y_i))^2 \geq l_1(\overline{X} - \overline{Y})^2$$

After rearranging terms in the left-hand side, we have:

$$\sum_{i=1}^{l_1}((\overline{X} - \overline{Y}) - (\Delta x_i - \Delta y_i))^2 \geq l_1(\overline{X} - \overline{Y})^2$$

Then, we expand the inequality using the binomial theorem:

$$\sum_{i=1}^{l_1}((\overline{X} - \overline{Y})^2 - 2(\overline{X} - \overline{Y})(\Delta x_i - \Delta y_i)$$
$$+ (\Delta x_i - \Delta y_i)^2) \geq l_1(\overline{X} - \overline{Y})^2$$

By using distributive law and summation properties, we have:

$$l_1(\overline{X} - \overline{Y})^2 - 2(\overline{X} - \overline{Y})\sum_{i=1}^{l_1}(\Delta x_i - \Delta y_i)$$
$$+ \sum_{i=1}^{l_1}(\Delta x_i - \Delta y_i)^2 \geq l_1(\overline{X} - \overline{Y})^2$$

We know that $x_i = \overline{X} - \Delta x_i$, which means that $\Delta x_i = \overline{X} - x_i$, and the same applies for Δy_i.

$$\sum_{i=1}^{l_1}(\Delta x_i - \Delta y_i) = \sum_{i=1}^{l_1}((\overline{X} - x_i) - (\overline{Y} - y_i))$$
$$= (\sum_{i=1}^{l_1}\overline{X} - \sum_{i=1}^{l_1}x_i) - (\sum_{i=1}^{l_1}\overline{Y} - \sum_{i=1}^{l_1}y_i)$$
$$= (l_1\overline{X} - \sum_{i=1}^{l_1}x_i) - (l_1\overline{Y} - \sum_{i=1}^{l_1}y_i)$$
$$= (\sum_{i=1}^{l_1}x_i - \sum_{i=1}^{l_1}x_i) - (\sum_{i=1}^{l_1}y_i - \sum_{i=1}^{l_1}y_i)$$
$$= 0 - 0 = 0$$

We substitute 0 into $\sum_{i=1}^{l_1}(\Delta x_i - \Delta y_i)$ in the inequality:

$$l_1(\overline{X} - \overline{Y})^2 - 0 + \sum_{i=1}^{l_1}(\Delta x_i - \Delta y_i)^2 \geq l_1(\overline{X} - \overline{Y})^2$$

Then by subtracting $n(\overline{X} - \overline{Y})^2$ from both sides, we have:

$$\sum_{i=1}^{l_1}(\Delta x_i - \Delta y_i)^2 \geq 0$$

This always holds true, so it completes the proof.

Step 2: Following the same method as in *Step 1*, we will show here that $MINDIST_v$ lower bounds the DR_v distance, that is:

$$\sqrt{\sum_{j=1}^{w}((\overline{x}_j - \overline{y}_j)^2 \times l_j)} \geq \sqrt{\sum_{i=j}^{w}(dist(\hat{x}_j, \hat{y}_j)^2 \times l_j)}$$

To prove the above inequality, it is sufficient to prove that $MINDIST_v$ in each segment lower bounds the DR_v distance in the segment. Without loss of generality, let us take the first segment S_1, and assume that its size is l_1. Thus, it is sufficient to prove the following inequality:

$$\sqrt{\sum_{i=1}^{1}((\overline{x}_i - \overline{y}_i)^2) \times l_1} \geq \sqrt{\sum_{i=1}^{1}(dist(\hat{x}_1, \hat{y}_1)^2 \times l_1)}$$

The above inequality can be written as: $l_1(\overline{X} - \overline{Y})^2 \geq l_1(dist(\hat{X}, \hat{Y}))^2$. There are two possible scenarios for the symbols representing X and Y.

Case 1: the symbols representing X and Y are either the same, or consecutive from the alphabet a, i.e. $|(\hat{X} - \hat{Y})| \leq 1$. In this case the *MINDIST* value is 0. Therefore, the inequality becomes:

$$l_1(\overline{X} - \overline{Y})^2 \geq 0$$

which always holds true.

Case 2: the symbols representing X and Y are at least two alphabets apart, i.e. $|(\hat{X} - \hat{Y})| > 1$. Let us assume that X is at a higher region than Y, i.e. $\hat{X} > \hat{Y}$, otherwise, in the case where $\hat{X} < \hat{Y}$, it can be demonstrated in the same way.

$$dist(\hat{X}, \hat{Y}) = \beta_{\hat{X}-1} - \beta_{\hat{Y}}$$

By substituting into the inequality, we have:

$$l_1(\overline{X} - \overline{Y})^2 \geq l_1(\beta_{\hat{X}-1} - \beta_{\hat{Y}})^2$$

By removing l_1 from both sides, we have:

$$|\overline{X} - \overline{Y}| \geq |\beta_{\hat{X}-1} - \beta_{\hat{Y}}|$$

Since $\hat{X} > \hat{Y}$ and $|(\hat{X} - \hat{Y})| > 1$, we can drop the absolute value notation and rearrange the terms:

$$\overline{X} - \beta_{\hat{X}-1} \geq \overline{Y} - \beta_{\hat{Y}}$$

We know that: $\beta_{\hat{X}-1} \leq \overline{X} < \beta_{\hat{X}}$ and $\beta_{\hat{Y}-1} \leq \overline{Y} < \beta_{\hat{Y}}$ which implies that $\overline{X} - \beta_{\hat{X}-1} \geq 0$ and $\overline{Y} - \beta_{\hat{Y}} < 0$.

Then, the inequality always holds true, and this completes the proof.

8   Experiments

In this section, we report the results of experimental studies on the proposed ASAX segmentation approaches, *i.e.* ASAX_EN, ASAX_SAE and ASAX_DP.

8.1   Datasets and Experimental Settings

We compared the ASAX_EN and ASAX_SAE representations with the existing SAX representation on datasets selected for their particular (lack of) uniformity. Notice that SAX and its extensions in the literature use a fixed-size segmentation of the time domain.

The approaches are implemented in Python programming language and Numba JIT compiler is used to optimize machine code at runtime[1]. The experimental evaluation was conducted on a machine using Ubuntu 18.04.5 LTS operating system with 20 Gigabytes of main memory, and an Intel Xeon(R) 3,10 GHz processor with 4 cores.

We carried out our experiments on several real world datasets from the UCR Time Series Classification Archive [6]. Table 2 gives basic information about the datasets: name, type, length of the time series (number of values). Almost all selected datasets have non-uniform distributions over time domain (see Fig. 10), else SyntheticControl that has a quasi uniform distribution.

For each approach, the length w of the approximate representations is reduced to 10% of the original time series length. For the variable-size segmentation algorithms, ASAX_SAE is initialized by splitting the time domain into segments of length 2 and for ASAX_EN we set the default cardinality value to 32.

Table 2. Datasets basic information

Name	Type	Time series length
AllGestureWiimoteZ	Sensor	500
ECG200	ECG	90
ECG5000	ECG	140
ECGFiveDays	ECG	130
Fungi	HRM	200
GesturePebbleZ1	Sensor	450
MedicalImages	Image	90
SonyAIBORobotSurface1	Sensor	70
SyntheticControl	Simulated	60

In the experiments, we measure the precision of the compared approaches in similarity search, by applying a k-Nearest Neighbor (k-NN) search, as detailed in Subsect. 8.2. For ASAX variable-size segmentation algorithms, we measure the time cost of the variable-size segmentation in Subsect. 8.3.

---

[1] Our code is available at: https://github.com/lamiad/ASAX.

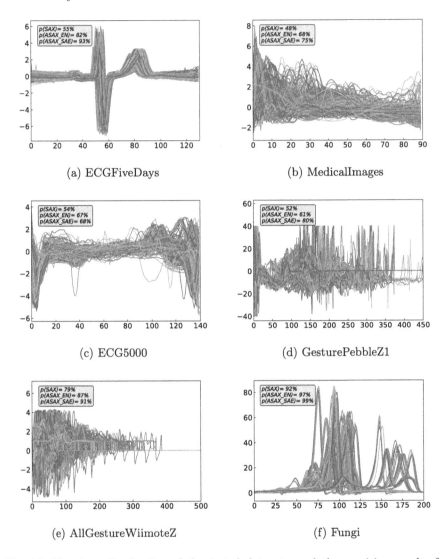

(a) ECGFiveDays

(b) MedicalImages

(c) ECG5000

(d) GesturePebbleZ1

(e) AllGestureWiimoteZ

(f) Fungi

Fig. 10. The data distribution of the tested datasets, and the precision results for each dataset. p(SAX), p(ASAX_EN) and p(ASAX_SAE) show the precision of SAX, ASAX_EN and ASAX_SAE respectively.

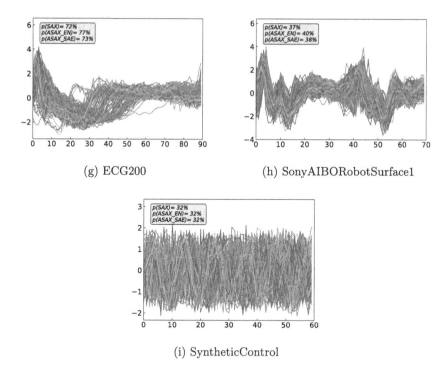

(g) ECG200   (h) SonyAIBORobotSurface1

(i) SyntheticControl

Fig. 10. (*continued*)

8.2 Precision of K-Nearest Neighbor Search

In this part of experiments, we compare the quality of ASAX and SAX representations on different datasets described in Table 2 by measuring the precision of the approximate k-NN search for both of the two approaches. The precision reported for each dataset represents the average precision for a set of arbitrary random queries taken from this dataset. The search precision for each query Q from a dataset D is calculated as follows:

$$p = \frac{|AppkNN(Q, D) \cap ExactkNN(Q, D)|}{k}$$

where *AppkNN(Q,D)* and *ExactkNN(Q,D)* are the sets of approximate k nearest neighbors and exact k nearest neighbors of Q from D, respectively. *AppkNN(Q,D)* is obtained using DR_f distance measure for SAX and DR_v for the ASAX representation and the set *ExactkNN(Q,D)* contains the k-NN of Q using the euclidean distance *ED*. *AppkNN(Q,D)* and *ExactkNN(Q,D)* use a linear search that consists in computing the distance from the query point Q to every other point in D, keeping track of the "best so far" result.

The precision results are reported in Fig. 10 where each dataset is plotted with the precision obtained (as percentage) for all approaches. The plots show the shape of the different time series of each dataset and we can notice that the distribution of time series over the time domain varies from one dataset to another. There are some datasets for which the distribution is quite balanced, those which undergo some variations and others whose variation increases a lot. We have noticed that the more the distribution of the data is unbalanced the more the gain is important. Let us take for example the *ECGFiveDays* dataset presented in Fig. 10a and *SyntheticControl* shown in Fig. 10i. On the first one, we were able to achieve a precision of 93% for ASAX_SAE, 82% for ASAX_EN while it is 55% for SAX, which is a significant gain in precision. This higher precision for our approaches is due to the variable-size segmentation which creates segments in the parts that undergo a significant variation (from time point 45 to 95 in *ECGFiveDays*), allowing ASAX_SAE and ASAX_EN to perform a better distribution of the segments according to information gain by creating several segments in the parts that undergo a significant variation that produces more accurate times series representations leading to a better result for the approximate kNN search.

For *SyntheticControl* we can see that the precision of the approximate k-NN search is the same for the three approaches which is 32%. In this dataset, the shape of the time series is balanced over the time, and the segmentations obtained by ASAX_SAE, ASAX_EN and SAX are the same, resulting in equivalent precision.

From the results, we can observe that ASAX_SAE approach performs better than ASAX_EN for most datasets, especially for the datasets with high variation.

Globally, the results suggest the effectiveness of our approaches and their advantage over traditional SAX when applied to time series, especially those with unbalanced distribution over the time domain.

Using *ECGFiveDays* dataset, Fig. 11 shows the precision gain of ASAX_EN and ASAX_SAE compared to SAX, for different number of segments $w = [10,13,26,65]$. The initial length of the time series in the dataset is around 130.

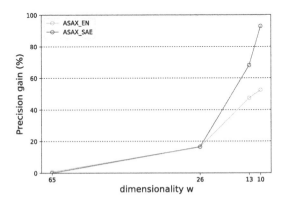

Fig. 11. Precision gain of ASAX_EN and ASAX_SAE compared to SAX on the *ECG-FiveDays* dataset, for different values of segments $w = [10,13,26,65]$.

The precision gain is computed by dividing the difference between the precision of ASAX_EN (or ASAX_SAE) and SAX, over the precision of SAX.

The results illustrate that ASAX_SAE performs better than ASAX_EN for all values of w. They also show that for small values of w the precision gain is higher. The reason is that in these cases the loss of information with SAX is much higher than our approaches. This suggests the interest of using our approaches for high dimentionality reduction.

8.3   Execution Time of Variable-Size Segmentation Algorithms

This subsection presents the time cost of the variable-size segmentation for our proposed algorithms. Figure 12 reports the segmentation time of ASAX_EN and ASAX_SAE on the datasets of our experiments. It does not concern SAX since SAX divides the time domain into segments of fixed size which does not require any computation beforehand. The segmentation time depends on both the number of time series in the dataset and their length. We can observe that the time cost of ASAX_SAE is always less than the one for ASAX_EN.

Let us now compare the variable-size segmentation time cost of the improved algorithm ASAX_DP with that of the basic algorithm ASAX_SAE. Figure 13 reports the performance gains of ASAX_DP compared to ASAX_SAE, in logarithmic scale. The variable-size segmentation time for the two methods is evaluated for the same datasets used previously. We can observe that ASAX_DP is much more efficient and allows to have significant performance gains.

Figure 14 reports the computation time of variable-size segmentation for ASAX_DP and ASAX_SAE over *AllGestureWiimoteZ* dataset, by varying the time series length. The runtime increases with the length of time series and, as one could expect. The basic approach ASAX_SAE takes much more time than

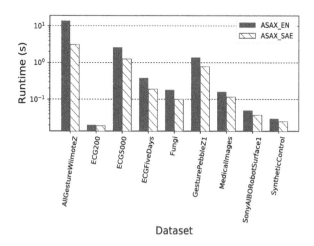

Fig. 12. Logarithmic scale. Runtime of ASAX_SAE and ASAX_EN segmentation algorithms for each dataset

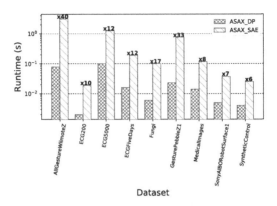

Fig. 13. Logarithmic scale. ASAX_DP's performance gain on ASAX_SAE in segmentation time for each dataset

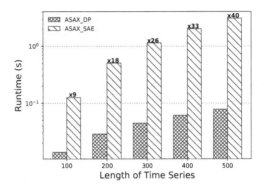

Fig. 14. Logarithmic scale. Variable-size segmentation time for ASAX_DP and ASAX_SAE as a function of time series length, over the *AllGestureWiimoteZ* dataset.

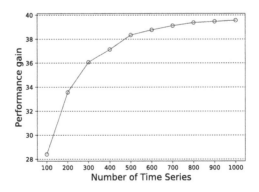

Fig. 15. ASAX_DP's performance gain on ASAX_SAE in segmentation time as a function of dataset size, over the *AllGestureWiimoteZ* dataset.

ASAX_DP. Depending on time series length, ASAX_DP shows performance gains that can reach ×40 for the 1000 time series with length 500 of the *AllGestureWiimoteZ* dataset.

Figure 15 illustrate ASAX_DP's performance gain on ASAX_SAE in segmentation time for the same dataset, by varying the number of time series. As seen, the performance gains vary significantly depending on the number of time series.

9 Conclusion

We addressed the problem of approximating time series, and proposed ASAX_EN and ASAX_SAE, new techniques for segmenting time series before their transformation into symbolic representations. Our solutions can reduce significantly the error incurred by possible splittings at different steps of the representation calculation, by taking into account the sum of absolute errors (ASAX_SAE) or the entropy (ASAX_EN). We also proposed an efficient algorithm, called ASAX_DP, for improving the execution time of our segmentation approach, by means of dynamic programming. We evaluated the performance of our segmentation approach through experiments using several real world datasets. The results suggest that the more the data distribution in the time domain is unbalanced (non-uniform), the greater is the precision gain of ASAX_EN and ASAX_SAE. For example, for the *ECGFiveDays* dataset that has a non-uniform distribution in the time domain, the precision of ASAX_SAE is 93% and 82% for ASAX_EN compared to 55% for SAX. Furthermore, the results illustrate the effectiveness of our dynamic programming algorithm ASAX_DP, *e.g.*, up to ×40 faster than the basic ASAX_SAE algorithm over *AllGestureWiimoteZ* dataset.

References

1. Agrawal, R., Faloutsos, C., Swami, A.: Efficient similarity search in sequence databases. In: Lomet, D.B. (ed.) FODO 1993. LNCS, vol. 730, pp. 69–84. Springer, Heidelberg (1993). https://doi.org/10.1007/3-540-57301-1_5
2. Camerra, A., Shieh, J., Palpanas, T., Rakthanmanon, T., Keogh, E.J.: Beyond one billion time series: indexing and mining very large time series collections with i SAX2+. Knowl. Inf. Syst. **39**(1), 123–151 (2014)
3. Chakrabarti, K., Keogh, E., Mehrotra, S., Pazzani, M.: Locally adaptive dimensionality reduction for indexing large time series databases. ACM Trans. Database Syst. **27**(2), 188–228 (2002)
4. Chan, K., Fu, A.W.: Efficient time series matching by wavelets. In: International Conference on Data Engineering (ICDE) (1999)
5. Cole, R., Shasha, D., Zhao, X.: Fast window correlations over uncooperative time series. In: International Conference on Knowledge Discovery and Data Mining (KDD), pp. 743–749 (2005)
6. Dau, H.A., et al.: Hexagon-ML: the UCR time series classification archive (2018). https://www.cs.ucr.edu/~eamonn/time_series_data_2018/

7. Djebour, L., Akbarinia, R., Masseglia, F.: Variable size segmentation for efficient representation and querying of non-uniform time series datasets. In: 37th ACM/SIGAPP Symposium on Applied Computing (SAC), pp. 395–402. ACM (2022)

8. Elsworth, S., Güttel, S.: ABBA: adaptive brownian bridge-based symbolic aggregation of time series. Data Min. Knowl. Discov. **34**(4), 1175–1200 (2020)

9. Faloutsos, C., Ranganathan, M., Manolopoulos, Y.: Fast subsequence matching in time-series databases. In: International Conference on Management of Data (SIGMOD) (1994)

10. Huijse, P., Estévez, P.A., Protopapas, P., Principe, J.C., Zegers, P.: Computational intelligence challenges and applications on large-scale astronomical time series databases. IEEE Comput. Int. Mag. **9**(3), 27–39 (2014)

11. Kashino, K., Smith, G., Murase, H.: Time-series active search for quick retrieval of audio and video. In: ICASSP (1999)

12. Keogh, E.J., Chakrabarti, K., Pazzani, M.J., Mehrotra, S.: Dimensionality reduction for fast similarity search in large time series databases. Knowl. Inf. Syst. **3**(3), 263–286 (2001)

13. Lin, J., Keogh, E., Lonardi, S., Chiu, B.: A symbolic representation of time series, with implications for streaming algorithms. In: International Conference on Management of Data (SIGMOD) (2003)

14. Lin, J., Keogh, E., Wei, L., Lonardi, S.: Experiencing sax: a novel symbolic representation of time series. Data Min. Knowl. Discov. **15**(2), 107–144 (2007)

15. Linardi, M., Palpanas, T.: ULISSE: ultra compact index for variable-length similarity search in data series. In: International Conference on Data Engineering (ICDE) (2018)

16. Linardi, M., Zhu, Y., Palpanas, T., Keogh, E.J.: Matrix profile X: VALMOD - scalable discovery of variable-length motifs in data series. In: International Conference on Management of Data (SIGMOD) (2018)

17. Linardi, M., Zhu, Y., Palpanas, T., Keogh, E.J.: VALMOD: a suite for easy and exact detection of variable length motifs in data series. In: International Conference on Management of Data (SIGMOD) (2018)

18. Lkhagva, B., Suzuki, Y., Kawagoe, K.: New time series data representation esax for financial applications. In: Workshops of International Conference on Data Engineering (ICDE) (2006)

19. Palpanas, T.: Data series management: the road to big sequence analytics. SIGMOD Rec. **44**(2), 47–52 (2015)

20. Rakthanmanon, T., et al.: Searching and mining trillions of time series subsequences under dynamic time warping. In: International Conference on Knowledge Discovery and Data Mining (KDD) (2012)

21. Raza, U., Camerra, A., Murphy, A.L., Palpanas, T., Picco, G.P.: Practical data prediction for real-world wireless sensor networks. IEEE Trans. Knowl. Data Eng. **27**(8), 2231–2244 (2015). https://doi.org/10.1109/TKDE.2015.2411594

22. Shasha, D.: Tuning time series queries in finance: case studies and recommendations. IEEE Data Eng. Bull. **22**(2), 40–46 (1999)

23. Shieh, J., Keogh, E.: iSAX: indexing and mining terabyte sized time series. In: International Conference on Knowledge Discovery and Data Mining (KDD) (2008)

24. Soldi, S., et al.: Long-term variability of AGN at hard X-rays. Astron. Astrophys. A&A **563**(A57), 16 (2014). https://doi.org/10.1051/0004-6361/201322653. https://hal.archives-ouvertes.fr/hal-01171251

25. Sun, Y., Li, J., Liu, J., Sun, B., Chow, C.: An improvement of symbolic aggregate approximation distance measure for time series. Neurocomputing **138**, 189–198 (2014)
26. Yahyaoui, H., Al-Daihani, R.: A novel trend based sax reduction technique for time series. Expert Syst. Appl. **130**, 113–123 (2019)
27. Ye, L., Keogh, E.J.: Time series shapelets: a new primitive for data mining. In: International Conference on Knowledge Discovery and Data Mining (KDD) (2009)
28. Yin, H., Yang, S.Q., Zhu, X.Q., Ma, S.D., Zhang, L.M.: Symbolic representation based on trend features for knowledge discovery in long time series. Front. Inf. Technol. Electron. Eng. **16**, 744–758 (2015)
29. Zhang, H., Dong, Y., Xu, D.: Entropy-based symbolic aggregate approximation representation method for time series. In: IEEE Joint International Information Technology and Artificial Intelligence Conference (ITAIC), pp. 905–909 (2020)
30. Zoumpatianos, K., Palpanas, T.: Data series management: fulfilling the need for big sequence analytics. In: International Conference on Data Engineering (ICDE) (2018)

Semantic Similarity in a Taxonomy by Evaluating the Relatedness of Concept Senses with the Linked Data Semantic Distance

Anna Formica[(✉)] [iD] and Francesco Taglino [iD]

Istituto di Analisi dei Sistemi ed Informatica "A. Ruberti" Consiglio Nazionale delle Ricerche (IASI-CNR), via dei Taurini 19, 00185 Rome, Italy
{anna.formica,francesco.taglino}@iasi.cnr.it

Abstract. This paper addresses the information-theoretic definition of semantic similarity based on the notion of *information content*, and presents an evolution of a novel approach for evaluating semantic similarity in a taxonomy. Such an approach takes into account not only the *generic sense* of a concept but also its *intended sense* in a given context. In particular, a method for computing the semantic relatedness of concepts in RDF knowledge graphs is used for evaluating the relevance of the intended sense of a concept with respect to its generic sense. The experiment of this work shows that the relatedness method based on *triple patterns* adopted in this paper leads to higher correlation values with human judgment with respect to the ones obtained according to the original proposal that is based on a *triple weights* relatedness measure.

Keywords: Semantic similarity · Information content · Taxonomy · Semantic relatedness · Concept sense · Context

1 Introduction

The information-theoretic definition of semantic similarity introduced by Lin in [20] has been extensively investigated over the years [8], and relies on the *information content* approach proposed by Resnik [26,27]. In the literature, in general, the measures originating from it have shown higher correlation values with human judgment (HJ) than other proposals [3,6,11].

In [14] a novel approach has been presented that allows semantic similarity to be computed by taking into account not only the information contents of the concepts but also the *context*, i.e., the meanings of the concepts in the given application domain. As shown in the mentioned paper, the context (or *perspective* [20]) is fundamental in evaluating semantic similarity, and different contexts can lead to different similarity degrees among the same concepts. The role of the context is more evident if we focus on *siblings*, i.e., concepts of the taxonomy

---

The original version of this chapter was revised: the characters > and < were corrected. The correction to this chapter is available at
https://doi.org/10.1007/978-3-662-66863-4_7

© Springer-Verlag GmbH Germany, part of Springer Nature 2023, corrected publication 2023
A. Hameurlain and A. M. Tjoa (Eds.): TLDKS LIII, LNCS 13840, pp. 66–89, 2023.
https://doi.org/10.1007/978-3-662-66863-4_3

with the same parent, which share the same information content. Note that also the approach proposed by Lin [20] is based on the notion of perspective, but it does not allow to evaluate similarity by addressing a single perspective at a time, and the information-theoretic definition of similarity between concepts is interpreted as "a weighted average of their similarities computed from different perspectives".

In this work, analogously to [14], we distinguish the notion of *generic sense* of a concept, i.e., the sense of the concept that is not related to any specific context, from its *intended sense*, i.e., the meaning of the concept in a specific context. In order to compute semantic similarity, an important contribution consists in evaluating also concept relatedness [15], which allows non-taxonomic relations between concepts to be captured. With this regard, in this paper we present an evolution of the original method proposed in [14], by refining the evaluation of the semantic relatedness between the generic sense and the intended sense of a given concept. In particular, in the aforementioned paper, semantic relatedness was computed by adopting the *Information Content-based Measure* (*ICM*) and, in particular, the *combIC* strategy [29], whereas here we rely on the $LDSD_{cw}$ measure, which belongs to the *Linked Data Semantic Distance* (*LDSD*) family [23]. These are both knowledge-based approaches for computing semantic relatedness of concepts in *Resource Description Framework* (RDF) knowledge graphs. Essentially, with respect to the *ICM* proposal that leverages *triple weights*, the *LDSD* family focuses on *triple patterns*. In the experiment presented in this paper, besides the *combIC* and the $LDSD_{cw}$ measures, the comparison also involves the following knowledge-based relatedness methods: $ASRMP_m$ [9], *Wikipedia Link-based Measure* (*WLM*) [34], *Exclusivity-based measure* (*ExclM*) [16], and *Linked Open Data Description Overlap* (*LODOverlap*) [37]. The new experimental results show that, in order to evaluate semantic similarity in a taxonomy, the $LDSD_{cw}$ relatedness measure proposed by [23] is, on average, the best strategy. In particular, it leads to an average increment of the average Pearson's correlation with human judgement of about 0.05. Overall, by also considering the average with the Spearman's correlation, $LDSD_{cw}$ outperforms the other methods. Therefore, the contribution of this paper consists in (i) the comparison of some among the most representative knowledge-based relatedness methods, and (ii) the identification of the approach that allows semantic similarity in a taxonomy to be evaluated by improving the correlation with human judgment with respect to the previous proposal of the authors [14].

The paper is organized as follows. In Sect. 2 the problem is informally recalled, and in Sect. 3 the enriched similarity measure is presented. In particular, in Sect. 3, the *ICM* method and the *LDSD* family of measures are recalled. In Sect. 4 the new experiment is presented. The related work follows in Sect. 5, and the conclusion is given in Sect. 6.

2   Semantic Similarity in a Taxonomy

In this section, the method is informally presented [14]. In particular, below the approaches of Resnik and Lin are illustrated by using a simple example about siblings and, successively, the proposed measure is addressed.

2.1   Similarity Between Siblings: An Example

According to Resnik [26,27], the notion of semantic similarity between concepts organized according to a taxonomy relies on concept frequencies in text corpora, e.g., huge collections of text samples of American English. The basic assumption of the approach is the following: the more information two concepts share the more similar they are. Then, the similarity between concepts is given by the maximum information content shared by them, which is represented by the information content of their *least common subsumer* (i.e., the most specific concept in the taxonomy that is more general than the two). The root of the taxonomy is the concept whose information content is null by definition, since it represents the most abstract concept.

For the sake of simplicity, in this section we address an example involving siblings, i.e., concepts that in the taxonomy are direct descendants of the same node (parent). Figure 1 shows a fragment of a taxonomy where the concept *person* is the parent of the three concepts *student*, *employee*, and *planter* (children).

Fig. 1. A simple taxonomy

The similarity between siblings is given by the information content associated with their parent, which is the maximum one shared by them. For this reason siblings, in pairs, all have the same semantic similarity degrees. Therefore, in the example, the maximum information content shared by the pairs (*employee*, *student*) and (*employee*, *planter*) is the one associated with their parent, *person*, and the following holds:

$$sim(employee, student) = sim(employee, planter)$$

where *sim* stands for the similarity degree of the pair. Of course, this value also coincides with the one of the pair (*student*, *planter*).

As a result, according to Resnik, siblings are indistinguishable from a similarity point of view, and the approach does not allow to capture further semantic aspects of the concepts, in order to have different pairs of siblings with different similarity degrees.

In [20], the notion of semantic similarity proposed by Resnik has been refined by also addressing the information contents of the compared concepts and, therefore, the related concept frequencies (or probabilities). Let us consider again the pairs of concepts (*employee*, *student*) and (*employee*, *planter*). Assume that the frequency of the concept *student* in a text corpus is greater than the one of the concept *planter* (but the opposite hypothesis can be taken as well). According to this assumption, the similarity degree between the concepts *employee* and *student* is greater than the one between *employee* and *planter* (see Sect. 3 where the similarity measure of Lin is formally recalled in Eq. 3), i.e.:

$$sim(employee, student) > sim(employee, planter).$$

Therefore, following this approach, given a set of sibling concepts in a taxonomy, one of them, in this case *employee*, is more similar to the "most frequent" sibling in a given corpus, i.e., *student* in the example. With respect to the previous approach, pairs of siblings do not have the same similarity degrees, however similarity is evaluated by considering only concept frequencies and, in particular, the more frequent two siblings are, the more similar they are. Indeed, as mentioned in the Introduction, this approach relies on concept *generic senses*, i.e., meanings that are not related to any specific context.

2.2   The Use of Perspectives

Consider again the taxonomy of Fig. 1, and now suppose we have an application domain for which an important requirement for people is to spend several hours per day in a building. According to this perspective, we expect *employee* to be more similar to *student* than to *planter*, because an *employee* and a *student* are both characterized by the mentioned requirement better than the concepts *employee* and *planter*. Therefore, we expect that the following holds:

$$sim(employee, student) > sim(employee, planter).$$

This is not the case if we consider another perspective, or application domain, where for instance it is more important to focus on people's income. Of course, in this second case, we expect that *employee* will be more similar to *planter* than to *student*, since the first two concepts share some form of *payment*. Therefore, in this second case, it is reasonable to expect the following:

$$sim(employee, student) < sim(employee, planter).$$

For these reasons, we propose to compute semantic similarity by also addressing the meanings that concepts have in the given domain, i.e., their *intended senses* in that domain. For instance, consider in Fig. 2 an extension of the fragment of the taxonomy shown in Fig. 1, where the concept *building* has *office* and *college* as children, and *payment* is the parent of *reward* and *salary*. Now, in line with the first perspective illustrated above, suppose we have an application domain,

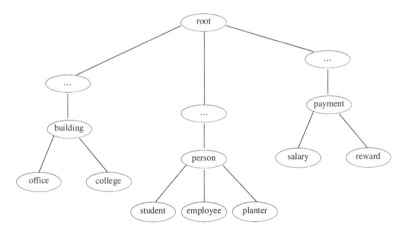

Fig. 2. A simple taxonomy including concept senses

say D_1, where it is important to characterize people on the basis of the time they spend in an edifice per day. Let $\mathcal{S}_{D_1}$ be the function associating the concepts of the taxonomy with their intended senses in the domain D_1, defined as follows:

$$\mathcal{S}_{D_1}(employee) = office$$

$$\mathcal{S}_{D_1}(student) = college$$

$$\mathcal{S}_{D_1}(planter) = reward$$

In the proposed approach, concept similarity is evaluated by addressing not only the maximum information content shared by the compared concepts, but also the one shared by their intended senses. Therefore, consider again the pairs of siblings of our example. The intended senses of the concepts *employee* and *student* are *office* and *college*, respectively, which have *building*, their parent, as maximum shared information content (see Fig. 2). Whereas, with regard to *employee* and *planter*, the most specific concept in the taxonomy that is more general than their meanings *office* and *reward* is the root, whose information content is null by definition. For this reason, this approach leads to what we expect, i.e.:

$$sim(employee, student) > sim(employee, planter).$$

In order to address the second scenario, where earnings are more relevant than workplaces, consider another application domain, say D_2, for which the intended sense of *employee* is defined by the function $\mathcal{S}_{D_2}$ as follows:

$$\mathcal{S}_{D_2}(employee) = salary$$

while keeping the same definition for the concepts *student* and *planter*, i.e.:

$$\mathcal{S}_{D_2}(student) = college$$

$$\mathcal{S}_{D_2}(planter) = reward.$$

In this second perspective, since *salary* and *reward* share *payment* as concept with maximum information content, whereas *salary* and *college* share only the root (see Fig. 2), the following holds:

$$sim(employee, student) < sim(employee, planter).$$

The similarity measure relying on this approach is formally recalled below.

3   The Proposed Method

In the next subsection, the proposed semantic similarity method is formally presented. As shown below, it requires a semantic relatedness measure in order to evaluate the relatedness between the generic sense and the intended sense of a concept. With respect to the work presented in [14], in this paper the focus is on semantic relatedness rather than semantic similarity. For this reason, in this section, the *ICM* approach, and the *LDSD* family of measures for evaluating semantic relatedness of concepts are recalled.

3.1   The Enriched Semantic Similarity Measure

Consider a set of concepts C, a random variable X taking values in C, and a function Pr:

$$Pr : X \rightarrow [0, 1]$$

such that, for any $c \in C$, $Pr(X = c)$ is the *probability* associated with the concept c computed on the basis of the relative concept *frequency*, $freq(c)$, evaluated from large collections of multidisciplinary texts, such as the Brown Corpus of American English:

$$Pr(X=c) = freq(c)/N$$

where N is the total number of concepts in the corpus. The *information content* of a concept c, $ic(c)$, is computed as:

$$ic_{Pr(X)}(c) = -log Pr(X = c) \tag{1}$$

that, for the sake of simplicity, can also be written as:

$$ic(c) = -logPr(c) \qquad (2)$$

According to this notion, specificity is a good proxy for relevance, and the less the probability associated with a concept, the higher its information content.

In particular, let C be the set of concepts of an ISA taxonomy (taxonomy for short), and $c_i, c_j \in C$. Then, the semantic similarity $sim(c_i, c_j)$, is defined as follows [20]:

$$sim(c_i, c_j) = \frac{2 \times ic(lcs(c_i, c_j))}{ic(c_i) + ic(c_j)} \qquad (3)$$

where lcs stands for the concept that is the *least common subsumer* (the most informative subsumer in [26]) of the concepts c_i, c_j in the taxonomy.

The information content approach recalled above, as well as the similarity methods originating from it, does not consider the semantic similarity of the meanings of the concepts according to a given context. In this direction, in [14] an enrichment of this approach has been proposed, by characterizing the meanings of the compared concepts with respect to a given application domain, as recalled below.

Suppose we have an application domain, say D_k, the semantic similarity of the concepts $c_i, c_j \in C$, indicated as $sim_{D_k}(c_i, c_j)$, is defined as:

$$sim_{D_k}(c_i, c_j) = sim(c_i, c_j) \times (1 - \omega_k) + sim(\mathcal{S}_{D_k}(c_i), \mathcal{S}_{D_k}(c_j)) \times \omega_k \qquad (4)$$

where sim is a similarity measure (for example the one in Eq. 3), ω_k is a weight, $0 \le \omega_k \le 1$, defined by the domain expert according to D_k, and $\mathcal{S}_{D_k}$ is a function from C to C, referred to as the *intended sense* function, associating a concept with its meaning according to D_k, i.e.:

$$\mathcal{S}_{D_k} : C \to C$$

and:

$$\mathcal{S}_{D_k}(c) = \begin{cases} s & \text{if } s \in C \text{ is the } intended \ sense \text{ of } c \text{ in } D_k \\ c & \text{otherwise} \end{cases}$$

Note that the weight ω_k, depending on D_k, allows a balance between the roles of the generic senses and intended senses of the concepts in the given domain, according to their relatedness in such a context [15]. With regard to evaluating the semantic relatedness of concepts, in the following we focus on knowledge-based methods. Knowledge-based methods mainly depend on the availability of a formal knowledge base, such as a knowledge graph, an ontology, or a taxonomy. In particular, we consider the methods for evaluating semantic relatedness of resources in RDF knowledge graphs, where concepts are represented by the nodes of the graph. RDF is a family of specifications designed as a standard model for data interchange on the Web. It is used for the conceptual description or modeling of information of Web resources, each identified by a Uniform Resource Identifier (URI). RDF is based upon the idea of making statements about resources by means of expressions in the form of triples following a *subject − predicate − object* pattern. The subject denotes the resource that is being described, and the predicate expresses a relation between the subject and the object, which can be a resource or a literal (e.g., a string, a number).

Let $R = \{r_1, r_2, ..., r_n\}$ be a finite set of URIs each representing a resource, and $L = \{l_1, l_2, ..., l_m\}$ a finite set of literals, an RDF triple has the form:

$$\langle s, p, o \rangle$$

where $s \in R$ is the subject, $p \in R$ is the predicate, and $o \in R \cup L$ is the object. An RDF knowledge graph is a set of RDF triples, where subjects and objects are nodes, and predicates are directed arcs (also called links, edges or arrows).

In this paper we recall two methods for evaluating semantic relatedness of resources in RDF knowledge graphs, that are the *Information Content-based Measure* proposed by Schuhmacher et al. in [29], and the family of measures for semantic distance defined by Passant in [23], named *Linked Data Semantic Distance*. The former requires the association of weights with the paths connecting the compared resources, and has been adopted in [14]. The latter relies on the identification of path patterns satisfying specific conditions in the knowledge graph.

3.2 Information Content-Based Measure

The method presented in [29], here referred to as *Information Content-based Measure (ICM)*, is based on the computation of the weights of the triples occurring in the undirected paths connecting the compared resources, up to a given length. Such a weight is evaluated on the basis of the information content notion given in Sect. 3, as explained below.

Suppose the random variable X of Eq. 1 describes the predicate of a triple, then the weight of the triple depends only on the probability associated with that predicate. Consequently, two triples with the same predicate have the same weight. However, it can be intuitively assessed that two triples having the same predicate, but different objects, in general, convey different amounts of information. This is the case of the following two triples extracted from DBpedia, representing information about Dante Alighieri, that are specified as follows:

$$\langle dbr\text{:}Dante\_Alighieri, rdf\text{:}type, dbo\text{:}Person \rangle$$

$$\langle dbr\text{:}Dante\_Alighieri, rdf\text{:}type, dbo\text{:}Writer \rangle$$

Both these triples have the same predicate, i.e., *rdf:type*, but since writer is a term more specific than person, the latter represents a more accurate and richer piece of information. For this reason, in order to compute the weight of a triple, both the predicate and the object of the triple are considered, and in the following we assume they are described by the random variables X and Y, respectively.

In [29], given the triple $t = \langle r_s, p, r_o \rangle$, the authors propose the following three strategies for computing the weight of t.

- *Joint Information Content (jointIC)*. In the case of the *jointIC* strategy, the weight of the triple t, $w_{jointIC}(t)$, is computed according to Eq. 5:

$$w_{jointIC}(t) = ic(p) + ic(r_o|p) \tag{5}$$

where $ic(p) = ic_{Pr(X)}(X = p)$ is the information content associated with probability that the random variable X assumes the value p, and

$$ic(r_o|p) = ic_{Pr(Y),Pr(X)}(Y = r_o|X = p)$$

is the information content associated with the conditional probability that the variable Y assumes the value r_o, supposing that the variable X assumes the value p. Note that $w_{jointIC}(t)$ is equivalent to the information content of the joint probability $Pr(p, r_o)^1$, that is the probability that the variables X and Y assume the values p and r_o, respectively. It represents the likelihood of randomly selecting, from the considered RDF knowledge graph, a triple with p and r_o as predicate and object, respectively. Therefore, Eq. 5 can be also written as $w_{jointIC}(t) = ic(p, r_o)$, emphasizing that the triples that contribute to the computation of *jointIC* are those with predicate p and object r_o.
- *Combined Information Content (combIC)*. The *combIC* strategy aims at mitigating the possible penalization of the *jointIC* measure, in the case of infrequent objects that occur with infrequent predicates, as shown by Eq. (6):

$$w_{combIC}(t) = ic(p) + ic(r_o) \tag{6}$$

where, with respect to Eq. 5, $ic(r_o)$ is evaluated independently of the predicate p. In fact, the *combIC* approach is applied while making an independence assumption between the predicate and the object. Consequently, the weight of the triple t results in the sum of the information contents of the predicate and the object.
- *Information Content and Pointwise Mutual Information (ICPMI)*. According to the *ICPMI* strategy, the weight of the triple t can be defined by Eq. 7:

$$w_{ICPMI}(t) = ic(p) + PMI(p, r_o) \tag{7}$$

where:

$$PMI(p, r_o) = log\frac{Pr(p, r_o)}{Pr(p)Pr(r_o)} \tag{8}$$

---

[1] $ic(p) + ic(r_o|p) = ic(Pr(X = p)) + ic(Pr(Y = r_o|X = p)) = -log(Pr(X = p)) - log(Pr(Y = r_o|X = p)) = -log(Pr(X = p)Pr(Y = r_o|X = p)) = -log(Pr(X = p), Pr(Y = r_o)) = ic(Pr(X = p), Pr(Y = r_o)) = ic(Pr(p, r_o)) = ic(p, r_o).$

In particular, PMI measures the mutual dependence between the two random variables describing the predicate and the object of a triple, and can be seen as a measure of the deviation from independence between the two outcomes. With respect to the previous strategies, by means of the addendum PMI, $ICPMI$ represents a balance between the assumptions of full dependence ($jointIC$) and independence ($combIC$) between predicates and objects. In Eq. 7, the information content of the predicate is summed with PMI in order to bias the weight towards less frequent, and thus more informative, predicates.

Once one of the strategies above has been adopted, consider two resources r_a and r_b, and the maximum length $h > 0$ of the paths to be considered, the semantic relatedness between r_a and r_b, $ICM_h(r_a, r_b)$, is computed according to Eq. 9:

$$ICM_h(r_a, r_b) = \frac{1}{\min\limits_{P \in \mathcal{P}^h} \sum\limits_{t_i \in P} (w_{max} - w(t_i))} \tag{9}$$

where:

- $\mathcal{P}^h$ is the set of the undirected paths connecting r_a and r_b with length less than or equal to h.
- t_i is the i-th triple in the path P of the set $\mathcal{P}^h$.
- $w(t)$ is the weight of the triple t, and w_{max} is the maximum weight a triple in the graph can assume, according to one of the above three strategies.

In the case $r_a \equiv r_b$ the semantic relatedness between the resources is assumed to be equal to 1. On the basis of the results of the experimentation presented in [29], the measure obtained according to $combIC$ outperforms the other two, and it is the measure that has been adopted in the experiment presented in [14].

3.3   Linked Data Semantic Distance

In [23], the author proposes a theoretical definition of Linked Data and shows how relatedness between resources can be evaluated by using the semantic distance measure introduced by Rada [25]. With respect to the traditional approach of Rada, which focuses on hierarchical relations, the proposed distance takes into account any kind of links. In particular, a family of measures for semantic distance has been defined, named *Linked Data Semantic Distance* (*LDSD*). Among the measures belonging to this family, below we recall the three most representative ones, the first focusing on direct links, the second on indirect links[2], and the third on a combination of both direct and indirect links between the compared resources.

---

[2] A direct link is an arc connecting two adjacent nodes, whereas an indirect link is a path with length greater than 1.

– $LDSD_{dw}$. The first measure is the *direct weighted LDSD* distance, indicated as $LDSD_{dw}$, which considers only the incoming and outgoing direct links between the resources to be compared. In particular, given a graph $\mathcal{G}$, let C_d be a function that computes the number of direct and distinct links between resources in the graph as follows. Given two resources r_a, r_b and the predicate p_j, $C_d(p_j, r_a, r_b) = 1$ if there exists a link labeled with p_j from the resource r_a to the resource r_b, i.e., a triple $\langle r_a, p_j, r_b \rangle$, otherwise $C_d(p_j, r_a, r_b) = 0$. Furthermore, $C_d(p_j, r_a)^3$ is the total number of links labeled with the predicate p_j from r_a to any node (i.e., the total number of resources that can be reached from r_a via p_j). Therefore, given the resources r_a and r_b, $LDSD_{dw}(r_a, r_b)$ is defined according to Eq. 10:

$$LDSD_{dw}(r_a, r_b) = \frac{1}{1 + \sum_{p_j \in W} \frac{C_d(p_j, r_a, r_b)}{1 + log(C_d(p_j, r_a))} + \sum_{p_j \in Z} \frac{C_d(p_j, r_b, r_a)}{1 + log(C_d(p_j, r_b))}} \tag{10}$$

where $W \subseteq R$ is the set of the predicates p such that $C_d(p, r_a, r_b) = 1$, and $Z \subseteq R$ is the set of the predicates p such that $C_d(p, r_b, r_a) = 1$.

– $LDSD_{iw}$. The *indirect weighted LDSD* is the second measure, that is indicated as $LDSD_{iw}$. It basically considers all the path patterns in the graph identified by those resources linked to both the compared resources via the same predicate. Let C_{io} and C_{ii} be functions that compute the number of indirect and distinct links between resources, outgoing and incoming respectively, as follows. Given two resources r_a, r_b and a predicate p_j, $C_{io}(p_j, r_a, r_b) = 1$ if there exists a resource r_n that satisfies both $\langle r_a, p_j, r_n \rangle$, and $\langle r_b, p_j, r_n \rangle$, otherwise $C_{io}(p_j, r_a, r_b) = 0$. Analogously, $C_{ii}(p_j, r_a, r_b) = 1$ if there exists a resource r_n that satisfies both $\langle r_n, p_j, r_a \rangle$, and $\langle r_n, p_j, r_b \rangle$, otherwise $C_{ii}(p_j, r_a, r_b) = 0$. Furthermore, let $C_{io}(p_j, r_a)$ and $C_{ii}(p_j, r_a)^4$ be the total number of resources indirectly linked to r_a via the predicate p_j, outgoing and incoming respectively. Hence, given the resources r_a and r_b, $LDSD_{iw}(r_a, r_b)$ addresses the indirect incoming and outgoing links between the resources, and is defined according to Eq. 11.

$$LDSD_{iw}(r_a, r_b) = \frac{1}{1 + \sum_{p_j \in U} \frac{C_{io}(p_j, r_a, r_b)}{1 + log(C_{io}(p_j, r_a))} + \sum_{p_j \in V} \frac{C_{ii}(p_j, r_a, r_b)}{1 + log(C_{ii}(p_j, r_a))}} \tag{11}$$

where $U \subseteq R$ is the set of the predicates p such that $C_{io}(p, r_a, r_b) = 1$, and $V \subseteq R$ is the set of the predicates p such that $C_{ii}(p, r_a, r_b) = 1$.

---

[3] In the original work [23], this function is defined as $C_d(p_j, r_a, n)$, where n represents the value of the function $C_d(p_j, r_a)$.

[4] Analogously to the function C_d, in [23], these two functions are defined as $C_{io}(p_j, r_a, n)$ and $C_{ii}(p_j, r_a, n)$, respectively.

- $LDSD_{cw}$. Finally, the author proposes the *combined weighted LDSD* distance between the resources r_a and r_b, indicated as $LDSD_{cw}(r_a, r_b)$, that is a combination of the previous distances, the direct and indirect ones, defined as follows:

$$LDSD_{cw}(r_a, r_b) = \frac{1}{1 + f_1 + f_2} \tag{12}$$

where:

$$f_1 = \sum_{p_j \in W} \frac{C_d(p_j, r_a, r_b)}{1 + log(C_d(p_j, r_a))} + \sum_{p_j \in Z} \frac{C_d(p_j, r_b, r_a)}{1 + log(C_d(p_j, r_b))}$$

$$f_2 = \sum_{p_j \in U} \frac{C_{io}(p_j, r_a, r_b)}{1 + log(C_{io}(p_j, r_a))} + \sum_{p_j \in V} \frac{C_{ii}(p_j, r_a, r_b)}{1 + log(C_{ii}(p_j, r_a))}$$

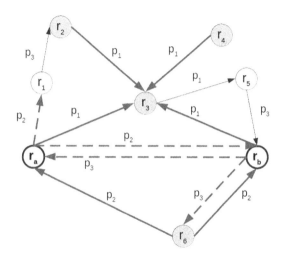

Fig. 3. Example of nodes and arcs involved in evaluating the relatedness between r_a and r_b according to the $LDSD_{cw}$ measure

For instance, consider the knowledge graph $\mathcal{G}$ shown in Fig. 3, containing 8 nodes standing for resources, linked with directed edges labeled with 3 possible predicates, namely, p_1, p_2, and p_3.

In order to evaluate the relatedness between the resources r_a and r_b, we need to compute the terms f_1 and f_2 in Eq. 12, each related to different links in the graph. Concerning the term f_1, the direct links between r_a and r_b, i.e., $\langle r_a, p_2, r_b \rangle$ and $\langle r_b, p_3, r_a \rangle$, determine $C_d(p_2, r_a, r_b) = 1$ and $C_d(p_3, r_b, r_a) = 1$, respectively. Furthermore, the sets $\{\langle r_a, p_2, r_b \rangle, \langle r_a, p_2, r_1 \rangle\}$ and $\{\langle r_b, p_3, r_a \rangle, \langle r_b, p_3, r_6 \rangle\}$ imply $C_d(p_2, r_a) = 2$ and $C_d(p_3, r_b) = 2$, respectively. The links above are highlighted with dashed gray arrows in the figure. With regard to the term f_2, the sets of links $\{\langle r_6, p_2, r_a\rangle, \langle r_6, p_2, r_b\rangle\}$ and $\{\langle r_a, p_1, r_3\rangle, \langle r_b, p_1, r_3\rangle\}$ allow us to evaluate $C_{ii}(p_2, r_a, r_b) = 1$ and $C_{io}(p_1, r_a, r_b) = 1$, respectively. In fact, the first set represents an indirect path between r_a and r_b, where the arcs are incoming to the compared resources, and are both outgoing from r_6 and labelled with same predicate p_2. Analogously, the links in the second set identify an indirect path where the arcs are outgoing from the two resources, and are both incoming to r_3 and labelled with the same predicate p_3. Finally, $C_{io}(p_1, r_a) = 3$ thanks to the following three sets of links $\{\langle r_a, p_1, r_3\rangle, \langle r_2, p_1, r_3\rangle\}$, $\{\langle r_a, p_1, r_3\rangle, \langle r_4, p_1, r_3\rangle\}$, and $\{\langle r_a, p_1, r_3\rangle, \langle r_b, p_1, r_3\rangle\}$, and $C_{ii}(p_2, r_a) = 1$ because of the presence in the graph of the set of links $\{\langle r_6, p_2, r_a\rangle, \langle r_6, p_2, r_b\rangle\}$. These links have been highlighted with gray arrows in Fig. 3.

Note that the distance defined according to Eq. 12 is not symmetric. According to the results given in [23], the $LDSD_{cw}$ measure performs better than $LDSD_{dw}$ and $LDSD_{iw}$, and this is the measure that has been used in the new experiment presented in this paper.

4   The Experiment

In this section the experiment is presented by illustrating first the experimental context and the assumptions made and, successively, the obtained results.

4.1   Experimental Context and Assumptions

As mentioned in [14], the measure addressed in this paper relies on a novel approach for which the experimentation requires, besides the dataset composed of pairs of concepts, further pairs of concepts representing the concept senses. Therefore, in order to compare the new experimental results with the ones of the original proposal, the Miller&Charles ($M\&C$) dataset [22] has been addressed and, for each pair of concepts of this dataset, all the pairs of concepts of the same dataset have been considered as possible contexts. Then, the same six information content based approaches discussed in [14] have been analyzed and, in particular, besides Resnik (sim_R) and Lin (sim_L), also Jiang and Conrath ($sim_{J\&C}$) [18], Pirrò ($sim_{P\&S}$) [24], Adhikari et al. (sim_A) [3], and the measure proposed by Adhikari et al. with the information content model computed as Meng ($sim_{A\&M}$) [2]. The Wu and Palmer method ($sim_{W\&P}$) [35] has also been addressed, as representative of the edge-counting approach [25].

Consider the 28 pairs of concepts of the $M\&C$ dataset, and for each pair the same dataset in order to associate with it 28 possible application domains D_k, $k = 1...28$, in the following referred to as contexts (therefore we have $28 \times 28 = 784$ similarity scores). For instance, for the pair of concepts ($coast, shore$) the 28 contexts are:

$$\mathcal{S}_{D_1}(coast) = car$$
$$\mathcal{S}_{D_1}(shore) = automobile$$

$\mathcal{S}_{D_2}(coast) = gem$
$\mathcal{S}_{D_2}(shore) = gewel$

...

$\mathcal{S}_{D_{28}}(coast) = rooster$
$\mathcal{S}_{D_{28}}(shore) = voyage.$

As mentioned in Sect. 3, in general, the intended senses of concepts are supposed to be estimated by domain experts, together with the related weight ω_k in the given context D_k (see Eq. 4). In the experiment presented in [14], in order to quantify such a weight, which represents the relevance of a pair of senses with respect to the pair of contrasted concepts, we used the *combIC* method proposed in [29], whereas in this experiment, besides the $LDSD_{cw}$ measure, we compared the results also with the ones obtained by relying on the following relatedness methods: $ASRMP_m$ [9], *Wikipedia Link-based Measure (WLM)* [34], *Exclusivity-based measure (ExclM)* [16], and *Linked Open Data Description Overlap (LODOverlap)* [37]. In particular, in the experiment, given a pair of concepts c_i, c_j and a context D_k, we assume that ω_k is defined as follows:

$$\omega_k = (r_1 + r_2)/2$$

where $r_1 = rel(c_i, \mathcal{S}_{D_k}(c_i))$ and $r_2 = rel(c_j, \mathcal{S}_{D_k}(c_j))$, and rel is the relatedness degree computed according to one of the above mentioned methods in DBpedia.

It is important to recall that in order to perform the experiment, given a pair of concepts, a disambiguation step has to be performed. In fact, it is well-known that in Wikipedia, and consequently in DBpedia, terms are addressed with the possible meanings they have, i.e., a term is associated with multiple senses. For this reason, in the experiment disambiguation is necessary in order to address senses in line with the *HJ* evaluation in the *M&C* experiment. For instance, *crane* in Wikipedia has two main senses, that are *bird* and *machine*, therefore when paired for instance with *implement*, it is disambiguated by using the sense *machine*.

In the experiment, in associating a given pair of concepts with a pair of possible concept senses, in some cases the weigh ω_k, for a given context D_k, is null. In addition, there are some particular situations for which both the concept senses do not have any relevance with the concepts to be compared, i.e., both the values r_1, r_2 above are null. In other words, for some pairs of concepts, there are contexts (or perspectives) that do not apply to both the compared concepts, i.e., they do not correspond to any specific point of view. For this reason, in the experimentation these contexts have been ignored. This is for instance the case of the pair of concepts $(coast, shore)$, when associated with the pairs of senses $(brother, monk)$, or (boy, lad). The same also holds in the case of concept senses with low similarity values, such as for instance the pair $(chord, smile)$, or $(noon, string)$. Therefore, in order to analyze significant contexts, a threshold for *HJ* has been introduced, in this case equal to 0.5 (in the scale from 0 to 4).

Table 1. Average Pearson's correlations in the 28 contexts according to the experiment presented in [14] based on *CombIC*

$concept_1$, $concept_2$	sim_R	$sim_{W\&P}$	sim_L	$sim_{J\&C}$	$sim_{P\&S}$	sim_A	$sim_{A\&M}$
Car, Automobile	0.84	0.77	0.86	0.85	0.87	0.87	0.87
Gem, Jewel	0.76	0.68	0.79	0.77	0.82	0.82	0.83
Journey, Voyage	0.90	0.81	0.91	0.90	0.92	0.92	0.92
Boy, Lad	0.85	0.75	0.89	0.85	0.92	0.89	0.89
Coast, Shore	0.82	0.79	0.87	0.85	0.81	0.88	0.88
Asylum, Madhouse	0.88	0.75	0.90	0.89	0.92	0.89	0.88
Magician, Wizard	0.80	0.69	0.85	0.87	0.89	0.86	0.85
Midday, Noon	0.86	0.71	0.88	0.88	0.88	0.87	0.87
Furnace, Stove	0.63	0.45	0.61	0.57	0.64	0.66	0.67
Food, Fruit	0.78	0.52	0.81	0.82	0.82	0.84	0.84
Bird, Cock	0.83	0.69	0.86	0.84	0.85	0.88	0.88
Bird, Crane	0.78	0.72	0.82	0.80	0.84	0.84	0.84
Tool, Implement	0.77	0.62	0.81	0.80	0.82	0.80	0.80
Brother, Monk	0.78	0.70	0.82	0.83	0.89	0.86	0.86
Crane, Implement	0.72	0.63	0.75	0.72	0.77	0.76	0.77
Lad, Brother	0.80	0.73	0.87	0.83	0.90	0.88	0.88
Journey, Car	0.89	0.84	0.90	0.88	0.90	0.91	0.91
Monk, Oracle	0.76	0.63	0.80	0.75	0.84	0.83	0.83
Food, Rooster	0.75	0.53	0.81	0.84	0.81	0.79	0.80
Coast, Hill	0.67	0.63	0.76	0.69	0.76	0.73	0.73
Forest, Graveyard	0.78	0.71	0.81	0.76	0.81	0.84	0.84
Monk, Slave	0.75	0.66	0.79	0.74	0.82	0.82	0.82
Coast, Forest	0.75	0.67	0.79	0.76	0.79	0.77	0.77
Lad, Wizard	0.77	0.72	0.85	0.79	0.88	0.86	0.85
Chord, Smile	0.74	0.71	0.85	0.80	0.89	0.82	0.81
Glass, Magician	0.87	0.85	0.92	0.92	0.90	0.89	0.88
Noon, String	0.93	0.85	0.94	0.92	0.94	0.94	0.94
Rooster, Voyage	0.90	0.85	0.90	0.93	0.93	0.92	0.91
Avg Correl.	0.80	0.70	0.84	0.82	0.85	0.84	0.84

Table 2. Average Pearson's correlations in the 28 contexts according to the new experiment based on $LDSD_{cw}$

$concept_1, concept_2$	sim_R	$sim_{W\&P}$	sim_L	$sim_{J\&C}$	$sim_{P\&S}$	sim_A	$sim_{A\&M}$
Car, Automobile	0.95	0.94	0.95	0.95	0.96	0.96	0.96
Gem, Jewel	0.91	0.90	0.93	0.92	0.95	0.95	0.94
Journey, Voyage	0.95	0.93	0.96	0.99	0.99	0.96	0.95
Boy, Lad	0.85	0.75	0.89	0.83	0.93	0.90	0.89
Coast, Shore	0.89	0.88	0.92	0.87	0.92	0.94	0.94
Asylum, Madhouse	0.90	0.80	0.90	0.90	0.93	0.92	0.92
Magician, Wizard	0.91	0.90	0.95	0.94	0.96	0.96	0.95
Midday, Noon	0.98	0.98	0.98	0.99	0.99	0.99	0.99
Furnace, Stove	0.55	0.42	0.51	0.50	0.59	0.57	0.57
Food, Fruit	0.68	0.09	0.79	0.92	0.85	0.75	0.74
Bird, Cock	0.92	0.83	0.92	0.92	0.94	0.95	0.94
Bird, Crane	0.88	0.86	0.87	0.90	0.93	0.92	0.91
Tool, Implement	0.99	0.99	0.99	0.99	0.99	0.99	0.99
Brother, Monk	0.68	0.63	0.68	0.70	0.88	0.90	0.90
Crane, Implement	0.78	0.75	0.82	0.82	0.85	0.83	0.83
Lad, Brother	0.83	0.76	0.85	0.82	0.89	0.86	0.86
Journey, Car	0.96	0.93	0.97	0.98	0.97	0.97	0.97
Monk, Oracle	0.75	0.63	0.78	0.71	0.85	0.86	0.85
Food, Rooster	0.74	0.13	0.81	0.92	0.84	0.76	0.76
Coast, Hill	0.65	0.63	0.72	0.54	0.68	0.76	0.79
Forest, Graveyard	0.76	0.69	0.78	0.75	0.80	0.86	0.86
Monk, Slave	0.77	0.69	0.79	0.74	0.85	0.86	0.86
Coast, Forest	0.82	0.77	0.85	0.82	0.86	0.87	0.87
Lad, Wizard	0.83	0.72	0.87	0.80	0.90	0.90	0.89
Chord, Smile	0.62	0.72	0.83	0.94	0.95	0.79	0.81
Glass, Magician	0.91	0.87	0.94	0.93	0.94	0.93	0.93
Noon, String	0.99	0.99	0.99	0.99	0.99	0.99	0.99
Rooster, Voyage	0.99	0.99	0.99	0.99	0.99	0.99	0.99
Avg Correl	0.84	0.76	0.87	0.86	0.90	0.89	0.89

Table 3. Averages of the average Pearson's correlations with different relatedness methods

	sim_R	$sim_{W\&P}$	sim_L	$sim_{J\&C}$	$sim_{P\&S}$	sim_A	$sim_{A\&M}$	Avg.
CombIC	0.80	0.70	0.84	0.82	0.85	0.84	0.84	**0.81**
$LDSD_{cw}$	0.84	0.76	0.87	0.86	0.90	0.89	0.89	**0.86**
$ASRMP^a_m$	0.85	0.75	0.86	0.84	0.89	0.88	0.88	**0.85**
WLM	0.79	0.73	0.82	0.82	0.86	0.84	0.84	**0.82**
ExclM	0.85	0.78	0.85	0.85	0.87	0.88	0.88	**0.85**
LODOverlap	0.86	0.67	0.81	0.77	0.83	0.86	0.86	**0.81**

4.2   Experimental Results

In Table 1, for reader's convenience, the average Pearson's correlations for all the 28 pairs according to the experimental results given in [14] are given, where the relatedness degrees have been computed by leveraging the semantic relatedness measure presented in [29]. In Table 2, the values have been obtained by relying on the semantic relatedness approach proposed in [23], with an average increment of the average correlations with human judgement of about 0.05 (0.86 vs 0.81).

This is shown in Table 3, where the averages of these values have been compared with the corresponding values obtained by relying on the $ASRMP_m$ [9], *WLM* [34], *ExclM* [16], and *LODOverlap* [37] relatedness measures mentioned above. Analogously, in Tables 4 and 5 the averages Spearman's correlations according to the *CombIC* and $LDSD_{cw}$ approaches are shown, respectively, and in Table 6 the averages of such values have been compared with the corresponding values of the other methods. Overall, according to Tables 3 and 6, $LDSD_{cw}$ shows the best averages values $((0.86 + 0.79)/2 = 0.83)$. Below, the key features underlying the compared methods are recalled. According to $ASRMP^a_m$, the key idea is to evaluate all the directed paths connecting the resources to be compared, of length equal to m. This does not hold in the case of the *WLM* method, which is inspired by the *Normalized Google Distance* measure. Indeed, *WLM* relies on the information gathered by the nodes that are adjacent to the compared resources and, in particular, on those with incoming links to them. Analogously, in the case of *LODOverlap* only the nodes that are adjacent to the compared resources are addressed, although the method also considers those with outgoing links from the compared resources. The remaining approaches shown in Table 3 (and Table 6) focus on the undirected links between the compared resources. In particular, as described in Sect. 3.2, *CombIC* is based on the computation of the information contents of both the predicates and the objects of the triples. The *ExclM* method focuses on a given number of undirected paths and, in particular, it is based on a path weighting function that allows the selection of the undirected paths between the compared resources with the greatest weights. As illustrated in Sect. 3.3, in $LDSD_{cw}$ the undirected paths with links incoming to, or outgoing from, the compared resources are addressed. In addition, with respect to the other methods, $LDSD_{cw}$ aims at verifying the existence of path patterns, i.e., specific configurations of paths in the graph. Such patterns involve further resources, on the basis of the names of the triples' predicates, by taking into account the combination of both the adjacent and the non-adjacent nodes to the compared resources.

As a result, the combination of the measure defined in Eq. 4 with the $LDSD_{cw}$ method proposed in [23] provides on average the best strategy in order to evaluate semantic similarity in a taxonomy by addressing the concept intended senses in a given context.

Table 4. Average Spearman's correlations in the 28 contexts according to the experiment presented in [14] based on *CombIC*

$concept_1, concept_2$	sim_R	$sim_{W\&P}$	sim_L	$sim_{J\&C}$	$sim_{P\&S}$	sim_A	$sim_{A\&M}$
Car, Automobile	0.81	0.80	0.84	0.85	0.85	0.84	0.86
Gem, Jewel	0.80	0.77	0.83	0.82	0.84	0.87	0.87
Journey, Voyage	0.89	0.87	0.90	0.86	0.92	0.92	0.92
Boy, Lad	0.85	0.81	0.91	0.85	0.92	0.85	0.85
Coast, Shore	0.94	0.85	0.93	0.90	0.92	0.93	0.91
Asylum, Madhouse	0.83	0.89	0.91	0.85	0.93	0.87	0.85
Magician, Wizard	0.92	0.86	0.89	0.90	0.91	0.87	0.87
Midday, Noon	0.87	0.89	0.91	0.91	0.92	0.87	0.87
Furnace, Stove	0.65	0.38	0.63	0.50	0.67	0.66	0.66
Food, Fruit	0.85	0.58	0.84	0.81	0.89	0.83	0.81
Bird, Cock	0.84	0.82	0.88	0.82	0.86	0.85	0.84
Bird, Crane	0.83	0.83	0.88	0.85	0.87	0.86	0.85
Tool, Implement	0.80	0.78	0.84	0.77	0.84	0.82	0.81
Brother, Monk	0.82	0.71	0.83	0.83	0.93	0.82	0.81
Crane, Implement	0.69	0.67	0.73	0.74	0.79	0.73	0.75
Lad, Brother	0.71	0.68	0.80	0.66	0.69	0.75	0.73
Journey, Car	0.69	0.58	0.71	0.78	0.77	0.71	0.72
Monk, Oracle	0.77	0.59	0.65	0.67	0.70	0.76	0.75
Food, Rooster	0.85	0.64	0.85	0.86	0.89	0.86	0.87
Coast, Hill	0.62	0.72	0.70	0.69	0.65	0.70	0.71
Forest, Graveyard	0.81	0.79	0.84	0.84	0.88	0.83	0.83
Monk, Slave	0.70	0.59	0.62	0.62	0.67	0.63	0.63
Coast, Forest	0.82	0.78	0.86	0.88	0.92	0.86	0.82
Lad, Wizard	0.64	0.59	0.64	0.54	0.72	0.59	0.59
Chord, Smile	0.58	0.76	0.78	0.99	0.99	0.76	0.76
Glass, Magician	0.85	0.85	0.85	0.91	0.89	0.81	0.77
Noon, String	0.92	0.88	0.92	0.94	0.86	0.94	0.93
Rooster, Voyage	0.79	0.73	0.82	0.86	0.90	0.83	0.82
Avg Correl.	0.79	0.74	0.81	0.80	0.84	0.81	0.80

Table 5. Average Spearman's correlations in the 28 contexts according to the new experiment based on $LDSD_{cw}$

concept$_1$, concept$_2$	sim$_R$	sim$_{W\&P}$	sim$_L$	sim$_{J\&C}$	sim$_{P\&S}$	sim$_A$	sim$_{A\&M}$
Car, Automobile	0.83	0.87	0.88	0.87	0.88	0.89	0.90
Gem, Jewel	0.84	0.87	0.89	0.91	0.92	0.90	0.91
Journey, Voyage	0.93	0.91	0.91	0.86	0.91	0.97	0.97
Boy, Lad	0.81	0.79	0.88	0.84	0.90	0.84	0.85
Coast, Shore	0.94	0.85	0.92	0.90	0.90	0.93	0.92
Asylum, Madhouse	0.78	0.86	0.89	0.88	0.89	0.81	0.81
Magician, Wizard	0.93	0.88	0.89	0.90	0.91	0.88	0.88
Midday, Noon	0.88	0.89	0.91	0.92	0.92	0.88	0.88
Furnace, Stove	0.62	0.38	0.56	0.48	0.64	0.63	0.61
Food, Fruit	0.81	0.56	0.83	0.83	0.89	0.82	0.81
Bird, Cock	0.85	0.79	0.86	0.79	0.88	0.85	0.86
Bird, Crane	0.84	0.79	0.86	0.84	0.89	0.83	0.83
Tool, Implement	0.76	0.71	0.80	0.71	0.76	0.78	0.80
Brother, Monk	0.74	0.69	0.79	0.80	0.94	0.80	0.81
Crane, Implement	0.67	0.66	0.72	0.68	0.76	0.72	0.72
Lad, Brother	0.69	0.61	0.75	0.72	0.78	0.74	0.71
Journey, Car	0.71	0.60	0.74	0.82	0.80	0.75	0.77
Monk, Oracle	0.75	0.57	0.74	0.70	0.86	0.81	0.80
Food, Rooster	0.75	0.61	0.78	0.82	0.87	0.79	0.78
Coast, Hill	0.58	0.71	0.66	0.66	0.63	0.72	0.74
Forest, Graveyard	0.73	0.60	0.73	0.77	0.80	0.81	0.81
Monk, Slave	0.72	0.68	0.72	0.69	0.78	0.80	0.78
Coast, Forest	0.74	0.70	0.79	0.84	0.85	0.79	0.77
Lad, Wizard	0.65	0.60	0.61	0.58	0.76	0.64	0.62
Chord, Smile	0.46	0.65	0.73	0.99	0.99	0.67	0.67
Glass, Magician	0.78	0.74	0.78	0.82	0.86	0.73	0.72
Noon, String	0.91	0.90	0.91	0.96	0.83	0.94	0.92
Rooster, Voyage	0.78	0.78	0.83	0.87	0.89	0.84	0.82
Avg Correl	0.77	0.72	0.80	0.80	0.85	0.81	0.80

The data concerning the new experiment are available in [31] where, with respect to the experiment presented in [14], also the Spearman's correlations have been given and analyzed.

Table 6. Averages of the average Spearman's correlations with different relatedness methods

	sim_R	$sim_{W\&P}$	sim_L	$sim_{J\&C}$	$sim_{P\&S}$	sim_A	$sim_{A\&M}$	Avg.
CombIC	0.79	0.74	0.81	0.80	0.84	0.81	0.80	**0.80**
LDSD$_{cw}$	0.77	0.72	0.80	0.80	0.85	0.81	0.80	**0.79**
ASRMP$_m^a$	0.78	0.72	0.78	0.77	0.81	0.77	0.76	**0.77**
WLM	0.74	0.71	0.78	0.80	0.83	0.78	0.76	**0.77**
ExclM	0.77	0.72	0.77	0.74	0.78	0.73	0.74	**0.75**
LODOverlap	0.78	0.73	0.80	0.79	0.83	0.80	0.79	**0.79**

5 Related Work

Within the several similarity measures that have been proposed in the literature [8], in this paper we restrict our attention to the methods based on the information content (IC) approach, which has been employed in different research areas, such as Natural Language Processing [4], Semantic Web [11,21], Formal Concept Analysis [12,32], Geographical Information Systems [10,13,28], and different application domains, such as health [1], and network security [33], just to mention a couple of examples. The IC approach, although recognized as "the state of the art on semantic similarity" [3,6], has shown some limitations. In particular, one objection to the early IC based measures relies on the use of large-scale corpora [3,5,6,17,36]. In fact, evaluating IC on the basis of statistical information taken from textual corpora requires a huge amount of manual effort at level of both the design and the maintenance of the corpus. For this reason, in the literature, an evolution of the IC notion has been extensively investigated, referred to as *intrinsic information content* (IIC), although there is a lack of a statistically significant difference between the performances of the IIC models and the corpus-based ones [19]. In particular, the IIC is evaluated independently of textual corpora, and in accordance with the intrinsic structure of the taxonomy, i.e., on the basis of the number of hyponyms and/or hypernyms of the concepts. Along this direction, Adhikari et Al. propose a method in [3] (sim_A in our experiment), arguing that by relying only on the maximum among the ICs of the least common subsumers leads to ignore some common subsumers that can be relevant in order to evaluate semantic similarity. For this reason, in the mentioned paper, the IC is estimated according to an IIC approach by introducing a new notion, referred to as *Disjoint Common Subsumers*. A variant of this approach based on Meng model has also been proposed in [2], that shows slightly better performances than the other measure ($sim_{A\&M}$ in this paper). Both the models they present achieve high correlation values when applied to the state-of-the-art measures addressed in our experiment. Analogously, in [24] an IIC approach for semantic similarity has been proposed by relying on the Tversky linear contrast model [30], which addresses both concept commonalities and differences, showing high correlation with human judgment with respect to the state-of-the-art ($sim_{P\&S}$ in this work).

It is worth mentioning that according to Resnik [26] (sim_R), concept similarity in a taxonomy is computed by considering only concept commonalities, therefore it shows some limitations since pairs of concepts having the same least common subsumers have the same similarity degrees. According to [7], the proposal of Lin [20] (sim_L) can be reconducted to the Tversky linear contrast model of similarity recalled above. In particular, also in [20] the importance of observing an object from different perspectives is emphasized, but the proposed resulting similarity degrees are considered as weighted averages of the similarity values obtained from such perspectives. As a result, this approach does not allow to estimate concept similarity by considering a single specific perspective at a time. Successively, in [18], in the late 1990s, a proposal combining the IC with the edge-counting approach has been presented ($sim_{J\&C}$), showing better performances with respect to the previous methods. The notion of sense has been addressed by Resnik in [27], where semantic similarity is used to identify and select the appropriate sense of a concept when it appears in a group of related terms. However, the mentioned paper addresses word sense disambiguation in the field of computational linguistics, where semantic similarity is not the objective of the work but it allows the association of a noun with the right sense in a given context. On the contrary, we use the concept intended senses to improve the computation of semantic similarity.

It is important to note that, with respect to the existing literature, in this paper we do not address a new IC or IIC computing model, and our proposal is independent of it. In fact, although the IIC approaches show a high accuracy in the similarity evaluation, they do not involve concept meaning and, in particular, the related similarity measures do not address the intended senses of concepts according to a given application domain.

6   Conclusion and Future Work

In this work the novel approach for evaluating semantic similarity in a taxonomy presented in [14] has been refined. In particular, in order to compute the relatedness of the generic sense of a concept with its intended sense, some among the most representative methods for computing semantic relatedness proposed in the literature have been compared. Among them, the *Linked Data Semantic Distance* approach proposed by Passant in [23] has shown the best performances. As a result, in order to evaluate semantic similarity in a taxonomy, looking for specific path patterns in the knowledge graph has a direct impact on the correlation with human judgment, and outperforms the previous approach of the authors based on triple weights.

As a future work, we are planning to extend this proposal by defining the intended sense of a concept as a *set* of concepts, rather than a single one (singleton). This assumption would allow us to benefit from the *SemSim* semantic similarity method [11] in order to easily perform the disambiguation step by comparing the sets of concept senses.

References

1. Abdelrahman, A.M.B., Kayed, A.: A survey on semantic similarity measures between concepts in health domain. Am. J. Comput. Math. **5**, 204–214 (2015)
2. Adhikari, A., Singh, S., Mondal, D., Dutta, B., Dutta, A.: A novel information theoretic framework for finding semantic similarity in wordnet. CoRR, arXiv:1607.05422, abs/1607.05422 (2016)
3. Adhikari, A., Dutta, B., Dutta, A., Mondal, D., Singh, S.: An intrinsic information content-based semantic similarity measure considering the disjoint common subsumers of concepts of an ontology. J. Assoc. Inf. Sci. Technol. **69**(8), 1023–1034 (2018)
4. Ajumder, G.O.M., Akray, P.A.P., Elbukh, A.L.G.: Measuring semantic textual similarity of sentences using modified information content and lexical taxonomy. Int. J. Comput. Linguist. Appl. **7**(2), 65–85 (2016)
5. Banu, A., Fatima, S.S., Khan, K.: Information content based semantic similarity measure for concepts subsumed by multiple concepts. Int. J. Web Appl. **7**(3), 85–94 (2015)
6. Batet, M., Sànchez, D.: Leveraging synonymy and polysemy to improve semantic similarity assessments based on intrinsic information content. Artif. Intell. Rev. **53**(3), 2023–2041 (2020)
7. Cazzanti, L., Gupta, M.R.: Information-theoretic and set-theoretic similarity, pp. 1836–1840. IEEE International Symposium on Information Theory, Seattle, WA (2006)
8. Chandrasekaran, D., Mago, V.: Evolution of semantic similarity - a survey. ACM Comput. Surv. **54**(2), Article 41 (2021)
9. El Vaigh, C.B., Goasdoué, F., Gravier, G., Sébillot, P.: A novel path-based entity relatedness measure for efficient collective entity linking. In: Pan, J.Z., et al. (eds.) ISWC 2020. LNCS, vol. 12506, pp. 164–182. Springer, Cham (2020). https://doi.org/10.1007/978-3-030-62419-4_10
10. Formica, A., Pourabbas, E.: Content based similarity of geographic classes organized as partition hierarchies. Knowl. Inf. Syst. **20**(2), 221–241 (2009)
11. Formica, A., Missikoff, M., Pourabbas, E., Taglino, F.: Semantic search for matching user requests with profiled enterprises. Comput. Ind. **64**(3), 191–202 (2013)
12. Formica, A.: Similarity reasoning in formal concept analysis: from one- to many-valued contexts. Knowl. Inf. Syst. **60**(2), 715–739 (2019)
13. Formica, A., Mazzei, M., Pourabbas, E., Rafanelli, M.: Approximate query answering based on topological neighborhood and semantic similarity in openstreetmap. IEEE Access **8**, 87011–87030 (2020)
14. Formica, A., Taglino, F.: An enriched information-theoretic definition of semantic similarity in a taxonomy. IEEE Access **9**, 100583–100593 (2021)
15. Hadj Taieb, M.A., Zesch, T. Aouicha, M.B.: A survey of semantic relatedness evaluation datasets and procedures. Artif. Intell. Rev. **53**, 4407–4448 (2020)
16. Hulpuş, I., Prangnawarat, N., Hayes, C.: Path-based semantic relatedness on linked data and its use to word and entity disambiguation. In: Arenas, M., et al. (eds.) ISWC 2015. LNCS, vol. 9366, pp. 442–457. Springer, Cham (2015). https://doi.org/10.1007/978-3-319-25007-6_26
17. Jeong, S., Yim, J.H., Lee, H.J., Sohn, M.M.: Semantic similarity calculation method using information contents-based edge weighting. J. Internet Serv. Inf. Secur. **7**(1), 40–53 (2017)

18. Jiang, J.J., Conrath, D.W.: Semantic similarity based on corpus statistics and lexical taxonomy. In: Proceedings of International Conference on Research Computational Linguistics (ROCLING X), Taiwan (1997)
19. Lastra-Dìaz, J.J., Garcìa-Serrano, A.: A new family of information content models with an experimental survey on WordNet. Knowl.-Based Syst. **89**, 509–526 (2015)
20. Lin, D.: An information-theoretic definition of similarity. In: Proceedings of the International Conference on Machine Learning, Madison, Wisconsin, USA, pp. 296–304. Morgan Kaufmann (1998)
21. Meymandpour, R., Davis, J.G.: A semantic similarity measure for linked data: an information content-based approach. Knowl.-Based Syst. **109**, 276–293 (2016)
22. Miller, G.A., Charles, W.G.: Contextual correlates of semantic similarity. Lang. Cognit. Process. **6**(1), 1–28 (1991)
23. Passant, A.: Measuring semantic distance on linking data and using it for resources recommendations. In: Proceedings of the AAAI Spring Symposium on Linked Data Meets Artificial Intelligence (2010)
24. Pirrò, G.: A semantic similarity metric combining features and intrinsic information content. Data Knowl. Eng. **68**(11), 1289–1308 (2009)
25. Rada, R., Mili, H., Bichnell, E., Blettner, M.: Development and application of a metric on semantic nets. IEEE Trans. Syst. Man Cybern. **9**, 17–30 (1989)
26. Resnik, P.: Using information content to evaluate semantic similarity in a taxonomy. In: Proceedings of the Int. Joint Conference on Artificial Intelligence, Montreal, Quebec, Canada, August 20–25, pp. 448–453. Morgan Kaufmann (1995)
27. Resnik, P.: Semantic Similarity in a taxonomy: an information-based measure and its application to problems of ambiguity in natural language. J. Artif. Intell. Res. **11**, 95–130 (1999)
28. Schwering, A.: Approaches to semantic similarity measurement for geo-spatial data: a survey. Trans. GIS **12**(1), 5–29 (2008)
29. Schuhmacher, M., Ponzetto, S.P.: Knowledge-based graph document modeling. In: Proceedings of the 7th ACM International Conference on Web Search and Data Mining, (WSDM), New York, USA, pp. 543–552 (2014)
30. Tversky, A.: Features of similarity. Psychol. Rev. **84**, 327–352 (1977)
31. Taglino, F., Formica, A.: Semantic similarity with concept senses. Mendeley Data, V1 (2022). https://data.mendeley.com/datasets/994p293zcf
32. Wang, F., Wang, N., Cai, S., Zhang, W.: A similarity measure in formal concept analysis containing general semantic information and domain information. IEEE Access **8**, 75303–75312 (2020)
33. Weller-Fahy, D.J., Borghetti, B.J., Sodemann, A.A.: A Survey of Distance and similarity measures used within network intrusion anomaly detection. IEEE Commun. Surv. Tutor. **17**(1), 70–91 (2015)
34. Witten, I.H., Milne, D.: An effective, low-cost measure of semantic relatedness obtained from Wikipedia links.. In: Proceedings of AAAI Workshop on Wikipedia and Artificial Intelligence: an Evolving Synergy, pp. 25–30. AAAI Press, Chicago, USA (2008)
35. Wu, Z., Palmer, M.: Verb semantics and lexical selection. In: Proceedings of the 32nd Annual Meeting of the Associations for Computational Linguistics, Las Cruces, New Mexico, pp. 133–138 (1994)
36. Zhang, X., Sun, S., Zhang, K.: An information content-based approach for measuring concept semantic similarity in wordnet. Wireless Pers. Commun. **103**(1), 117–132 (2018). https://doi.org/10.1007/s11277-018-5429-7

37. Zhou, W., Wang, H., Chao, J., Zhang, W., Yu, Y.: LODDO: using linked open data description overlap to measure semantic relatedness between named entities. In: Pan, J.Z. et al. (eds.) Proceedings of Joint International Semantic Technology Conference, JIST 2011 (2012)

Constituency-Informed and Constituency-Constrained Extractive Question Answering with Heterogeneous Graph Transformer

Mingzhe Du[1(✉)][iD], Mouad Hakam[2][iD], See-Kiong Ng[1,2][iD], and Stéphane Bressan[1,2][iD]

[1] Institute of Data Science, National University of Singapore, Singapore, Singapore
{mingzhe,seekiong,steph}@nus.edu.sg
[2] School of Computing, National University of Singapore, Singapore, Singapore
e1002601@u.nus.edu

Abstract. Large neural language models are achieving exceptional performance in question answering and other natural language processing tasks. However, these models can be costly to train and difficult to interpret. In this paper, we propose to investigate whether incorporating explicit linguistic information can boost model performance while improving model interpretability.

We present a novel constituency-informed and constituency-constrained question answering model called SyHGT-CN. The linguistics-informed model integrates the symbolic information contained in constituency trees with the statistical knowledge of a neural language model. The integration of the linguistics graphic structures with the transformer-based neural language model is achieved by the adjunction to the latter of a heterogeneous graph neural network, in which the former is encoded.

We comparatively and empirically show, with the SQuAD2.0 benchmark, that the proposed approach is more accurate than a constituency-oblivious BERT and the constituency-informed SyHGT-C model.

Keywords: Question answering · Linguistics-informed natural language processing · Transformer · Graph neural network

1 Introduction

The integration of statistical machine learning with symbolic knowledge and reasoning "opens relevant possibilities towards richer intelligent systems" remarked the authors of [5] arguing for a principled integration of machine learning and reasoning. Nevertheless, most existing neural language models are still plundering the benefits of statistical learning before they attempt to explicitly exploit old-fashion symbolic knowledge of the linguistic structures. While the success of transformer-based neural language models is attributed to the self-attention mechanism [40] that they implement, the question arises whether the adjunction of a focused attention mechanism guided by structures representing symbolic linguistic information [3] can further improve the performance of neural language models.

© Springer-Verlag GmbH Germany, part of Springer Nature 2023
A. Hameurlain and A. M. Tjoa (Eds.): TLDKS LIII, LNCS 13840, pp. 90–106, 2023.
https://doi.org/10.1007/978-3-662-66863-4_4

Zhu et al., in [45], successfully leveraged heterogeneous graph transformers [10] to incorporate linguistics information into neural language models and guide natural language processing tasks. Indeed, linguists and computational linguists [3,27] commonly formalize linguistics information, whether morphology, syntax, semantics, or pragmatics information, by means of graphic structures such as morphology trees, dependency graphs, constituency parse trees, and graphs of semantic relations. Zhu et al. devised a family of models, SyHGT, that adjoins a graph neural network representation of the syntactic structure of the question and context, for instance, the constituency parse tree in the case of SyHGT-C, to the neural language model for the task of extractive question answering.

We revisit SyHGT-C, the constituency-informed model of [45], and devise, present, and evaluate a novel, not only constituency-informed but also constituency-constrained, model, SyHGT-CN, a syntax-informed heterogeneous graph neural network constituency node model for extractive question answering. The originality of SyHGT-CN is that its output is also constituency-constrained. SyHGT-CN departs from existing neural extractive question answering models in that it leverages the constituency tree to return a node instead of a start and end position to represent the answer's span.

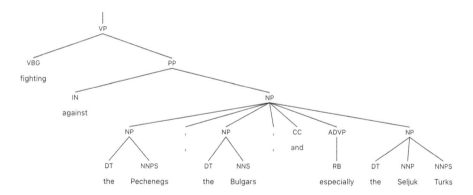

Fig. 1. Constituency parse tree of the phrase *"fighting against the Pechenegs, the Bulgars, and especially the Seljuk Turks."*

The Constituency parse tree of the phrase *"fighting against the Pechenegs, the Bulgars, and especially the Seljuk Turks"* is shown in Fig. 1. A constituency parse tree is a tree-based representation of the structure of a sentence stemming from the rules of an underlying generative context-free grammar [1]. For instance, the rule $VP \rightarrow V + NP$ states that a verb phrase can be formed by combining a verb and a noun phrase and yields a tree $VP(V(verb), NP(proper\ noun))$. The same rules that generatively define valid sentences are used to extract the syntactical structure of a given sentence according to the grammar. The constituency parse tree organizes the words of a sentence into nested constituents based on their grammatical category [15]. The example in Fig. 1 uses the categories and tags of the Penn Tree bank [26] made of nonterminals, representing phrases, and part-of-speech tags. The categories, and their corresponding tags, include noun phrases, NP, determiners, DT, nouns, NN, plural nouns, NNS, proper nouns, NNP, plural proper nouns, NNPS, and adverbial phrases, ADVP, for instance. In a constituency parse tree, the words of the sentence are always included as terminal nodes. Typically, each word has a parent node that contains its part-of-speech tag (noun, verb, adjective, etc.) [30].

The potential advantages of a constituency-informed and constituency-constrained question answering model are therefore twofold. First, the constituency information may improve the accuracy of the model in complex situations in which the question, context, and answer involve complex grammatical structures. Second, the constraint that the model can only return a node of the constituency tree guarantees the grammatical integrity of the answer.

For instance, the SQuAD2.0 question *"Who was the Normans' main enemy in Italy, the Byzantine Empire and Armenia?"* with the context *"Soon after the Normans began to enter Italy, they entered the Byzantine Empire and then Armenia, fighting against the Pechenegs, the Bulgars, and especially the Seljuk Turks.[...]"* has the ground truth answer *"the Pechenegs, the Bulgars, and especially the Seljuk Turks"*. The constituency-oblivious BERT question answering model finds the answer *"Pechenegs"*, which is both semantically inaccurate and grammatically incorrect, while the novel approach that we present here, informed and constrained by the constituency parse tree, finds the correct answer.

In the remainder of the paper, we briefly synthesize the relevant related work, present the proposed constituency-informed and constituency-constrained question answering model, SyHGT-CN, and comparatively evaluate the performance of a linguistics-oblivious BERT-based question answering model, to which we refer as BERT, of the original constituency-informed question answering model, SyHGT-C, and of the proposed constituency-informed and constituency-constrained question answering model, SyHGT-CN, with the Stanford Question Answering Dataset (SQuAD2.0) [33].

2   Background and Related Work

2.1   Transformers and Heterogeneous Graph Transformers

The Transformer architecture is a revolutionary network design that relies solely on attention mechanisms, eliminating the need for recurrence and convolutions [40]. This unique approach allows for faster and more efficient processing, making it a highly sought-after tool in deep learning. The attention mechanisms utilized in the Transformer architecture enable the model to focus selectively on relevant information, allowing it to capture long-term dependencies and complex patterns in data effectively. This innovative architecture has been widely adopted in natural language processing tasks, such as machine translation, summarisation, and question answering [14].

BERT, Bidirectional Encoder Representations from Transformers, is a widespread deep-learning model that considers a word's entire context rather than its parts [4].

The heterogeneous Graph Transformer (HGT) is a graph neural network architecture specifically designed to deal with large-scale heterogeneous and dynamic graphs [10]. This unique architecture utilizes an independent attention mechanism capable of handling the heterogeneity of the graph. Unlike other architectures that parameterize each edge type, the heterogeneous graph transformer utilizes a heterogeneous mutual attention approach that breaks down each edge based on its meta-relation triplet. This allows nodes and edges of different types to maintain their specific representation spaces while still allowing for connected nodes of different types to interact, pass, and aggregate messages without being hindered by their distribution gaps [10].

Since most transformer models operate in high-dimensional embedding spaces, heterogeneous graph transformers can propagate and aggregate new embeddings with the same dimension, regardless of whether the original embeddings represent tokens, words, or other language units [44].

2.2   Question Answering

Question answering [2] is a sub-field of both natural language processing [13] and information retrieval [24]. Question answering is concerned with designing and implementing algorithms, tools, and systems for automatically answering questions in natural language. Among the different types of question answering tasks, extractive question answering refers to the extraction from a document or paragraph, called context or passage, the correct answer to a question as a continuous span of text [33,34,38,46].

Early question answering systems typically employed syntactic analysis and rule-based approaches to generate answers [12]. With the rise of natural language processing and machine learning techniques, modern question answering systems have become more sophisticated and efficient, incorporating more advanced algorithms and data-driven approaches to provide more accurate and comprehensive answers. The follow-up models explored the influence of feature engineering and network structure on the results based on the pioneering works [37].

Subsequently, advancements in computing hardware and software frameworks have paved the way for the success of neural networks, which do not rely on intensive feature engineering. By learning inductive bias on massive training samples, neural networks have achieved overwhelming performance improvements in extractive question answering tasks. As an early representative of neural language models, BERT and its variants have become the standard backbone model for extractive question answering tasks for eleven natural language processing benchmarks [4].

The emergence of large-scale language models, such as BERT [4] and its successors [8,17], has brought epoch-making performance improvements to most natural language processing tasks, including question answering tasks [17,38]. Although these self-supervised models, as shown by Goldberg et al. [6], can implicitly learn pertinent linguistics information and, as argued by Manning et al. in [23], can recover the rich latent structure of human language, Kuncoro et al., in [16], demonstrate that BERT still benefits from supplementary syntactic information for various structured prediction tasks.

Based on the original BERT work, Jawahar et al. probed each layer of BERT models. They found that lower layers captured surface features, middle layers captured syntactic features, and upper layers captured semantic features [11]. The upper layers were found to model the long-distance dependencies, making them crucial to performance in downstream tasks. However, it was also found that syntactic information is diluted in these upper layers. Kuncoro et al. extended BERT to account for syntactic information by modifying its pre-training objective [16]. By utilizing another syntactic language model as a learning signal, the researchers added a new component called "syntactic bias" to vanilla BERT, enhancing its grammar understanding capabilities to adapt to the nuances and complexities of natural language.

Vashishth et al. utilized dependency trees and graph convolutional networks to develop syntax-based embeddings that encode functional grammar similarity instead of topical similarity [39]. The syntax-based embeddings were found to encode information complementary to ELMo [29] embeddings that only relied on sequential context. Zhang et al. proposed a syntax-guided network (SG-Net), a question answering model that used dependency trees as explicit syntactic constraints for a self-attention layer [29]. The syntax-guided attention mechanism filled the flaws of traditional attention mechanisms since the syntax guidance offered more explicit attentive signals and reduced the impact of noise. Therefore, SG-NET was particularly effective with longer questions as it could select vital parts. Zhu et al. introduced syntactic information into the extractive question answering pipeline by importing constituency trees and dependency graphs [45]. The heterogeneous mutual attention nature of heterogeneous graph transformers supports the seamless integration of the high-dimensional text representation space with the adjunctive syntactic graph structures. This enables nodes and edges of different types to maintain their individual representation spaces while still allowing for connected nodes of different types to interact, pass, and aggregate messages without being hindered by their distribution gaps [10].

Graph neural networks operate directly on graphs and can capture dependencies between vertices. This work shows the utility of syntax and graph neural networks in learning better representations [44]. Unlike traditional graph neural networks, a heterogeneous graph transformer can handle a heterogeneous graph, which consists of multiple types of vertices connected by different relations [10].

In the same vein as the approach by Mao et al. [25], we bridged traditional rule-based systems and new neural models by integrating symbolic knowledge into statistical machine learning. Furthermore, we explicitly incorporate constituency trees into the extractive question answering pipeline, such that constituency linguistic information can not only provide additional knowledge to the model but also normalize the selection of answers. This keeps our approach rooted linguistically instead of solely relying on pre-trained language models that are not explainable.

As far as we know, the integration of heterogeneous syntax information and constituent node prediction for extractive question answering has yet to be explored in natural language processing. By leveraging the unique capabilities of a heterogeneous graph transformer, we can unlock new levels of performance and accuracy in the extractive question answering task.

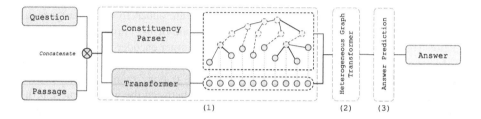

Fig. 2. There are three primary components in our proposed approach, namely (1) graph construction, (2) graph processing, and (3) answer prediction. The purple vertices are the last hidden embeddings of transformer models. The dashed green vertices are constituency nodes. (Color figure online)

3   Methodology

3.1   The Task

Extractive question answering takes as input a question $q = \{q_0, q_1, \cdots, q_n\}$ and a passage $p = \{p_0, p_1, \cdots, p_m\}$ from which the task predicts a single answer span $a = \langle a_{start}, a_{end} \rangle$, represented as a pair of indices into p, where n is the question length and m is the context length. The specific objective of this task is to learn the function $f(q, p) \rightarrow a$ from a training dataset of $\langle q, p, a \rangle$ triplets [18, 33].

In most extractive question answering pipelines, answer prediction is modelled as locating the beginning and end of the answer from a given passage. However, this paradigm cannot explicitly learn syntactic knowledge. The two indices are generated independently without guaranteeing that the generated answer, whose span they delimitate, conforms to grammatical rules.

We propose SyHGT-CN, a constituency-informed and constituency-constrained architecture, extending the constituency-informed SyHGT-C model [45].

We need to create and process linguistic, graphic structures connecting the language model embeddings of the tokens of the question and passage. This non-Euclidean graph structure cannot be used directly by the neural language model [32]. However, the insertion of a heterogeneous graph transformer layer to the question answering pipeline allows a relatively straightforward implementation combining the statistical and symbolic information [10]. By inserting the graph neural network between the neural language model and the output layer, we can process the graph before making a prediction. Figure 2 depicts, SyHGT-CN, the proposed approach, with its three main components: graph construction, graph processing, and answer prediction.

3.2   Graph Creation Modules

The question and the context are concatenated and then input into a tokeniser. The tokeniser splits the text into individual tokens and feeds them to a transformer encoder that generates a representation embedding for each. This process allows the creation of embedded representations of each token in the conjoined sequence. In the next step, the tokens and their embedded representations are added to the heterogeneous graph as pre-terminal nodes, becoming the cornerstone of the entire graph network. Section Transformer Encoder elaborates on the transformer encoder details.

Meanwhile, the constituency parser parses the connected sequence and generates the corresponding constituency tree. The nodes of the tree are span segments divided according to given grammatical rules, and the edges between the nodes represent the affiliation relationship of the nodes. Section Constituency Graph introduced the context of the constituency tree.

After obtaining embedded representations of each token and the corresponding constituency tree, Section Token Alignment discusses connecting the pre-terminal nodes added to the graph with the constituency tree.

Transformer Encoder. SyHGT-CN requires a natural language representation model as its initial encoder, which produces embedding vectors for the text input. The Bidirectional Encoder Representations from Transformers (BERT), see Vaswani et al. [40] and Devlin et al. [4], is used for implementation and performance evaluation in this paper.

The question q and context p are concatenated with the appropriate BERT-specific special tokens to form the sequence: [CLS] q [SEP] p [SEP]. The sequence is fed into BERT to acquire the token embeddings $T = t_1, ..., t_n$, which are the hidden states of the input sequence at the last layer, where n is the number of tokens.

Constituency Graph. Constituency analysis iteratively decomposes sentences into constituent or sub-phrases: clauses, phrases, and words. These constituents belong to one of several categories, such as noun phrase (NP), verb phrase (VP), as well as parts of speech [30]. Explicitly, given an input sentence, constituency analysis builds a tree in which leaves or terminal vertices correspond to input words, and the internal or non-terminal vertices are constituents.

The vertices in the constituency tree are grouped into three categories, token vertices, lexeme vertices, and constituent vertices. Token vertices correspond to common tokens, and Lexeme vertices represent lexemes that need to be recomposed from the token vertices of their sub-words. Constituent vertices represent constituents. Inner nodes and the root of the constituency tree are virtual, lexeme, constituency, and vertices.

The edges in the constituency tree are grouped into three categories, morphology edges, part-of-speech edges, and constituent edges. Morphology edges connect token vertices corresponding to sub-words to lexeme vertices. Part-of-speech edges connect the part-of-speech vertices to lexemes vertices. Constituency edges connect low-level constituents to high-level constituents.

Token Alignment. The use of distinct algorithms in the transformer tokenizer and the constituency tree parser may lead to a slight discrepancy between the embedding sequence produced by the transformer encoder and the underlying pre-terminal nodes of the constituency tree. This mismatch can hinder the effectiveness of the downstream heterogeneous graph transformer that relies on the accurate alignment of these two components. To address this issue, it is necessary to adopt a cohesive post-processing step to ensure the alignment of the embedding sequence with the pre-terminal nodes of the constituency tree.

Suppose the token sequence of the question text is $q = \{q_{t1}, q_{t2}, \cdots, q_{tn}\}$, the token sequence of the passage is $p = \{p_{t1}, p_{t2}, \cdots, p_{tm}\}$. After adding a few BERT-specific tokens, the final concatenation S is represented in Eq. (1). The bottom pre-terminals C of the Constituency tree depicts in Eq. (2).

$$S = \{[CLS], q_{t1}, q_{t2}, \cdots, q_{tn}, [SEP], p_{t1}, p_{t2}, \cdots, p_{tm}, [SEP]\} \tag{1}$$

$$C = \{q_{t1}, q_{t2}, \cdots, q_{tn}, p_{t1}, p_{t2}, \cdots, p_{tm}\} \tag{2}$$

The objective of token alignment is to find the corresponding embedded representation for each pre-terminal node in the constituency tree $TA(S) \rightarrow C$, where the relationship can be one-to-one or one-to-many. for example, token "morn##" and token "##ing" may belong to one constituency pre-terminal"morning". We harnessed a greedy matching algorithm to detect if the pre-terminal node overlaps the current sequence token from left to right. The method is both simple and efficient, but for a small number of data, a mismatch in the token alignment could cause all subsequent tokens not to match. As a result, we temporarily skip all data with this abnormal token alignment to avoid potential issues.

3.3 Graph Processing

The heterogeneous graph transformer takes the constructed graphs as input and passes its outputs to the linear layer. The output from the linear layer is the probability that a node is an answer to the question. The maximum score determines the final predicted answer span.

Graph neural networks, proposed by the authors of [35], are neural models that capture the dependence of graphs via message passing following the edges between the vertices in a graph [42,44]. Specifically, the target for a graph neural network layer is to yield contextualized representations for each vertex via aggregating the information from its surrounding vertices. By stacking multiple layers, the obtained representations of the vertices can be fed into downstream tasks, such as vertex classification, graph classification, link prediction, etc.

Recent years have witnessed the emerging success of graph neural networks for modelling structured data. However, most GNNs are designed for homogeneous graphs, in which all vertices and edges belong to the same types, making them infeasible to represent heterogeneous structures [10]. Relational Graph Convolutional Network (R-GCN) first proposed relation-specific transformation in the message passing steps to deal with various relations [36]. Subsequently, several works focused on dealing with the heterogeneous graph [41,43].

Inspired by the architecture design of Transformer [40], Hu et al. [10] presented the heterogeneous Graph Transformer that incorporates the self-attention mechanism in a general graph neural network structure that can deal with a heterogeneous graph.

Given a heterogeneous graph $G = (V, E)$, each vertex $v \in V$ and each edge $e \in E$ are associated with their type $c \in C$ and $r \in R$. The process in one heterogeneous graph transformer layer can be decomposed into three steps: heterogeneous mutual attention calculation, heterogeneous message passing, and target-specific aggregation.

For a source vertex s of type c_s and a target vertex t of type c_t connected by an edge $e = (s, t)$ of type r_e, we first calculate a query vector Q_t and a key vector K_s, with the output from the previous heterogeneous graph transformer layer, by two vertex type-specific linear projections $W_{c_t}^Q$ and $W_{c_s}^K$, as shown in Eq. (3) and (4), where, $h_s^{(l-1)}$ and $h_t^{(l-1)}$ denote the representations of vertex s and vertex t by the $(l-1)$-th heterogeneous transformer layer, separately.

$$Q_t = W_{c_t}^Q h_t^{(l-1)} \tag{3}$$

$$K_s = W_{c_s}^K h_s^{(l-1)} \tag{4}$$

Then, we calculate a similarity score by taking the dot product of Q_t with K_s. An edge type-specific linear projection $W_{r_e}^A$ is utilized in case there are multiple types of edges between the same vertex type pair, while μ is a predefined vector indicating the general significance of each edge type. The obtained score is normalized by the square root of the dimension of key vector d_{K_s}. After the scores for all neighbours of t have been computed, a softmax function is applied to yield the normalized attention weights A_t for neighbour aggregation, as shown in Eq. (5).

$$A_t = \underset{\forall s \in N_t}{softmax}(\frac{\mu K_s W_{r_e}^A Q_t^T}{\sqrt{d_{K_s}}}) \tag{5}$$

In parallel to the mutual attention calculation, the representation of source vertex s from the previous heterogeneous graph transformer layer $h_s^{(l-1)}$, is fed into another linear projection $W_{c_s}^M$ to produce a message vector M_s. The message vector is shown in Eq. (6), where another projection $W_{r_e}^M$ is added to incorporate the edge dependency.

$$M_s = W_{c_s}^M h_s^{(l-1)} W_{r_e}^M \tag{6}$$

With the attention weights A_t and message vector M_s yielded by previous steps, we aggregate the information from all the neighbours to t, as shown in Eq. (7), where $W_{c_t}^C$ is another linear projection mapping the aggregated representation back to t's type-specific feature space, followed by a non-linear activation operation.

$$h_t^{(l)} = \sigma(W_{c_t}^C \sum_{s \in N_t} A_t M_s) + h_t^{(l-1)} \tag{7}$$

By conducting the residual connection operation [7], a highly contextualized representation $h_t^{(l)}$ for the target vertex t by the current l-th heterogeneous graph transformer layer is produced that can be fed into the following module for downstream tasks.

3.4   Answer Prediction

Recent works have mainly adopted the SQuAD paradigm in the answer prediction phase to predict individual probabilities of where answers start and end in a given passage. This approach, known as index-level prediction, has become the paradigm of extractive question answering. Motivated by the approach presented in the SyHGT paper [45], which integrates syntactic information into the extractive question answering pipeline, we propose a novel span-level prediction method. This approach directly selects the nodes of the constituent tree as the potential answer, engaging the model to explicitly learn the syntactic structure information while ensuring that the output always retains proper grammar.

   Unlike independently predicting the start and end positions of the answer, we believe that using a "span-level prediction" approach provides a more intuitive and human-like way to perform extractive question answering tasks. When asked to find the answer to a question in a given passage, people often search for word fragments rather than trying to identify each index [38]. Additionally, most human answers are complete sentences or at least a phrase that follows grammatical rules [28]. With this idea in mind, we restrict our model's output to a specific node from the given constituency tree. This approach ensures that the generated answers are grammatically correct and coherent.

   After propagation by the heterogeneous graph transformer layers, the output representations h for the vertices are passed to the linear layer with the learned parameter W_p and bias b_p. The probability distribution y_p, shown in Eq. (8) indicates the probability of each vertex being the answer span of the given question.

$$y_p = softmax(W_p h + b_p) \tag{8}$$

We use cross-entropy loss (CE) [9] as our initial training objective, as shown in Eq. (9), where y_p' is the ground truth node position of the answer.

$$\mathcal{CE} = -y_p' \log y_p \tag{9}$$

Since the number of non-answer nodes is far greater than the number of answer nodes, in order to balance the proportion of positive (answer node) and negative samples(non-answer node), we adopted "focal loss" and "soft label" to alleviate class-imbalance, as defined in Eq. (10).

$$\mathcal{FL} = -\alpha(1 - y_p')^\beta \log y_p \tag{10}$$

   Focal Loss is a modification of CE that attempts to handle the issue of class imbalance by assigning more weight to difficult examples (answer nodes) and less weight to easy examples (non-answer nodes) [20]. The above Eq. (9) is enhanced with the inclusion of hyperparameters α and β (see in Eq. (10), which can be adjusted for further calibration. α is a weighted term that has a value of α for the positive class and $1 - \alpha$ for the negative class. β can also be understood as a relaxation parameter. The higher the value of β, the more emphasis is placed on hard examples while less loss is propagated from easy examples. According to a study in [21], a value of $\beta = 2$ yields the best results.

To converge the model prediction to the ground-truth answer node, we did not set the label of the ground-truth answer node to 1 and the labels of other non-answer nodes to 0. Instead, we employed the edit distance [19] to calculate the overlap distance between each node and the ground truth answer and then normalized them to the range from 0 to 1, which are set as the soft labels to guide the model further to find the correct answer.

Span-level prediction also has certain drawbacks. One major issue is that compared to index-level prediction, span-level prediction requires the alignment of the output representation embeddings of the transformer encoder with the nodes of the constituency parse tree, which increases the model complexity and lengthens the processing time. Additionally, since most current extractive question answering benchmarks follow the index-level prediction format, evaluating the performance of SyHGT-CN on these existing benchmarks may be biased if the ground-truth answer does not conform to grammatical rules (not a complete constituency node). Because the output answer is limited to a specific node of the constituency tree, the exact match score of SyHGT-CN is lower than the empirical scenario.

4 Performance Evaluation

We present the experimental setup and the results of a comparative empirical performance evaluation.

4.1 Experimental Setup

We use a pre-trained BERT model in its public PyTorch implementation from the *Transformers* library[1], as the base encoder. With keeping its default settings and a maximum input length of 384, we initialize the weights from the saved models available at *Hugging Face*[2]. We then fine-tune the weights during training. We use the standard case-sensitive BERT base model, also known as *bert-base-cased* model. We use the *PyTorch-geometric* library[3] to implement the heterogeneous graph transformer.

We use the constituency parser of the Stanza library [31] (formerly StanfordNLP) to parse the questions and contexts of SQuAD 2.0. Thanks to the token alignment discussed in Sect. 3.2, each pre-terminal node corresponds to one or more consecutive tokens, and its initial embedding is initialized with the mean of the embeddings of the corresponding tokens.

The training utilizes an AdamW optimizer [22] and a learning rate of 2e-5. We stack two heterogeneous graph transformer layers with four attention heads in each. The model is trained with a mini-batch size of 64 for five epochs. All experiments are conducted on an NVIDIA A100 SXM4 server.

The empirical evaluation is conducted with SQuAD 2.0 [33]. SQuAD 2.0 follows in the footsteps of its predecessor SQuAD, with a focus on improving models' ability to handle unanswerable questions. To achieve this, the dataset combines previous SQuAD

---

[1] https://github.com/huggingface/transformers.

[2] https://huggingface.co/.

[3] https://github.com/rusty1s/pytorch_geometric.

Table 1. Comparative empirical performance with SQuAD2.0.

Method	EM	F1
BERT	71.78	75.41
SyHGT-C	72.55	75.87
SyHGT-CN	**73.82**	**77.11**

data with a new collection of over 50,000 adversarially-written unanswerable questions. These questions were carefully crafted by crowdworkers to be relevant to the accompanying paragraph and to contain a plausible answer that matches the type of information being asked for.

We use the F1 score and the exact match score to comparatively evaluate the performance of the models. The F1 Score measures the normalized average overlap between the predicted and ground-truth answers, while the exact match score assesses whether the prediction exactly matches the ground truth. These metrics comprehensively evaluate the model's ability to predict answers accurately [33,34].

4.2   Results

The main experiment results are presented in Table 1. Table 1 shows the F1 score (F1) and the exact match score (EM) for the three models: a linguistics-oblivious BERT-based question answering model (BERT), the original constituency-informed question answering model (SyHGT-C), and of the proposed constituency-informed and constituency-constrained question answering model (SyHGT-CN) for the Stanford Question Answering Dataset.

We observe a minor improvement of 0.77 in the exact match score and of 0.46 in the F1 score for SyGHT-C compared to the BERT baseline, and a more substantial improvement of 2.04 in the exact match score and of 1.70 in the F1 score for SyGHT-CN compared to the BERT baseline.

The results above also account for ground truth answers in SQuAD that do not correspond to the node of the constituency tree. This may be due to either the fact that some SQuAD answers are ungrammatical or to the particular constituency parser that we are using for this evaluation. When exclusively considering SQuAD answers that correspond to nodes of the constituency tree, according to the parser that we use, SyHGT-CN yields an impressive exact match score of 83.03 and an F1 score of 80.00. Compared with the performance, exact match score 71.19, F1 score 75.24, of the baseline model.

5   Conclusion

We have presented a novel constituency-informed and constituency-constrained question answering model, SyHGT-CN.

The linguistics-informed model integrates the symbolic information contained in constituency trees with the statistical knowledge of a neural language model. The integration of the linguistics graphic structures with the transformer-based neural language model is achieved by the adjunction to the latter of a heterogeneous graph neural network, in which the former is encoded.

We devised a simple but efficient alignment method that takes advantage of the inherent hierarchical structure of constituency trees to align token embeddings in a simple but effective manner. This mechanism enables the subsequent creation of a heterogeneous graph representing the constituency trees of the question and context. The constituency trees of the question and context not only inform the answering machine learning model but also constrains its output to be a span corresponding to a valid subtree.

A comparative empirical evaluation with SQuAD2.0 shows that the proposed approach yields substantial improvement of up to ten points of the exact match score and of up to nearly five points of the F1 score over the BERT baseline.

This work suggests a generalisable approach, combining neural language models and heterogeneous graph neural networks, to the development of novel linguistics-informed solutions, leveraging linguistics graphic structures, to question answering and other natural language processing tasks.

Acknowledgements. This research is supported by the National Research Foundation, Singapore under its Industry Alignment Fund - Pre-positioning (IAF-PP) Funding Initiative. Any opinions, findings and conclusions or recommendations expressed in this material are those of the authors and do not reflect the views of the National Research Foundation, Singapore.

References

1. Charniak, E.: Statistical parsing with a context-free grammar and word statistics. In: Kuipers, B., Webber, B.L. (eds.) Proceedings of the Fourteenth National Conference on Artificial Intelligence and Ninth Innovative Applications of Artificial Intelligence Conference, AAAI 1997, IAAI 1997(July), pp. 27–31, 1997. Providence, Rhode Island, USA, pp. 598–603. AAAI Press/The MIT Press (1997). http://www.aaai.org/Library/AAAI/1997/aaai97-093.php
2. Cimiano, P., Unger, C., McCrae, J.P.: Ontology-Based Interpretation of Natural Language. Synthesis Lectures on Human Language Technologies, Morgan & Claypool Publishers (2014). https://doi.org/10.2200/S00561ED1V01Y201401HLT024
3. Dawson, H., Phelan, M.: Language Files: Materials for an Introduction to Language and Linguistics. Ohio State University Press (2016). https://books.google.com.sg/books?id=wSP_jgEACAAJ
4. Devlin, J., Chang, M., Lee, K., Toutanova, K.: BERT: pre-training of deep bidirectional transformers for language understanding. In: Burstein, J., Doran, C., Solorio, T. (eds.) Proceedings of the 2019 Conference of the North American Chapter of the Association for Computational Linguistics: Human Language Technologies, NAACL-HLT 2019, Minneapolis, MN, USA, 2–7 June 2019, vol. 1, (Long and Short Papers), pp. 4171–4186. Association for Computational Linguistics (2019). https://doi.org/10.18653/v1/n19-1423
5. d'Avila Garcez, A.S., Gori, M., Lamb, L.C., Serafini, L., Spranger, M., Tran, S.N.: Neural-symbolic computing: an effective methodology for principled integration of machine learning and reasoning. FLAP. **6**(4), 611–632 (2019). https://collegepublications.co.uk/ifcolog/?00033

6. Goldberg, Y.: Assessing BERT's syntactic abilities. CoRR abs/1901.05287 (2019). arxiv:1901.05287

7. He, K., Zhang, X., Ren, S., Sun, J.: Deep residual learning for image recognition. In: 2016 IEEE Conference on Computer Vision and Pattern Recognition (CVPR), pp. 770–778 (2016). https://doi.org/10.1109/CVPR.2016.90

8. He, P., Liu, X., Gao, J., Chen, W.: DEBERTA: decoding-enhanced BERT with disentangled attention. In: 9th International Conference on Learning Representations, ICLR 2021, Virtual Event, Austria, 3–7 May 2021. OpenReview.net (2021). https://openreview.net/forum?id=XPZIaotutsD

9. Ho, Y., Wookey, S.: The real-world-weight cross-entropy loss function: modeling the costs of mislabeling. IEEE Access **8**, 4806–4813 (2020). https://doi.org/10.1109/ACCESS.2019.2962617

10. Hu, Z., Dong, Y., Wang, K., Sun, Y.: Heterogeneous graph transformer. In: Huang, Y., King, I., Liu, T., van Steen, M. (eds.) WWW 2020: The Web Conference 2020, Taipei, Taiwan, 20–24 April 2020, pp. 2704–2710. ACM/IW3C2 (2020). https://doi.org/10.1145/3366423.3380027

11. Jawahar, G., Sagot, B., Seddah, D.: What does BERT learn about the structure of language? In: Korhonen, A., Traum, D.R., Màrquez, L. (eds.) Proceedings of the 57th Conference of the Association for Computational Linguistics, ACL 2019, Florence, Italy, July 28–August 2 2019, vol. 1, Long Papers, pp. 3651–3657. Association for Computational Linguistics (2019). https://doi.org/10.18653/v1/p19-1356

12. Jr., B.F.G., Wolf, A.K., Chomsky, C., Laughery, K.: Baseball: an automatic question-answerer. In: Bauer, W.F. (ed.) Papers presented at the 1961 western joint IRE-AIEE-ACM computer conference, IRE-AIEE-ACM 1961 (Western), Los Angeles, California, USA, 9–11 May 1961, pp. 219–224. ACM (1961). https://doi.org/10.1145/1460690.1460714

13. Jurafsky, D., Martin, J.H.: Speech and Language Processing: An Introduction to Natural Language Processing, Computational Linguistics, and Speech Recognition. 2nd Edition. Prentice Hall series in artificial intelligence, Prentice Hall, Pearson Education International (2009). https://www.worldcat.org/oclc/315913020

14. Kalyan, K.S., Rajasekharan, A., Sangeetha, S.: AMMUS : a survey of transformer-based pretrained models in natural language processing. CoRR abs/2108.05542 (2021). arxiv:2108.05542

15. Kuhl, P.K.: Learning and representation in speech and language. Current Opinion Neurobiol. **4**(6), 812–822 (1994). https://doi.org/10.1016/0959-4388(94)90128-7, https://www.sciencedirect.com/science/article/pii/0959438894901287

16. Kuncoro, A., Kong, L., Fried, D., Yogatama, D., Rimell, L., Dyer, C., Blunsom, P.: Syntactic structure distillation pretraining for bidirectional encoders. Trans. Assoc. Comput. Linguist. **8**, 776–794 (2020). https://doi.org/10.1162/tacl_a_00345

17. Lan, Z., Chen, M., Goodman, S., Gimpel, K., Sharma, P., Soricut, R.: ALBERT: a lite BERT for self-supervised learning of language representations. In: 8th International Conference on Learning Representations, ICLR 2020, Addis Ababa, Ethiopia, 26–30 April 2020. OpenReview.net (2020). https://openreview.net/forum?id=H1eA7AEtvS

18. Lee, K., Kwiatkowski, T., Parikh, A.P., Das, D.: Learning recurrent span representations for extractive question answering. CoRR abs/1611.01436 (2016). arxiv:1611.01436

19. Li, B., Zhou, H., He, J., Wang, M., Yang, Y., Li, L.: On the sentence embeddings from pre-trained language models. In: Webber, B., Cohn, T., He, Y., Liu, Y. (eds.) Proceedings of the 2020 Conference on Empirical Methods in Natural Language Processing, EMNLP 2020, Online, 16–20 November 2020, pp. 9119–9130. Association for Computational Linguistics (2020). https://doi.org/10.18653/v1/2020.emnlp-main.733
20. Li, X., et al.: Generalized focal loss: learning qualified and distributed bounding boxes for dense object detection. In: Larochelle, H., Ranzato, M., Hadsell, R., Balcan, M., Lin, H. (eds.) Advances in Neural Information Processing Systems 33: Annual Conference on Neural Information Processing Systems 2020, NeurIPS, December 2020, pp. 6–12, 2020. virtual (2020). https://proceedings.neurips.cc/paper/2020/hash/f0bda020d2470f2e74990a07a607ebd9-Abstract.html
21. Lin, T., Goyal, P., Girshick, R.B., He, K., Dollár, P.: Focal loss for dense object detection. In: IEEE International Conference on Computer Vision, ICCV 2017, Venice, Italy, 22–29 October 2017, pp. 2999–3007. IEEE Computer Society (2017). https://doi.org/10.1109/ICCV.2017.324
22. Loshchilov, I., Hutter, F.: Decoupled weight decay regularization. In: 7th International Conference on Learning Representations, ICLR 2019, New Orleans, LA, USA, 6–9 May 2019. OpenReview.net (2019). https://openreview.net/forum?id=Bkg6RiCqY7
23. Manning, C.D., Clark, K., Hewitt, J., Khandelwal, U., Levy, O.: Emergent linguistic structure in artificial neural networks trained by self-supervision. Proc. Natl. Acad. Sci. U.S.A. 117(48), 30046–30054 (2020). https://doi.org/10.1073/pnas.1907367117
24. Manning, C.D., Raghavan, P., Schütze, H.: Introduction to Information Retrieval. Cambridge University Press, Cambridge (2008). https://doi.org/10.1017/CBO9780511809071, https://nlp.stanford.edu/IR-book/pdf/irbookprint.pdf
25. Mao, J., Gan, C., Kohli, P., Tenenbaum, J.B., Wu, J.: The neuro-symbolic concept learner: Interpreting scenes, words, and sentences from natural supervision. In: 7th International Conference on Learning Representations, ICLR 2019, New Orleans, LA, USA, 6–9 May 2019. OpenReview.net (2019). https://openreview.net/forum?id=rJgMlhRctm
26. Marcus, M.P., Santorini, B., Marcinkiewicz, M.A.: Building a large annotated corpus of English: the Penn Treebank. Comput. Linguist. 19(2), 313–330 (1993). https://aclanthology.org/J93-2004
27. O'Grady, W., Archibald, J., Aronoff, M., Rees-Miller, J.: Contemporary Linguistics: An Introduction. Bedford/St. Martin's (2017). https://books.google.fr/books?id=51MovgAACAAJ
28. Palangi, H., Smolensky, P., He, X., Deng, L.: Question-answering with grammatically-interpretable representations. In: McIlraith, S.A., Weinberger, K.Q. (eds.) Proceedings of the Thirty-Second AAAI Conference on Artificial Intelligence, (AAAI-18), the 30th innovative Applications of Artificial Intelligence (IAAI-2018), and the 8th AAAI Symposium on Educational Advances in Artificial Intelligence (EAAI-18), New Orleans, Louisiana, USA, 2–7 February 2018, pp. 5350–5357. AAAI Press (2018). https://www.aaai.org/ocs/index.php/AAAI/AAAI18/paper/view/17090
29. Peters, M.E., et al.: Deep contextualized word representations. In: Walker, M.A., Ji, H., Stent, A. (eds.) Proceedings of the 2018 Conference of the North American Chapter of the Association for Computational Linguistics: Human Language Technologies, NAACL-HLT 2018, New Orleans, Louisiana, USA, June 1–6, 2018, vol. 1 (Long Papers), pp. 2227–2237. Association for Computational Linguistics (2018). https://doi.org/10.18653/v1/n18-1202
30. Petrov, S., Das, D., McDonald, R.T.: A universal part-of-speech tagset. In: Calzolari, N., et al. (eds.) Proceedings of the Eighth International Conference on Language Resources and Evaluation, LREC 2012, Istanbul, Turkey, 23–25 May 2012, pp. 2089–2096. European Language Resources Association (ELRA) (2012). http://www.lrec-conf.org/proceedings/lrec2012/summaries/274.html

31. Qi, P., Zhang, Y., Zhang, Y., Bolton, J., Manning, C.D.: Stanza: a python natural language processing toolkit for many human languages. In: Proceedings of the 58th Annual Meeting of the Association for Computational Linguistics: System Demonstrations (2020). https://nlp.stanford.edu/pubs/qi2020stanza.pdf
32. Qiu, X., Sun, T., Xu, Y., Shao, Y., Dai, N., Huang, X.: Pre-trained models for natural language processing: A survey. CoRR abs/2003.08271 (2020). https://arxiv.org/abs/2003.08271
33. Rajpurkar, P., Jia, R., Liang, P.: Know what you don't know: Unanswerable questions for squad. In: Gurevych, I., Miyao, Y. (eds.) Proceedings of the 56th Annual Meeting of the Association for Computational Linguistics, ACL 2018, Melbourne, Australia, 15–20 July 2018, vol. 2, Short Papers, pp. 784–789. Association for Computational Linguistics (2018). https://doi.org/10.18653/v1/P18-2124, https://aclanthology.org/P18-2124/
34. Rajpurkar, P., Zhang, J., Lopyrev, K., Liang, P.: Squad: 100, 000+ questions for machine comprehension of text. In: Su, J., Carreras, X., Duh, K. (eds.) Proceedings of the 2016 Conference on Empirical Methods in Natural Language Processing, EMNLP 2016, Austin, Texas, USA, 1–4 November 2016, pp. 2383–2392. The Association for Computational Linguistics (2016). https://doi.org/10.18653/v1/d16-1264
35. Scarselli, F., Gori, M., Tsoi, A.C., Hagenbuchner, M., Monfardini, G.: The graph neural network model. IEEE Trans. Neural Netw. 20(1), 61–80 (2009). https://doi.org/10.1109/TNN.2008.2005605
36. Schlichtkrull, M., Kipf, T.N., Bloem, P., van den Berg, R., Titov, I., Welling, M.: Modeling relational data with graph convolutional networks. In: Gangemi, A., et al. (eds.) ESWC 2018. LNCS, vol. 10843, pp. 593–607. Springer, Cham (2018). https://doi.org/10.1007/978-3-319-93417-4_38
37. Shen, D., Klakow, D.: Exploring correlation of dependency relation paths for answer extraction. In: Proceedings of the 21st International Conference on Computational Linguistics and 44th Annual Meeting of the Association for Computational Linguistics, pp. 889–896. Association for Computational Linguistics, Sydney, Australia, July 2006. https://doi.org/10.3115/1220175.1220287, https://aclanthology.org/P06-1112
38. Soares, M.A.C., Parreiras, F.S.: A literature review on question answering techniques, paradigms and systems. J. King Saud Univ. Comput. Inf. Sci. 32(6), 635–646 (2020). https://doi.org/10.1016/j.jksuci.2018.08.005
39. Vashishth, S., Bhandari, M., Yadav, P., Rai, P., Bhattacharyya, C., Talukdar, P.P.: Incorporating syntactic and semantic information in word embeddings using graph convolutional networks. In: Korhonen, A., Traum, D.R., Màrquez, L. (eds.) Proceedings of the 57th Conference of the Association for Computational Linguistics, ACL 2019, Florence, Italy, July 28–August 2 2019, vol. 1: Long Papers, pp. 3308–3318. Association for Computational Linguistics (2019). https://doi.org/10.18653/v1/p19-1320
40. Vaswani, A., et al.: Attention is all you need. In: Guyon, I., et al. (eds.) Advances in Neural Information Processing Systems 30: Annual Conference on Neural Information Processing Systems, December 2017, pp. 4–9, 2017. Long Beach, CA, USA, pp. 5998–6008 (2017). https://proceedings.neurips.cc/paper/2017/hash/3f5ee243547dee91fbd053c1c4a845aa-Abstract.html
41. Wang, X., et al.: Heterogeneous graph attention network. In: Liu, L., et al. (eds.) The World Wide Web Conference, WWW 2019, San Francisco, CA, USA, 13–17 May 2019, pp. 2022–2032. ACM (2019). https://doi.org/10.1145/3308558.3313562
42. Wu, Z., Pan, S., Chen, F., Long, G., Zhang, C., Yu, P.S.: A comprehensive survey on graph neural networks. IEEE Trans. Neural Netw. Learn. Syst. 32(1), 4–24 (2021). https://doi.org/10.1109/TNNLS.2020.2978386

43. Zhang, C., Song, D., Huang, C., Swami, A., Chawla, N.V.: Heterogeneous graph neural network. In: Teredesai, A., Kumar, V., Li, Y., Rosales, R., Terzi, E., Karypis, G. (eds.) Proceedings of the 25th ACM SIGKDD International Conference on Knowledge Discovery and Data Mining, KDD 2019, Anchorage, AK, USA, 4–8 August 2019, pp. 793–803. ACM (2019). https://doi.org/10.1145/3292500.3330961

44. Zhou, J., et al.: Graph neural networks: a review of methods and applications. AI Open **1**, 57–81 (2020). https://doi.org/10.1016/j.aiopen.2021.01.001

45. Zhu, F., Tan, L.Y., Ng, S., Bressan, S.: Syntax-informed question answering with heterogeneous graph transformer. In: Strauss, C., Cuzzocrea, A., Kotsis, G., Tjoa, A.M., Khalil, I. (eds.) Database and Expert Systems Applications - 33rd International Conference, DEXA 2022, Vienna, Austria, August 22–24, 2022, Proceedings, Part I. LNCS, vol. 13426, pp. 17–31. Springer, Cham (2022). https://doi.org/10.1007/978-3-031-12423-5_2

46. Zhu, F., Lei, W., Wang, C., Zheng, J., Poria, S., Chua, T.: Retrieving and reading: a comprehensive survey on open-domain question answering. CoRR abs/2101.00774 (2021). arxiv:2101.00774

FAPFID: A Fairness-Aware Approach for Protected Features and Imbalanced Data

Ginel Dorleon$^{(\boxtimes)}$ [ID], Imen Megdiche [ID], Nathalie Bricon-Souf [ID], and Olivier Teste [ID]

Toulouse Institute for Computer Science Research (IRIT), Toulouse, France
{ginel.dorleon,imen.megdiche,nathalie.bricon-souf,
olivier.teste}@irit.fr

Abstract. The use of automated decision-making based on machine learning algorithms has raised concerns about potential discrimination against minority group defined by protected features such as gender, race, etc. Particularly, in some areas with high social impact such as justice, job search or healthcare, it has been observed that using protected feature in machine learning algorithms can lead to unfair decisions that favor one group (privileged) over another group (unprivileged). In order to improve fairness in decision-making with regard to protected features, many machine learning approaches focus either on discarding the protected features or maintaining an overall accuracy performance for both unprivileged and privileged groups. However, we notice that these approaches have limited efficiency in the case where the protected features are useful for the learning model or when dealing with imbalanced data.

To overcome this limitation when dealing with such issues, we propose in this work FAPFID, a fairness-aware strategy based on the use of balanced and stable clusters. To do this, we divide our input data into stable clusters (subgroups) while ensuring that privileged and unprivileged groups are fairly represented in each cluster. Experiments on three real-world and biased datasets demonstrated that our proposed method outperforms state-of-the-art fairness-aware methods under comparison in terms of performance and fairness scores.

Keywords: Decision systems · Bias · Fairness · Machine learning · AI

1 Introduction

Nowadays, machine learning-based decision support systems have become increasingly automated while assisting human judgment with largely data-driven decisions. Since these systems are data-driven, they can be applied in a wide variety of applications such as transportation [30], recruitment or employment screening [32], healthcare [13], finance [1] and many more. However, concerns have been raised [42] that machine learning algorithms may lead to decisions against certain groups defined by sensitives or protected features such as gender, race, religion. In

© Springer-Verlag GmbH Germany, part of Springer Nature 2023
A. Hameurlain and A. M. Tjoa (Eds.): TLDKS LIII, LNCS 13840, pp. 107–125, 2023.
https://doi.org/10.1007/978-3-662-66863-4_5

areas with high social impacts such as justice, risk assessment, online purchase and delivery, loan application, there are already many cases [17,29,37,41] where discriminatory decisions have already been made against minority or unprivileged group with harmful consequences. Basically, two majors problems were identified [7,33] as the main cause of the unfairness in automated decision-making: the uncontrolled use of protected/sensitive features and the used of imbalanced datasets [23]. Protected or sensitive features, according to [12], are features that are of particular importance either for social, ethical or legal reasons when making decisions. According to [7], a dataset suffers from class imbalance when there is significant or extreme disproportion between the number of examples of each class in the dataset. By class in the dataset we mean, in the context of supervised machine learning and with a classification task in particular, the label or output we want to predict based on a set of inputs values. Based on a protected feature such as *gender*, a privileged group (male for example) would be more likely to receive an advantageous treatment than the unprivileged group (here, female for example). Such a behavior is not only undesirable but may have serious impact on the unprivileged group [34].

To this end, many machine learning approaches have proposed to help improving fairness in decision-making systems in areas where automated decision-making based on machine learning algorithms are used. Some of the proposed machine learning approaches [11] for fairness improvement with regard to protected features tend to remove them prior the learning model in order to obtain a fair outcome. However, while this strategy may work, we found that it is limited and can lead to a significant performance loss in the case where protected features are relevant for the learning task. Some other approaches [5,18] to improve fairness also tend to focus on maintaining an overall accuracy for both privileged and unprivileged. Again, we noticed that this strategy may not always work when using data that suffer from class imbalance. It has been proved [16,43] that overall accuracy is not always a good performance indicator when using imbalanced dataset since it tends to favor the majority group over the minority. Since most of fairness-related datasets suffer from class imbalance, addressing fairness with regards to protected features in machine learning algorithm also requires addressing the issue of imbalanced dataset.

Thus, in our work, we focused on these two issues, the use of protected features and class imbalance, that directly impact performance and fairness of machine learning algorithms. To this end, we propose FAPFID: A Fairness-aware Approach for Protected Features and Imbalanced Data. Our method allows to handle protected feature and class imbalance while ensuring an efficient and fair model for decision-making involving machine learning algorithms. Using the input dataset, our method creates a set of balanced and stable clusters while ensuring that both privileged and unprivileged groups are fairly represented in each cluster. Then an ensemble learning model is built upon the aggregated balanced and stable clusters which allow to obtain a cumulative and fair model.

Our contributions in this work can be summarized as follows:

- We define a cumulative-fairness approach for dealing with protected features in decision support, it is tested on a binary classification task using an ensemble learning strategy.
- The proposed approach is based on stable and balanced clusters, thus we propose a clustering stability algorithm to this end.
- Our method takes into consideration protected features and class imbalance while making fair decisions, so that the balanced-accuracy score remains high.
- Our method to achieve fairness is based on Equalized of Odds as fairness metric and it being tested on three real-world dataset suitable for fairness study and is easily adaptable to any social decision problems with regards to protected features and class imbalance.

The rest of this paper is organized as follows: in Sect. 2, we summarize the different existing methods to tackle the issues identified with their limitations. In Sect. 3, we introduce some basics concepts and definitions. We present our new approach in Sect. 4. The experimental results are described and analyzed in Sect. 5. Conclusions and future work are presented in Sect. 6.

2   Related Work

Many existing work have proposed various machine learning methods to deal with fairness issues related to the use of protected features and imbalanced data [2]. Here we look at those existing methods under these two categories and we also look at what previous work has defined in terms of fairness metrics.

Many definitions of fairness [14,39] have been proposed over the recent years. Most of the recent proposed methods use fairness definitions such as demographic parity [22,36,40]. This fairness metric suggests that a predictor is unbiased if the prediction ($\hat{y}$) is independent of the protected feature such that positive prediction rate between the two subgroups are the same. Other proposed methods have instead used other fairness metric such as equalized odds [15,27,31]. Unlike demographic parity, this fairness metric instead suggests that the true positive rate and the false positive rate will be the same for both unprivileged and privileged groups. However while each of these definition has merit, there is no consensus on which one is consequently the best, and this issue is beyond the scope of this article. Our goal is not to address the relative virtues of these definitions of fairness, but rather to assess the strength of the evidence presented by a set of subgroup that a model is unfair to a certain group based on a given metric and the best possible trade-off between fairness and performance.

For proposed methods that deal with fairness related to protected features, we notice several approaches [24,25]. Particularly, we notice the work in [9,11] where authors introduced naive approaches consisting of removing completely all protected features of the dataset to ensure fairness. However, we notice that these approaches may not solve the problem because there may be redundant features or even proxies to the protected [38]. As underlined by [42], some features known as proxies such as zip code, for example, can reveal the predominant race of a residential area. Thus, this can still lead to racial discrimination in a decision making problem such as loan application despite the fact that zip code appears to be a non-protected feature. We also notice the work of [19] where authors introduced a framework that combines pre-processing balancing strategy with post-processing decision boundary adjustment in order to deal with fairness related to protected features and class imbalance. In the pre-processing strategy, they created local subgroups where they performed random under-sampling technique to guarantee equitable representation between minority and majority groups. While this strategy may work on large datasets with thousands of instances, we notice that it suffers from a performance loss when used on a restricted dataset.

Given the limitations of the above approaches, there is a need for more in-depth research to overcome these limitations. Thus, we propose FAPFID, a new fairness-aware strategy that allows the obtaining of an efficient and fair models with regards to protected features and imbalanced data. We would like to recall here, as part of our approach, a given model is said to be "fair", or "equitable", if its results are independent of one or more given features, in particular those considered to be protected [21,28].

3   Basic Concepts and Definitions

In this paper, we consider an input dataset $S = \left(X_{m,n}, Y_{1,n} \right)$ that consists of n observations and m features. Let f be a learning model and its performance score $f[S]$ which will be used to predict a binary output $\hat{y} \in \{0,1\}$. Each sample $x_i \in X_{m,n}$ is associated to a protected feature P, for simplicity we consider that P is binary: $P \in \{P_0, P_1\}$. We consider P_0 to be an unprivileged group and P_1 a privileged group. For instance, $P =$ 'gender' could be the protected attribute with $P_0 =$ 'female', the unprivileged group, and $P_1 =$ 'male' the privileged one. Likewise, we consider $\hat{y} = 1$ to be the preferred outcome, assuming it represents the more desirable of the two possible outcomes.

Suppose for some samples we know the ground truth; i.e., the true value $y \in \{0,1\}$. Note that these outcomes may be statistically different between different groups, either because the differences are real, or because the model is somewhat biased. Depending on the situation, we may want our estimate $\hat{y}$ to take these differences into account or to compensate them.

Choice of Fairness Metric: In this work, we have used Equalized Odds (EqOd) as fairness metric since it is widely used and adopted by recent state-of-the-art method and other methods. EqOd measures the difference of true classified examples between privileged and unprivileged group in all classes [3]. That being said, prediction $\hat{y}$ is conditionally independent of the protected feature P, given the true value $y : Pr(\hat{y}|y, P) = Pr(\hat{y}|y)$. This means that the true positive rate and the false positive rate will be the same between the privileged and unprivileged groups. To compute the difference between classified instances of the two groups, EqOd is defined as follow:

$$EqOd = Pr(\hat{y} = 1|P_1, y = y_i) - Pr(\hat{y} = 1|P_0, y = y_i), y_i \in \{0,1\} \qquad (1)$$

A fair value for this metric is between $[-0.1, 0.1]$. The ideal value of this metric is 0. A value < 0 implies higher benefit for the privileged group and a value > 0 implies higher benefit for the unprivileged group.

Ensemble Learning Choice: We will use an ensemble learning strategy to help obtaining a final model. Ensemble learning helps improving machine learning results by combining several intermediate models. This approach allows the production of better predictive performance compared to a single model. For our ensemble learning strategy, we will use Bagging. Also known as bootstrap aggregating, Bagging is the aggregation of multiple versions of a predicted model. Each model is trained individually upon a subset, and combined using a majority voting process. Thus, we believe using an ensemble learning is an efficient technique to tackle imbalanced ratio towards protected feature as it divides the learning problem into multiple sub-problems and then combines their solutions (local models) into an final model. Intuitively, we found it easier to tackle the problem related to fairness in the subset with locals models rather than in a single and global model.

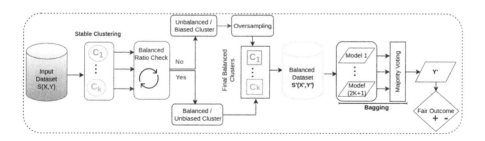

Fig. 1. FAPFID: the proposed approach with different steps

4   Proposed Approach

We introduce in this section our approach, shorten as FAPFID, to achieve fairness as illustrated in Fig. 1. It works as follows: first the input data is divided into K stable clusters by a clustering strategy; then we ensure that obtained clusters are balanced with respect to the protected feature in each cluster. In the case where some clusters are imbalanced, we apply an oversampling technique, SMOTE [6]. Then a final set of balanced clusters is constructed. The final ensemble is then divided into bags where we apply an ensemble learning strategy, Bagging. A learner is trained on each bag and then a final model is obtained by majority vote. Below we describe each step.

4.1 Stable Clustering

In this step, we use a strategy to ensure that the number of clusters that we obtain are stable, i-e optimal. For this, we define a stability strategy to strengthen our clustering solution.

Why Stable Clusters? Obtaining stable clusters is useful to maintain a great performance hence ensuring a reliable fairness. A stable clustering guarantees a better homogeneity within clusters and ensure that the instances are really in their respective clusters [8]. Thus, we establish a clustering stability strategy based on K-means to avoid that wrongly clustered instances impact the balancing strategy that we later perform. In order to guarantee the obtaining of stable clusters, we define a statistical setup. Our stability strategy aims to provide information on the variation of instances for different values of k between two clusterings solutions of sub-samples of the same dataset. Thus, for each value of k, we seek to obtain a stability rate by looking at the percentage of instances, points or pairs of points on which the two clusterings agree or disagree. The value of k whose instances variation percentage between the two clusterings is closer to zero will be the one that guarantees the best stability, and therefore the optimal value of k to choose.

Stability Strategy. Here we define our clustering stability approach which is based on K-means. The generic clustering algorithm receives as input a dataset $S = \left(X_{m,n}, Y_{1,n} \right)$ and an additional parameter K. It then assigns clusters to all samples of S. The dataset S is assumed to consist of n samples $1, \ldots, x_n$ that have been drawn independently from a probability distribution T on some space X.

Assume we agree on a way to compute distances $d(C, C')$ between clusterings C and C'. Then, for a fixed probability distribution T, a fixed number K of clusters and a fixed sample size n, the stability of the clustering algorithm is defined as the expected distance between two clusterings $C_K(S_z), C_K(S'_z)$ on different samples S_z, S'_z of size z, that is:

$$C_{stab}(K, z) = d(C_K(S_z), C_K(S'_z)) \tag{2}$$

Algorithm 1 below shows how we performed the stability analysis.

In line (8), since the two clusterings are defined on the same samples, then it is straightforward to compute a distance score between these clusterings using any of the well-known clustering distances such as the Rand index, Jaccard index, Hamming distance, Variation of Information distance [26]. All these distances estimate, in some way or the other, the percentage of points or pairs of points

---

Algorithm 1: Clustering stability algorithm

Input: a set **S** of samples, a clustering algorithm **A**, k_{max} clusters and z_{max} samples.
Output: Optimal value of **K**
1 **Begin**
2 **for** $k = 2 \ldots k_{max}$:
3   Generate z_{max} subsamples S_z ($z = 1, \ldots, z_{max}$) of S
4   **for** $z = 1 \ldots z_{max}$:
5   Split S_z into k clusters C_z using A
6   **end for**
7   **for** $z, z' = 1 \ldots z_{max}$:
8   Compute pairwise distance $d(C_z, C_{z'})$ using Jaccard index distance (4)
9   Compute stability as the mean distance between clustering C_z and $C_{z'}$
   as: $C_{stab}(k, z_{max}) = \frac{1}{z_{max}^2} \sum_{z,z'=1}^{z_{max}} d(C_z, C_{z'})$
10   Choose the parameter K with highest C_{stab}
11   **end for**
12 **end for**
13 **End**

---

on which the two clusterings C_z and $C_{z'}$ agree or disagree. In our experiments, we have used the Jaccard Index Distance [35].

Jaccard Index Similarity. The Jaccard similarity is a measure of how close two clusters, $C_z, C_{z'}$ are. The closer the clusters are, the higher the Jaccard similarity. We associate an actual distance measure to it, which is called the Jaccard distance. The Jaccard similarity of two clusters C_z and $C_{z'}$ is given by:

$$SIM(C_z, C_{z'}) = \frac{C_z \cap C_{z'}}{C_z \cup C_{z'}} \qquad (3)$$

The Jaccard distance $d(C_z, C_{z'})$ is then given by (4) and, it equals 1 minus the ratio of the sizes of the intersection and the union of the clusters C_z and $C_{z'}$.

$$d(C_z, C_{z'}) = 1 - SIM(C_z, C_{z'}) \qquad (4)$$

4.2 Balanced Check Ratio

The main goal here is to divide the clusters into balanced and imbalanced clusters. We compute the ratio rp (5) between privileged and unprivileged instances for each cluster:

$$rp = \frac{privileged}{unprivileged} \qquad (5)$$

Clusters with ratio $rp \neq 1$ are considered to be biased thus are sent to the oversampling stage to be oversampled using SMOTE [6]. We qualify these clusters as biased by the fact that the ratio $rp \neq 1$ reflects the presence of the demographic bias between privileged and non-privileged instances (group imbalance).

We apply the SMOTE strategy in a different way of what have being used. In the original paper where SMOTE has been introduced [6], it is applied globally to the minority class. However, SMOTE in our approach is only applied to protected features label, that means our clusters are balanced towards the unprivileged and privileged group and not the class label. Once the imbalanced clusters are oversampled, we construct a set of final balanced clusters that are therefore aggregated into a final set from which bags will be created to train different classification models.

4.3 Bagging

Estimating the number of bags b must be sufficient to construct enough learners, since we consider each bag as a sample of the training data. To ensure that all the clustered instances are at least in one of the bags, we estimate the number of bags b as: $b = 2K + 1$, K is the number of stable clusters obtained in Sect. 4.1 with Algorithm 1. Since we will consider a classification task, the final model will be chosen by a majority voting strategy.

4.4 Proposed Method

Using the basic concepts that we previously defined in Sect. 3, the algorithm defined below takes as inputs a clustering algorithm A, a set of samples S, K number of clusters, privileged group P_1, unprivileged group P_0 and a base classifier G. We start by initializing an empty set of balanced clusters M (2) which later will contains the final balanced clusters as explained in Sect. 4.2. Then split S into K clusters (the value of K is known for each dataset with Algorithm 1) using A to obtain C_i, $i = 1...K$ (3). For each C_i cluster, we compute the imbalance ratio between privileged group P_1 and unprivileged group (P_0) of clusters C_i. If the computed ratio is equal to 1, we add the current cluster C_i to M (4–6), that means this cluster is balanced toward privileged and unprivileged group. However, if the computed ratio is not equal to 1, we oversample the current cluster C_i using SMOTE [6] to obtain a balanced cluster C_i^{bal}. We add this balanced cluster C_i^{bal} to the final set M then we start over using a different value of i (7–11).

Once we have used all the values of K and obtain our final list of balanced cluster M, we create a balanced dataset X' from M (12). Then, we create b, ($b = 2 * K + 1$), number of bags from X'. For each bag X'_j extracted from X', we train a model using the base classifier G (14–16). The final output ensemble model E is obtained by a majority vote over G_j (17).

After obtaining the final ensemble model E, we then compute the performance scores based on accuracy and balanced-accuracy, and we compute the fairness score using Equalized of odds (EqOd).

Algorithm 2: Pseudo-code of the proposed method

Input: a clustering algorithm **A**, **S** samples, **K** number of clusters, privileged
group P_1 & P_0, a base classifier **G**

Output: Ensemble Model **E**

1 **Begin**
2   M← { } //*final set of balanced cluster*
3   Split **S** into **K** clusters C_i, $i = 1...K$ using **A**
4   **for** $i = 1...K$:
5   **if** rp $C_i(P_1)/C_i(P_0) = 1$:
6   M ← M ∪ $\{C_i\}$
7   **else**
8   C_i^{bal} ← SMOTE(C_i)
9   M ← M ∪ $\{C_i^{bal}\}$
10   **end if**
11   **end for**
12   Create X' from M
13   **for** $j = 1...2K + 1$:
14   Extract boostrap sample X'_j from X'
15   Fit $G_j(X'_j)$
16   **end for**
17   Output **E** : ensemble model of G_j
18 **End**

---

5   Experiment and Results

In this section we detail on the experimental approach, our goal, the learning
parameter, the dataset used, baseline and results.

5.1   Goal

We carried out an experimental approach with the goals of i) comparing our
method FAPFID to existing methods of fairness [5,19,20] and ii) assessing the
impacts of the imbalance ratio between P_0 and P_1 on the performance of FAPFID
(Sect. 5.7). In particular, for the first goal, the comparison was made based on
two criterion: performance and fairness score. For performance score, we have
used Accuracy and Balanced-Accuray. Accuracy summarizes the performance
of the classification task by dividing the total correct prediction over the total
prediction made by the model. It is the number of correctly predicted samples
out of all the samples. However, since all of the three datasets used are highly
imbalanced, we also use Balanced-accuracy [4] in order to shade more lights on
our model's evaluation on imbalanced datasets compared to the Accuracy. It is
the arithmetic mean of the true positive rate for each class.

5.2 Learning, Evaluation and Parameters

To evaluate and compare the proposed method to existing methods, we proceeded to a learning task by considering a binary classification problem over the three datasets that we described below in Sect. 5.3. For this binary classification problem, Decision Tree is used as base classifier. This choice is made in order to be consistent with the evaluation protocol for concurrent methods. For training and testing, first we use the classic train-test split strategy with a 70%-30% respectively then use k-fold validation on the train set, $2K + 1$ folds in total with K the number of clusters obtained for the used dataset. The folds are made by preserving the percentage of samples for each class.

5.3 Datasets

To evaluate our method, we carried out experiments using three well-known and real-world datasets [10]. They each contain known protected features, which allowed us to evaluate our method on appropriate cases. These datasets were chosen on the basis of the differences and the characteristics, i.e., number of instances, dimensionality and class imbalance. These datasets also provide an interesting benchmark, which is tough, for fairness evaluation as most of recent proposed fairness approaches in the literature have used them. Moreover, they facilitated our comparison with other competitors.

- **Adult census income** dataset [10] contains census data from the U.S whose task it to predict whether someone's income exceeds "50K/yr". After removing duplicate instances and instances with missing values, we ended up with $n = 45,175$ instances. Like our competitors, $P = gender$ was considered as protected feature with $P_0 = female$ and $P_1 = male$. Ratio between unprivileged and privileged instances is 2.23 and 3.53 between classes.
- **Bank dataset** [10] is related to direct marketing campaigns of a Portuguese banking institution with $n = 40,004$ instances. The task is to determine whether a person subscribes to the product (bank term deposit). As target class we consider people who subscribed to a term deposit. Again like our competitors, we consider $P = maritalstatus$ as protected feature with $P_0 = married$ and $P_1 = unmarried$. The dataset suffers from severe class imbalance with global ratio between unprivileged and privileged instances of 2.13. Imbalance ratio between classes is 7.57.
- **KDD census dataset** [10] is basically the same with Adult census, however the target field of this data, was drawn from the "total person income" field rather than the "adjusted gross income" and, therefore, behave differently than the original ADULT target field. This dataset is very skewed, the global ratio between unprivileged and privileged instances is 1.09. $P = gender$ was considered as protected feature with $P_0 = female$ and $P_1 = male$ like in the other methods used for comparison. This is a very skew dataset in terms of class imbalance, the ratio between classes is 15.11. More details on these datasets are given in Table 1.

Table 1. Experimental datasets used and characteristics. For each dataset, n instances: number of instances of each dataset, m Features: number of features, P Feature: protected feature, P Ratio: ratio between privileged (P_1) and unprivileged (P_0) group of the protected feature, Class ratio: ratio between class label of the dataset

	Adult income	Bank	KDD adult
n instances	45175	40004	299285
m features	14	16	41
P feature	Gender	Marital S	Gender
Privileged	Male	Unmarried	Male
Unprivileged	Female	Married	Female
P ratio	2.23	2.13	1.09
Class ratio	3.53	7.57	15.11
Majority label	1	1	1

5.4   Experimental Baseline

We compare our approach to three other recent state-of-the-art proposed methods tackling the problem of imbalance and protected attributes with the aim of improving fairness. The three other approaches used for comparison are:

- *AdaFair* [20]: This method is a fairness-aware boosting approach that adapts AdaBoost to fairness by changing the data distribution at each round based on the notion of cumulative fairness.
- *Fairness Aware Ensemble (FAE)* [19]: This strategy is fairness aware classification that combines pre-processing balancing strategies with post-processing decision boundary adjustment. They use a bagging approach to create sub-datasets while handling the imbalance by an undersampling strategy.
- *SMOTEBoost* [5]: This is an extension of AdaBoost for imbalanced data where new synthetic instances of the minority class are created using SMOTE [6] at each boosting round to compensate the imbalance. This strategy does not tackle the fairness problem, however we used its performance score to evaluate fairness and see if by addressing only the imbalance between classes, the fairness problem can be resolved.

5.5   Results Analysis

We present in the Tables 2, 3, 4 and 5 the results obtained with the different methods. For every dataset, first, we present the result for our stability algorithm that allows us to select the K numbers of stable clusters to use prior our learning strategy. Secondly, for predictive performance, we report on Balanced Accuracy (Bal. Acc.) and Accuracy, for fairness, we report Equalized of Odds (EqOd).

Cluster Stability. In Table 2 below, we report the results for our stability algorithm, the value of K and the stability rate for each dataset. For Adult

Income dataset, the best and stable value for K is 4 with a stability rate of 93%. This means, among all of possible values for K, we tried 12 values, $K = 4$ is the one that allowed us to obtain more consistent and stable clusters. For the other datasets, the respective stability rates are 90 and 93%

Table 2. Cluster stability

	Adult income	Bank	KDD adult
K value	4	5	4
Stability rate	93%	90%	93%

Adult Income Dataset. Performance results with the different approaches for this dataset is presented in Table 3. For predictive performance, we can see that three methods, our proposed one, AdaFair and FAE achieve the same and highest performance score of 83% for Accuracy. However, like we stated above, Accuracy is not as good when we are dealing with imbalanced data. Since this dataset suffers from class imbalance, Balanced-Accuracy is the metric that will tell us how good our model is in terms of performance score. For Balanced-Accuracy, our proposed method outperforms our competitors with a score of 83% as the highest, then FAE and SMOTEBoost both with 81%. We notice that our proposed method performance score is the same for Balanced-Accuracy and Accuracy, this is meaningful since it highlights our strategy of balancing with regards to the protected features in each subgroup prior training the classifier.

For fairness score, we see clearly that our proposed method has surpassed the other three methods used for comparison. Our proposed method has the lowest Equalized Odds score, 0.05 (the lower the better for EqOd) following by AdaFair with 0.08. In short, the proposed method outperforms our competitors on this dataset in terms of Balanced-Accuracy and Fairness score.

Table 3. Adult income: predictive and fairness performance, the best results are in bold.

Score	FAPFID	AdaFair	FAE	SMOTEBoost
Bal. Acc	**0.83**	0.78	0.81	0.81
Accuracy	**0.83**	**0.83**	**0.83**	0.80
EqOd	**0.05**	0.08	0.15	0.47

Bank Dataset. Performance results with the different approaches for this dataset is presented in Table 4. For predictive performance, our proposed method and SMOTEBoost achieve the same and highest performance score of 90% on Accuracy. However, since we are dealing with imbalanced data, we look at Balanced-Accuracy instead. For this, our proposed method achieves the highest score for Balanced-Accuracy, 88% following by the others with a Balanced-Accuracy score under 79%.

For fairness score, our proposed method has surpassed the other three methods used for comparison since it has the lowest Equalized Odds score, 0.06 following by FAE and SMOTEBoost with -0.12 and 0.12 respectively, which based on the definitions of Equalized Odds are not fair at all. Again, the proposed method outperforms our competitors on this dataset in terms of Balanced-Accuracy and Fairness score.

Table 4. Bank dataset: predictive and fairness performance, the best results are in bold.

Score	FAPFID	AdaFair	FAE	SMOTEBoost
Bal. Acc	**0.88**	0.77	0.78	0.74
Accuracy	**0.90**	0.87	0.83	**0.90**
EqOd	**0.06**	0.27	-0.12	0.12

KDD Adult Dataset. Performance results with the different approaches for this dataset is presented in Table 5. For predictive performance, we can see that FAE achieves the highest performance score of 95% for Accuracy following by SMOTEBoost, 94% then the proposed method, 92%. However, our proposed method has the highest Balanced-Accuracy score, 91% which is the one we look at if since this dataset is highly imbalanced. Despite the fact that FAE has the highest Accuracy score, it fails to provide a great Balanced-Accuracy score, it achieves the lowest score of 66%. That means, since this dataset is highly imbalanced, FAE has a higher predictive rate for one group at the expense of the other. FAPFID, our proposed approach instead, has a better fairness score, 0.01 which is the lowest here on this dataset.

In brief, FAPFID outperforms our competitors on this dataset in terms of Balanced-Accuracy and Fairness score.

Table 5. KDD adult: predictive and fairness performance, the best results are in bold.

Score	FAPFID	AdaFair	FAE	SMOTEBoost
Bal. Acc	**0.91**	0.84	0.66	0.76
Accuracy	0.92	0.86	**0.95**	0.94
EqOd	**0.01**	0.07	0.27	0.36

5.6   Discussion

The results on these three datasets show that our method performs well. Compared to the three other fairness-aware methods for dealing with protected feature and data imbalance, we clearly see that our a method has a higher score for Balanced-Accuracy and the lowest score for fairness evaluation. Even in the case where other methods achieve a higher or equal value for Accuracy, our method still outperforms them in terms of Balanced-accuracy and fairness core (EqOd). This is very interesting for handling social decisions problems guarantying a fair outcome for different groups.

In general, on these 3 datasets, we get satisfactory results and we have maintained a good level of performance (Balanced-accuracy) and the best fairness score (the lowest) in terms of Equalized of Odds.

5.7   Effects of Imbalance Ratio

The second goal of our experiments is to evaluate the effects of different imbalance ratios on the performance. Our method is able to achieve efficient and reliable results on the benchmarks datasets above. However, in this section, we investigate the effects of imbalance ratio between privileged and unprivileged group for a given dataset. The goal is to observe the evolution of performance

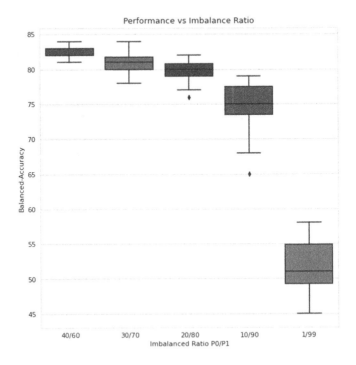

Fig. 2. Effects of imbalanced ratio on balanced-accuracy

scores of the proposed method with regards to different imbalance ratio. Thus, for a given dataset, we create 10 sub-samples where we maintain a fixed imbalance ratio between privileged and unprivileged group, then we report the balanced accuracy for these 10 sub-samples using box-plot.

Basically we proceed as follow: we consider a ratio of 40/60 between unprivileged (P_0) and privileged(P_1) group and create 10 sub-samples, i-e, each sub-sample is created with 40% of (P_0) and 60% of (P_1). We repeated this by varying the ratio such that we obtain different imbalanced ratios between privileged and unprivileged group. The different ratio that we used are: 30/70, 20/80, 10/90 and 1/99.

We report on Fig. 2 the results obtained with Adult Income dataset for performance using Balanced-Accuracy.

As we can see, there is a huge difference between performance scores for different ratio of imbalance. For an imbalance ratio of at least 20% (for P_0), our method still maintains a great averaged Balanced-Accuracy score of 80% at least. With an imbalanced ratio of 10/90, our method suffers from a decreasing in terms of Balanced-Accuracy. We also tested on an extreme case of imbalance ratio between P_0 and P_1: 1/99 where we observed a performance loss. This is because there are not enough P_0 in the cluster so the oversampling method used, SMOTE, can not generate as many meaningful samples for the under-represented group P_0.

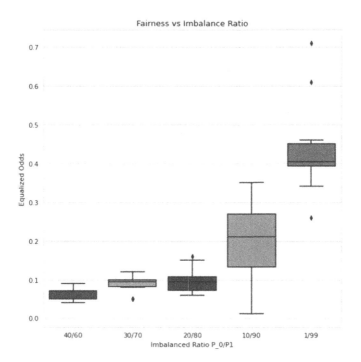

Fig. 3. Effects of imbalanced ratio on fairness

We also report on Fig. 3 the results obtained with Adult Income dataset for fairness using Equalized of Odds. For an imbalanced ratio between 20/80 and 40/60, we get satisfactory results in terms of fairness score with an average score under 0.1 which acceptable for Equalized Odds. However, starting at 10/90 to lower, our method has limited ability to maintain a high level of fairness on this dataset due to the limitations of the oversampling method used and the lack of data for the under-represented group. A limitation that we will later overcome in our future work.

6   Conclusion

In this article, we have proposed a fairness-aware ensemble learning method based on balanced and stables clusters. The proposed method achieves fairness with regards to protected features and class imbalance while maintaining a great performance score.

To do this, we divide the inputs dataset into stable clusters and ensure that privileged and unprivileged groups are fairly represented in each clusters. To obtain stable clusters, we introduce a stability clustering approach that helps maintaining a better homogeneity within clusters. To ensure that privileged and unprivileged instances are fairly represented in each cluster, we have used a novel strategy where we compute a balanced ratio rate within cluster and apply SMOTE only on clusters where the balanced ratio is $\neq 1$.

The performance of our method was experimentally evaluated on three well known biased datasets. Compared to three recent state-of-the-art fairness-aware methods, we obtain satisfactory results and the proposed approach outperforms our competitors in terms of performance (Balanced-Accuracy) and fairness (EqOd) scores. The comparative results obtained show our method's effectiveness in boosting fairness while maintaining a high level of performance.

For our future work, we will look forward to generalise our approach on datasets that are not part of this benchmark and improve our model's performance in dealing with datasets that suffer from a high (10/90) imbalance ratio.

Source Code: The full source code including data of our experiments is available on GitHub under request.

References

1. Amarasinghe, T., Aponso, A., Krishnarajah, N.: Critical analysis of machine learning based approaches for fraud detection in financial transactions. In: Proceedings of the 2018 International Conference on Machine Learning Technologies, pp. 12–17, ICMLT 2018. Association for Computing Machinery, New York, NY, USA (2018)
2. del Barrio, E., Gordaliza, P., Loubes, J.M.: Review of mathematical frameworks for fairness in machine learning (2020). https://doi.org/10.48550/ARXIV.2005.13755, https://arxiv.org/abs/2005.13755

3. Bellamy, R.K.E., et al.: AI fairness 360: an extensible toolkit for detecting, understanding, and mitigating unwanted algorithmic bias. ArXiv abs/1810.01943 (2018)

4. Brodersen, K.H., Ong, C.S., Stephan, K.E., Buhmann, J.M.: The balanced accuracy and its posterior distribution. In: 2010 20th International Conference on Pattern Recognition, pp. 3121–3124. IEEE (2010)

5. Chawla, N.V., Lazarevic, A., Hall, L.O., Bowyer, K.W.: SMOTEBoost: improving prediction of the minority class in boosting. In: Lavrač, N., Gamberger, D., Todorovski, L., Blockeel, H. (eds.) PKDD 2003. LNCS (LNAI), vol. 2838, pp. 107–119. Springer, Heidelberg (2003). https://doi.org/10.1007/978-3-540-39804-2_12

6. Chawla, N.V., Bowyer, K.W., Hall, L.O., Kegelmeyer, W.P.: SMOTE: synthetic minority over-sampling technique. J. Artif. Intell. Res. **16**(1), 321–357 (2002)

7. Chawla, N.V., Japkowicz, N., Kotcz, A.: Special issue on learning from imbalanced data sets. ACM SIGKDD Explor. Newsl. **6**(1), 1–6 (2004)

8. Dash, M., Liu, H.: Feature selection for clustering. In: Terano, T., Liu, H., Chen, A.L.P. (eds.) PAKDD 2000. LNCS (LNAI), vol. 1805, pp. 110–121. Springer, Heidelberg (2000). https://doi.org/10.1007/3-540-45571-X_13

9. Dorleon, G., Megdiche, I., Bricon-Souf, N., Teste, O.: Feature selection under fairness constraints. In: Proceedings of the 37th ACM/SIGAPP Symposium on Applied Computing, pp. 1125–1127 (2022)

10. Dua, D., Graff, C.: UCI machine learning repository (2017)

11. Dwork, C., Hardt, M., Pitassi, T., Reingold, O., Zemel, R.: Fairness through awareness. In: Proceedings of the 3rd Innovations in Theoretical Computer Science Conference, pp. 214–226, ITCS 2012. Association for Computing Machinery, New York, NY, USA (2012)

12. Fang, B., Jiang, M., Cheng, P., Shen, J., Fang, Y.: Achieving outcome fairness in machine learning models for social decision problems. In: Bessiere, C. (ed.) Proceedings of the Twenty-Ninth International Joint Conference on Artificial Intelligence, IJCAI 2020, pp. 444–450. ijcai.org (2020)

13. Farahani, B., Barzegari, M., Aliee, F.S.: Towards collaborative machine learning driven healthcare internet of things. In: Proceedings of the International Conference on Omni-Layer Intelligent Systems, pp. 134–140, COINS 2019. Association for Computing Machinery, New York, NY, USA (2019)

14. Garg, P., Villasenor, J., Foggo, V.: Fairness metrics: a comparative analysis. In: 2020 IEEE International Conference on Big Data (Big Data), pp. 3662–3666. IEEE (2020)

15. Ghassami, A., Khodadadian, S., Kiyavash, N.: Fairness in supervised learning: an information theoretic approach. In: 2018 IEEE International Symposium on Information Theory (ISIT), pp. 176–180. IEEE (2018)

16. Gu, Q., Zhu, L., Cai, Z.: Evaluation measures of the classification performance of imbalanced data sets. In: Cai, Z., Li, Z., Kang, Z., Liu, Y. (eds.) ISICA 2009. CCIS, vol. 51, pp. 461–471. Springer, Heidelberg (2009). https://doi.org/10.1007/978-3-642-04962-0_53

17. Hamilton, M.: The sexist algorithm. Behav. Sci. Law **37**(2), 145–157 (2019)

18. Hu, S., Liang, Y., Ma, L.T., He, Y.: MSMOTE: improving classification performance when training data is imbalanced. In: 2009 Second International Workshop on Computer Science and Engineering, vol. 2, pp. 13–17 (2009)

19. Iosifidis, V., Fetahu, B., Ntoutsi, E.: FAE: a fairness-aware ensemble framework. In: 2019 IEEE International Conference on Big Data (Big Data), pp. 108–110 (2019)

20. Iosifidis, V., Ntoutsi, E.: AdaFair: cumulative fairness adaptive boosting. In: CIKM 2019, pp. 781–790. Association for Computing Machinery, New York, NY, USA (2019)

21. Ji, D., Smyth, P., Steyvers, M.: Can i trust my fairness metric? Assessing fairness with unlabeled data and Bayesian inference. In: Larochelle, H., Ranzato, M., Hadsell, R., Balcan, M.F., Lin, H. (eds.) Advances in Neural Information Processing Systems, vol. 33, pp. 18600–18612. Curran Associates, Inc. (2020)

22. Jiang, Z., Han, X., Fan, C., Yang, F., Mostafavi, A., Hu, X.: Generalized demographic parity for group fairness. In: International Conference on Learning Representations (2021)

23. Kotsiantis, S., Kanellopoulos, D., Pintelas, P., et al.: Handling imbalanced datasets: a review. GESTS Int. Trans. Comput. Sci. Eng. **30**(1), 25–36 (2006)

24. Lahoti, P., et al.: Fairness without demographics through adversarially reweighted learning. Adv. Neural. Inf. Process. Syst. **33**, 728–740 (2020)

25. Martínez, N., Bertrán, M., Papadaki, A., Rodrigues, M.R.D., Sapiro, G.: Blind pareto fairness and subgroup robustness. In: ICML (2021)

26. Meilă, M.: Comparing clusterings by the variation of information. In: COLT (2003)

27. Mishler, A., Kennedy, E.H., Chouldechova, A.: Fairness in risk assessment instruments: post-processing to achieve counterfactual equalized odds. In: Proceedings of the 2021 ACM Conference on Fairness, Accountability, and Transparency, pp. 386–400 (2021)

28. Oneto, L., Chiappa, S.: Fairness in machine learning. In: Recent Trends in Learning From Data, pp. 155–196 (2020)

29. O'Reilly-Shah, V.N., Gentry, K.R., Walters, A.M., Zivot, J., Anderson, C.T., Tighe, P.J.: Bias and ethical considerations in machine learning and the automation of perioperative risk assessment. BJA: Br. J. Anaesth. **125**(6), 843 (2020)

30. Paparrizos, I., Cambazoglu, B.B., Gionis, A.: Machine learned job recommendation. In: Proceedings of the Fifth ACM Conference on Recommender Systems, RecSys 2011, pp. 325–328. Association for Computing Machinery, New York, NY, USA (2011)

31. Pleiss, G., Raghavan, M., Wu, F., Kleinberg, J., Weinberger, K.Q.: On fairness and calibration. In: Advances in Neural Information Processing Systems, vol. 30 (2017)

32. Qin, Z.T., Tang, J.: Deep reinforcement learning with applications in transportation. In: Proceedings of the 25th ACM SIGKDD International Conference on Knowledge Discovery & Data Mining, KDD 2019, pp. 3201–3202. Association for Computing Machinery, New York, NY, USA (2019)

33. Ristanoski, G., Liu, W., Bailey, J.: Discrimination aware classification for imbalanced datasets. In: Proceedings of the 22nd ACM international conference on Information & Knowledge Management, pp. 1529–1532 (2013)

34. Romei, A., Ruggieri, S.: A multidisciplinary survey on discrimination analysis. Knowl. Eng. Rev. **29**, 582–638 (2013)

35. Shameem, M.U.S., Ferdous, R.: An efficient k-means algorithm integrated with Jaccard distance measure for document clustering. In: 2009 First Asian Himalayas International Conference on Internet, pp. 1–6 (2009)

36. Singh, A., Joachims, T.: Fairness of exposure in rankings. In: Proceedings of the 24th ACM SIGKDD International Conference on Knowledge Discovery & Data Mining, pp. 2219–2228 (2018)

37. Sweeney, L.: Discrimination in online ad delivery (2013)

38. Teste, O.: Feature selection under fairness and performance constraints. In: Wrembel, R., Gamper, J., Kotsis, G., Tjoa, A.M., Khalil, I. (eds.) Big Data Analytics and Knowledge Discovery: 24th International Conference, DaWaK 2022, Vienna, Austria, 22–24 August 2022, Proceedings, vol. 13428, p. 125. Springer, Cham (2022). https://doi.org/10.1007/978-3-031-12670-3_11

39. Verma, S., Rubin, J.: Fairness definitions explained. In: Proceedings of the International Workshop on Software Fairness, pp. 1–7. FairWare 2018. Association for Computing Machinery, New York, NY, USA (2018)
40. Wadsworth, C., Vera, F., Piech, C.: Achieving fairness through adversarial learning: an application to recidivism prediction. arXiv preprint arXiv:1807.00199 (2018)
41. Washington, A.L.: How to argue with an algorithm: lessons from the COMPAS-ProPublica debate. Colo. Tech. LJ **17**, 131 (2018)
42. Yeom, S., Datta, A., Fredrikson, M.: Hunting for discriminatory proxies in linear regression models. In: Proceedings of the 32nd International Conference on Neural Information Processing Systems, NIPS 2018, pp. 4573–4583. Curran Associates Inc., Red Hook, NY, USA (2018)
43. Zhuang, L., Dai, H.: Reducing performance bias for unbalanced text mining. In: Sixth IEEE International Conference on Data Mining - Workshops (ICDMW 2006), pp. 770–774 (2006)

D-Thespis: A Distributed Actor-Based Causally Consistent DBMS

Carl Camilleri, Joseph G. Vella$^{(\boxtimes)}$, and Vitezslav Nezval

Computer Information Systems, Faculty of ICT, University of Malta, Msida, Malta
{carl.camilleri.04,joseph.g.vella,vitezslav.nezval}@um.edu.mt

Abstract. Data Consistency defines the validity of a data set according to some set of rules, and different levels of data consistency have been proposed. Causal consistency is the strongest type of consistency that can be achieved when data is stored in multiple locations, and fault tolerance is desired. D-Thespis is a distributed middleware that innovatively leverages the Actor model to implement causal consistency over an industry-standard relational database, whilst abstracting complexities for application developers behind a REST open-protocol interface. We propose the concept of elastic horizontal scalability, and propose systematic designs, algorithms and a correctness evaluation for a middleware that can be scaled to the needs of varying workloads whilst achieving causal consistency in a performant manner.

Keywords: Causal consistency · Distributed databases · Actor model · Middleware · High availability · Elastic horizontal scalability

1 Introduction

The CAP theorem [10,21] proves that having both availability and partition tolerance within disparate databases (DBs) that implement Strong Consistency (SC) [23] is not possible. SC is the strongest type of data consistency offered by traditional database management systems (DDBMSs).

Distributed data centres (DCs) have led to a wide adoption of DB setups that forego strong data consistency in favour of availability and partition tolerance to provide the scalability and high availability (HA) properties sought by enterprise-scale applications. Popular DB setups in this area offer Eventual Consistency (EC) [44], a weak data consistency model which guarantees that given no new WRITE operations, all sites (i.e. distributed partitions) of a DB eventually converge to the same state.

EC is relatively easy to implement, and does not suffer from the performance limitations of distributed algorithms, such as Paxos [28], that attempt to achieve a durability and consensus in a unreliable (distributed) environment. However, EC forgoes consensus, shifts data safety and consistency responsibilities to the application layer, giving rise to a new set of problems [19].

Causal Consistency (CC) [3] is weaker than SC, but stronger than EC, and has been proven to be the strongest type of consistency that can be achieved

© Springer-Verlag GmbH Germany, part of Springer Nature 2023
A. Hameurlain and A. M. Tjoa (Eds.): TLDKS LIII, LNCS 13840, pp. 126–165, 2023.
https://doi.org/10.1007/978-3-662-66863-4_6

in a fault-tolerant, distributed system [31]. Informally, CC implies that readers cannot find a version of a data element before all the operations that led to that version are visible [5]. Whilst CC is sufficiently strong, and sufficiently performant, for most enterprise applications [39], we believe its adoption in the industry is attenuated by a number of issues, including:

1. Lack of support for rich data modelling, with CC DBs supporting data sets based on the key-value data model, or abstract data types.
2. Programmer accessibility, given that existing CC DBs require engineering applications specifically around their semantics or client libraries, and do not sufficiently abstract the programmer from the complexities of distributed data management [9].
3. DBMS lock-in, with the CC DB storing data in native formats which are incompatible with other consumers.

In previous work, we presented Thespis [11], a middleware that achieves CC, stores the data in a relational database management system (RDBMS), and is accessible to application developers through intuitive APIs, abstracting the complexities of CC as much as possible.

In this paper, we describe D-Thespis, an approach that re-visits Thespis and proposes improvements in two main areas. Firstly, D-Thespis achieves "elastic horizontal scalability", so the middleware can be deployed in more than one machine in every DC, whilst at the same time allowing each DC to be autonomously configured. This differs from the standard notion of "horizontal scalability" through less flexible techniques, such as partitioning, that require the configuration of the DBMS (e.g., the number of partitions) to be defined a-priori and to be standardised across the different DCs. Secondly, D-Thespis aims to optimise the Thespis protocol by reducing the occurrence of false positives when identifying causal dependencies, and therefore improving the update visibility latency and reducing the time it takes for the effects of WRITE operations to be made available to clients (i.e., data consumers) in remote DCs.

The rest of the paper is organised as follows. We define useful terminology in Sect. 2. In Sect. 3, give a brief overview of related works in the literature, and a concise description of the Thespis architecture, whilst Sect. 4 specifies the objectives of our work. Section 5 elicits the requirements for a causally-consistent middleware that supports elastic horizontal scalability, with details of the architectural design given in Sect. 6. A correctness evaluation is then given in Sect. 7, followed by a discussion in Sect. 8 and we conclude in Sect. 9.

2   Definitions

This section provides definitions that are relevant throughout the rest of the paper.

Replica. A replica denotes a copy of a database. Our context assumes that each replica is a full copy of the database.

Data Centre/Site. A Data Centre (DC), or site, refers to a physical location that hosts one of the replicas of a database.

Distributed Database. A distributed database (DDB) is considered to be a database which resides in multiple sites.

Database Operation. A database operation denotes an activity that is performed by an application through some API offered by the DBMS.

Operation Latency. A DB's operation latency is the time elapsed between when a client submits an operation to when the result of that operation arrives back at the client (it is typically quoted in milliseconds).

System Throughput. The throughput achieved from a particular setup (i.e. system implementation installed on a specific infrastructure) is the number of operations served in a period of time (it is typically quoted in requests per second).

Data Freshness. Data freshness refers to how long it takes clients connected to a remote DC to be able to read the result of a DB operation that changes state e.g., a WRITE operation, in the local DC. In most implementations, data freshness is traded for throughput and operation latency optimisation. Thus, a client's higher throughput and lower latency are preferred over reading the latest changes from remote DCs.

Causal Consistency. A DDB instance is causally-consistent if all operations that are causally-related are seen in the same order across all the sites having access to the DDB [3]. Two operations a and b are deemed to be potentially causally-related, denoted by $a \rightarrow b$ (i.e. a leads to b), if at least one of three criteria holds [27]:

1. **Thread of Execution:** Given a process P, operations within the same process are causally-related i.e. $a \rightarrow b$ if P performs a, then it performs b.
2. **Reads from:** Given a WRITE operation a, if b reads the result of a, then $a \rightarrow b$.
3. **Transitivity:** If $a \rightarrow b$, and $b \rightarrow c$, then $a \rightarrow c$.

Conversely, the order of *concurrent* operations across the different sites is not guaranteed. Concurrent operations are those that are not related through causality, and are therefore essentially unrelated with respect to the data items read and/or written [3]. Two operations a and b are deemed to be concurrent if $a \nrightarrow b$ and $b \nrightarrow a$, and so can be replicated in any order across the DDB cluster, without violating CC.

Conflict Handling. For a DDB to support HA with low latency, WRITEs need to be accepted at any site without requiring co-ordination and consensus, at least in the critical path, with other sites [5]. A state of conflict causes data consistency between different sites to be broken. A conflict is declared when the same data element in two replica gets updated concurrently. Two operations on the same data element are conflicting if they write a different value, and are not related by causality [3] i.e. they are concurrent. Concurrent and conflicting operations, in the context of a DDB, can therefore be defined as follows:

– Let Θ_1 and Θ_2 define a WRITE operation on a data item identified by key k, in DC_1 and DC_2 respectively.

– Let $\Theta_1 = put(k, v_1)$.
– Let $\Theta_2 = put(k, v_2)$.

$\therefore \Theta_1$ and Θ_2 are concurrent and conflicting operations.

Various approaches for conflict detection and conflict resolution have been put forward [16, 26, 43]. The Last-Writer Wins (LWW) is a popular conflict resolution technique where the most recent update is retained in case of conflict. A database which offers CC as well as conflict detection and resolution, and therefore convergence, is said to provide *causal+ consistency* (CC+) [30].

3   Literature Review

3.1   Causally-Consistent Databases

In COPS [30], application clients are co-located with a cluster of servers that store a full replica of a DB. A WRITE operation is placed in a queue and sent to peer DCs, where it is stored if all its dependencies are also stored. Dependencies of a WRITE operation are tracked by a client-side library that tracks a *context identifier*. Within a *context*, dependencies of a WRITE operation are defined as the latest version of all keys that have so far been interacted with, guaranteeing causality. Conflicts are handled using a LWW approach.

COPS-GT [30] extends COPS with support for read-only transactions. Clients can request the values of a set of keys, rather than that of a single key, and the DDBMS returns a causally-consistent snapshot of the requested keys. COPS-GT, like COPS, uses a sequentially-consistent key-value store, but changes the client library, the DB and the semantics of the READ and WRITE operations. Keys are mapped to a set of versions, rather than one value as in COPS. Each version is mapped to a value and a set of dependencies, encoded as pairs of ⟨*key*, version⟩, thus supporting READ and WRITE operations in a transactional context.

Bolt-On [5] describes a custom middleware on top of Cassandra, a commercially-available EC DB with a columnar data model which handles replication. Bolt-On implements explicit causality, offloading dependency tracking to the client. Data items are tagged with a set of tuples, each indicating a process identifier and its monotonically-increasing identifier. The dependencies of a WRITE operation are the versions of the keys read to produce that operation. Each client holds an *interest set*, the keys that it needs to read, and a resolver process maintains a causally-consistent view of the keys within this set by fetching the latest versions of the data items and their dependencies.

GentleRain [17] provides CC over a key-value, multi-versioned, sharded and replicated DB. It depends on a custom replication protocol to propagate WRITEs across DCs. Dependency tracking is efficient, as the only meta-data stored with a WRITE operation is a timestamp and a server identifier. Any READ operation can only access versions of data that are created in the local DC, or versions that have been created in remote DCs and replicated across all DCs. This guarantees causality by ensuring that when reading a version, the items which have led to its creation (i.e. its dependencies) are present in all DCs.

Wren [37] takes a somewhat similar approach to Gentlerain [17], but uses Hybrid Logical Clocks [25] to timestamp events in a more reliable manner. Furthermore, Wren implements transactional CC, allowing clients to perform read transactions as well as running multiple WRITE operations atomically.

3.2   Thespis

Thespis [11] is a middleware that provides CC over a data repository as well as conflict detection and resolution, thus achieving CC+. Data is stored in a DB managed by a DBMS. The DBMS offers SC and a rich data model with effective querying and reporting capabilities but has no effective horizontal scalability. In fact, Thespis is built over an RDBMS. RDBMSs are widely used in production systems and offer a rich data model with effective querying and reporting capabilities for data management. Hence, although not mandatory for the Thespis middleware, its implementation assumes that: a) the main data handling engine is an RDBMS; and b) that the client is an application handling "objects", primarily instances of business domain models.

Thespis tackles several objectives: it enables the adoption of CC without requiring major application re-engineering, stores data in a format accessible to other systems that need to consume it (e.g. reporting modules), and considers efficiency such that performance overheads of CC guarantees do not outweigh the benefits of using a DDBMS. These objectives are tackled through the fusion several methodologies, including:

1. **The Actor Model** [24], which organises logic in terms of a hierarchical society of "experts" that communicate together via asynchronous message passing. An actor consists of a) a *mailbox* where incoming messages are queued; b) an actor's *behaviour*, or the behavioural logic that is executed in response to a received message; and c) an actor's *state*, i.e., the data stored by the actor at a given point in time. Actors process one message at a time, and exist in the context of Actor Systems [2], where hierarchies can form.
2. **Command Query Responsibility Segregation (CQRS)** [47], a software design pattern that applies the concept of Command Query Separation (CQS) [34] to maintain separate data models for READs and for WRITEs.
3. **Event Sourcing (ES)** [20], another pattern where data changes are captured as a sequence of events which, when stored in an event log and applied in order, provide a view of the system state at a particular point in time.

Figure 1 illustrates the Thespis middleware that offers an API allowing two operations, READ and WRITE. All operations employ the Actor model to deal with concurrency issues. Firstly, the actor-based implementation ascertains that READs happen concurrently. Secondly, it also ascertains that WRITEs on the same object, and in the same replica, happen in a set sequence. The hierarchical nature of Actor Systems is also exploited to reflect a causally-consistent view of the underlying database. The **Writer Actor** and **Reader Actor** are responsible for storing actor states and retrieving business objects from the underlying DB respectively. The **Replication Actor** is responsible for replicating actor state changes from one replica to the other. The core **Middleware** actor system holds a set of actors which provide a view of the underlying DB to the application. Finally the actor system adopts a "child-per-entity" approach, spawning one Entity Actor per type of business object (e.g., DB table), supervising dedicated Entity Instance Actors for each business object instance (e.g., a table's row). The state of the Entity Instance Actor is made up of two elements: the Entity Instance and the Event Log. The events in the Event Log can be applied to the Entity Instance governed by the Entity Instance Actor to retrieve the latest, and causally-consistent, version of the entity.

The middleware snapshots data changes in the DB only when received in all the DCs. WRITEs are captured in the middleware layer and, given a new version of an entity being created by any WRITE operation, a set of events representing the new state, compared to the previous version, are extracted.

Finally, the system incorporates a replication protocol, again implemented through the Actor model, which encapsulates two algorithms, one running on the *Originating Server* (i.e. the server where a new event is created), the other on the *Remote Server*, or the server which is receiving an event from an *Originating Server*. Key to the replication protocol, and to enforce causality, is the Stable Version Vector (SVV). The SVV is simply a vector of length M, where M is the number of peer DCs. Each element SVV_{DC} in the vector is the latest observed timestamp from the corresponding peer DC. Specifically, the vector element $SVV_{DC_N}[M]$ denotes the latest timestamp observed from DC M within DC N.

Results from our evaluation of an implementation of Thespis [11] show that this approach achieves CC+, availability and partition tolerance whilst achieving better performance than an RDBMS. Furthermore, and consistent with the PACELC theorem [1], Thespis can provide CC, and optimises operation latency under normal conditions whilst tolerating network partitions or site failures.

In subsequent work, we extend Thespis to support read-only transactions, through ThespisTRX [13]. This adds functionality to Thespis to allow multiple entities to be retrieved from the underlying DB, potentially in multiple operations, whilst preserving causality. We show that ThespisTRX solves problems such as Time-To-Check-Time-To-Use (TOCTOU) race conditions, whilst our empirical evaluation shows that read latency is similar in both Thespis and ThespisTRX. Another Thespis extension, ThespisDIIP [12], achieves preservation of integrity invariants for data values that must be satisfied according to a Linear Arithmetic Inequality constraint [6] in a distributed setup. Our empirical evaluations [12] show that, in ThespisDIIP, asynchronous operation latency is short enough to eliminate waiting time in the critical path of a typical enterprise application.

4 Objectives for D-Thespis

In this section, we identify the main objectives of D-Thespis. These are grounded in a critical evaluation of Thespis which we discussed briefly in Sect. 3.2. We outline aspects that present an opportunity for change, and also discuss other properties that complement the objectives of D-Thespis and can therefore be carried forward from Thespis.

4.1   Achieving Elastic Horizontal Scalability

The Thespis [11] middleware and its variants (ThespisTRX [14] and ThespisDIIP [12]) do not scale horizontally within a single DC. The Thespis middleware is also more memory bound than an RDBMS. Specifically, actors that are spawned to represent data entities within the DB reside in main memory, and this implicitly imposes much higher requirements on main memory than an RDBMS.

This does not detract from the applicability of Thespis. Firstly, the underlying RDBMS cannot be easily scaled horizontally or made highly available. Indeed, our attempts to achieve horizontal scalability and HA by an RDBMS through standard and established techniques showed that this rendered the setup unfeasible for applications with high-throughput data processing requirements [11]. Secondly, a single computer can nowadays have access to main memory storage where the capacity runs in the order of terabytes[1], and in fact in-memory databases have been developed specifically to exploit such an availability of main memory storage [32]. Works in the literature also indicate that many transactional applications are backed by DBs that fit completely in main memory [22,29]. Therefore, our approaches for a middleware that does not scale horizontally within each DC are still considered valid and applicable to transactional workloads that are typically served by an RDBMS.

Nonetheless, having the possibility to horizontally scale the middleware within a single DC brings several advantages. Firstly, machines that have access to copious amounts of main memory are typically considered, and priced as, premium machines (even in public cloud providers). Imposing the requirement to utilise premium machines to host the middleware goes against the objective of scaling an RDBMS with CC using commodity hardware. Secondly, the memory requirements of the middleware are directly impacted by the current workload: a workload that accesses a large number of records in a short period of time, or one which accesses records that comprise a large amount of data, will have more main memory requirements than a workload that, for example, accesses fewer records. For some transactional applications, the workload profile can change by as much as 30% over a period of time [18]. As such, it is foreseen that the memory requirements of the middleware can vary over different periods for any one installation, even if the size of the dataset within the RDBMS does not vary. For example, the middleware will need lower amounts of memory during a period where the information system experiences lower data requests. Therefore, having a middleware that scales horizontally, even within a single DC, allows the amount of main memory available to be elastically adjusted to the current needs of an application.

---

[1]   At the time of writing, a single *m2-megamem-416* in GCP can have more than 5.5 TB of RAM, and a single *u-24tb1.metal* instance in AWS can have more than 24.5 TB of RAM.

4.2   Improving Remote Update Visibility Latency

Thespis uses scalar, physical timestamps to track causality. Gentlerain [17] shows that this approach is correct and efficient in modelling CC, and our experiments [11] also confirm the adequacy and efficiency of this approach. However, it suffers from the issue of remote update visibility latency [4], or slowdown cascades [33]. i.e., the time taken for an update in a DC DC_x to be made available to clients connected to a remote DC DC_y [4]. The Thespis protocol, like Gentlerain, is therefore vulnerable to laggards and network partitions since it uses scalar timestamps to version events. We address this limitation in D-Thespis by adopting a similar approach to Cure [4] and CausalSpartan [36]. Thus, we improve update visibility latency by using version vectors of physical timestamps, rather than scalar timestamps, to record the timestamp of a WRITE operation.

4.3   Improving Operation Concurrency

By modelling all operations as calls to Actors, the Thespis protocol processes all types of operations on any single entity in the same DC sequentially. Whilst this is a correct and an efficient manner to handle the complexity of parallelism and concurrency on stateful entities, handling all READ and WRITE operations on a single data entity sequentially introduces unnecessary bottlenecks. The topic of allowing transaction concurrency without sacrificing correctness is well-studied, and has been shown to be effective in improving the performance of a DBMS, especially in the context of read-intensive workloads [35] and write-heavy workloads with a high contention, such as a workload that conforms to the Zipfian distribution [41]. Such types of workload distributions have been observed in real scenarios [46]. RDBMSs such as PostgreSQL and Oracle rely on Multi-Version Concurrency Control (MVCC) [8] algorithms to allow concurrent READ operations to access previous versions of a data element and not be blocked by each other, or by other WRITE operations [35]. In D-Thespis, we explore opportunities to adopt similar approaches to improve performance through operation concurrency without sacrificing any of the consistency guarantees of Thespis.

4.4   Maintaining the Thespis Approach

Several aspects of the Thespis protocol remain adequate for D-Thespis.

Firstly, D-Thespis continues to store data in an RDBMS, in keeping with the original objectives of Thespis. It therefore does not aim to achieve HA within a single DC, since the RDBMS does not have HA capabilities. Instead, like Thespis, D-Thespis achieves HA when deployed across several DCs.

Similarly, the DB is not sharded across several partitions in a single DC. This allows the D-Thespis protocol to be built upon the same assumptions as the Thespis protocol, which incorporates several simplifications when compared to systems that handle partitioned data sets [4,17,33,38]. It also allows autonomous infrastructural configuration at DC level i.e., the amount of machines running D-Thespis can differ across DCs, hence achieving elastic horizontal scalability.

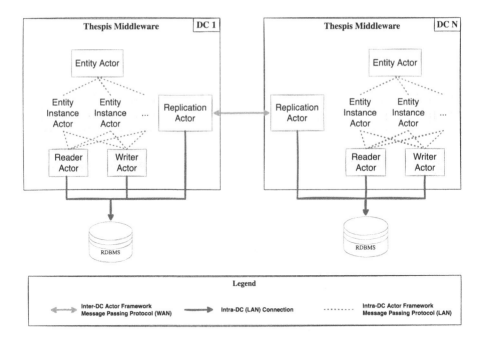

Fig. 1. Thespis system model: actor-based middleware for causal consistency

In D-Thespis we also retain the use of physical timestamps. Other works in the literature [36] identify the need of logical timestamps to address the impact of clock skew on WRITE operations in a distributed setup. D-Thespis assumes that each server running the middleware in a single DC has access to a *data centre clock*, which acts as the authority that provides physical timestamps to all D-Thespis servers in that DC. Values for the *data centre clock* can be taken from highly synchronised clocks, which are becoming more prevalent especially within public cloud infrastructures. For example, machines running in the Amazon Web Services (AWS) cloud have access to the *Amazon Time Sync service*[2] which provides a reference clock based on satellite and atomic clocks. Similarly, Azure provide *Time Sync*[3,4]. At the time of writing, time synchronisation services are free of charge in AWS and Azure, and most machine images are configured to use such services by default. Alternatively, a single server in each DC can act as the time authority. Although this represents a single point of failure for all D-Thespis servers in the same DC, a single DC running D-Thespis is not required to provide HA. With this approach, D-Thespis does not suffer from the impact of clock skew on WRITE operations [36].

Finally, D-Thespis implements CC+ correctly whilst assuming "sticky" clients i.e., any one particular client is connected to a single DC, and that clients do not move between DCs. This is carried over from Thespis, and is based on an impossibility result that shows that sticky clients are required for CC+ [36].

---

[2] https://aws.amazon.com/blogs/aws/keeping-time-with-amazon-time-sync-service/.

[3] https://docs.microsoft.com/en-us/azure/virtual-machines/windows/time-sync.

[4] https://docs.microsoft.com/en-us/azure/virtual-machines/linux/time-sync.

5   D-Thespis Requirements Analysis

This section describes the requirements for D-Thespis to be able to achieve the objectives set out in Sect. 4.

Introducing scalability in the Thespis middleware is beneficial, but it brings forth an element of complexity. Several approaches that worked well for a middleware that always runs on a single machine within each DC do not remain valid for a horizontally scalable setup, and these approaches need to be identified and addressed. We use the term *single-machine middleware* to refer to a middleware that can scale only vertically within a single DC but scales horizontally across different DCs (such as Thespis [11]), whilst the term *horizontally scalable middleware* is used to refer to a middleware that does not only scale horizontally across different DCs, but can also run on several machines within a single DC (such as the D-Thespis middleware being discussed in this paper).

The initial implementations of our design were based on the Akka.NET[5] toolkit. Results have shown that this was a good choice for a single-machine middleware. However, the results from the various empirical tests on Thespis cannot be deemed conclusive that this choice is proper for a horizontally scalable middleware. Section 5.4 discusses several alternative possibilities for the implementation of the Actor framework, with empirical evaluation showing that a one-size-fits-all approach is not an optimal solution.

Furthermore, horizontally scalable middleware has to assume a shared-nothing architecture [40], and therefore a few of our approaches in Thespis need to be revisited. Most importantly, Thespis relies on a physical, scalar clock to assign timestamps to events. The Thespis protocol hinges on assigning timestamps reliably for events happening in any DC. D-Thespis needs to make provisions for horizontally scaled deployments upon commodity hardware or within an infrastructure where a highly synchronised clock service is not available. Section 5.4 discusses how correctness can be maintained in a horizontally scaled setup where highly-synchronised clocks are not available.

A core objective of a horizontally scalable middleware is to handle larger workloads in each DC. This entails a larger amount of READ and WRITE operations. Thespis [11] is inspired by CQRS and Event Sourcing techniques, in that the effects of WRITE operations are stored as events. In Thespis, events are stored in the RDBMS. In the context of a sufficient amount of WRITE operations, the log of events generated by Thespis may outgrow the storage provided by a single machine, whilst the computational resources of a single machine can also become saturated, even before the middleware or the primary RDBMS (and therefore the DC). In D-Thespis, we seek to address this limitation by proposing alternative ways that make event storage also horizontally scalable in a single DC, as discussed in Sect. 5.2.

---

[5] https://getakka.net/.

5.1   Supporting a Horizontally Scalable Middleware

To achieve the required optimisations, D-Thespis incorporates an additional four components over the Thespis system model, specifically:

1. The Data Centre Clock
2. The Cluster Clock
3. A Scalable Event Log
4. A Version Cache

The *Data Centre Clock* is the authority which defines the physical timestamps within a particular DC. The D-Thespis protocol relies on the Data Centre Clock to enforce two guarantees, namely:

1. **Time Monotonicity**, and therefore produces values that always increment;
2. **Highly Synchronised**, and therefore that all servers within the same DC should have access to a source of physical timestamps that correctly reflect when an operation has happened, and its possible causal relationship to all other operations in the same DC.

Conversely, the protocol does not rely on Data Centre clocks within different DCs to be synchronised.

In D-Thespis, we aim to abstract the source of physical timestamps from the core implementation and support three ways of having a data centre clock.

Firstly, the *Server Data Centre Clock* refers to a configuration of D-Thespis that obtains timestamps from the physical clock of each server. This configuration is valid under several conditions, such as for servers that have highly synchronised clocks. Secondly, the *Database Data Centre Clock* refers to a configuration where D-Thespis takes its physical timestamps by running a relevant query on the underlying DBMS. This effectively assigns the RDBMS server as the source of truth for physical timestamps. Lastly, the *Middleware Data Centre Clock* is a configuration whereby D-Thespis runs a single instance of a bespoke component that exposes an endpoint through which D-Thespis components running on any other server in the same DC can obtain a timestamp.

The *Cluster Clock* is the authority which defines the values of the SVV within a particular DC. The SVV is a data structure that is carried forward from the Thespis protocol and is used for dependency tracking of remote events. In a single-machine middleware, the SVV can be represented by a data structure in the memory of the server hosting the middleware. However, in a horizontally scalable middleware, all servers within the same DC need to access and maintain a single instance of the SVV. D-Thespis aims to also abstract the source of the SVV from the core implementation, and supports two approaches for its implementation. The *Server Cluster Clock* refers to a configuration whereby the SVV is stored in memory. This is the most efficient implementation but it is only suitable for when D-Thespis is running in a single-machine configuration. When running in a horizontally scaled configuration, D-Thespis needs to use the *Middleware Cluster Clock*. Similar to the approach taken for the data centre clock, a single server hosts an instance of the *Server Cluster Clock*, which is then exposed to all the other servers within the same DC through remote procedure calls (RPC).

5.2 A Scalable Event Log

To achieve scalability and correctness, the D-Thespis protocol requires the event log storage layer to provide:

1. **Key-based multi-record lookups**, to allow efficient loading of all the events that pertain to a particular data entity (i.e., a particular record in the RDBMS referenced by its primary key);
2. **Key-based event queueing**, to allow the middleware to add events resulting from WRITE operations to the list pertaining to a particular data entity;
3. **Durability**, in that the event log needs to guarantee that once an event is saved, the operation is durable even in case of a hardware failure;
4. **Key-level Atomicity**, such that a request to add an event to the list pertaining to a particular data entity will either succeed or fail, without any in-between states;
5. **Key-level Isolation**, such that concurrent requests to add events to the list pertaining to a particular data entity are serialised and ordered correctly;
6. **Horizontal scalability**, such that the storage of events can scale across several machines.

The first five guarantees are inherently available when the event log is stored within the RDBMS, as in Thespis. Storing the event log in the RDBMS provides additional functionalities, such as the possibility to read a subset of events for a particular data entity, or the possibility to read the events in order. However, the approach for D-Thespis does not deem these as hard requirements for the event log storage layer.

5.3 Version Cache for Operation Concurrency

To achieve operation concurrency, the D-Thespis design incorporates a cache layer in each DC that stores the latest causally consistent version of a specific Data Entity inferred by a READ operation within the DC. All servers within the same DC connect to the same cache layer, and the D-Thespis READ and WRITE operations are tuned with cache maintenance functionality.

In a horizontally scaled setup, we also recognise the benefits of having this type of cache layer due to the potential contention in communication within a distributed Actor cluster. For example, in considering the scenario illustrated in Fig. 2, a client can request a data entity with identity "1". Suppose that the client request is routed by standard load balancing equipment to *Server*1, which is not responsible to store the Actor corresponding to data entity "1". In this case, the request is still served by *Server*1, but the READ operation is delegated to run on *Server*2. Inter-cluster communication for a distributed Actor model implementation is responsible for specific message delivery semantics (e.g., at

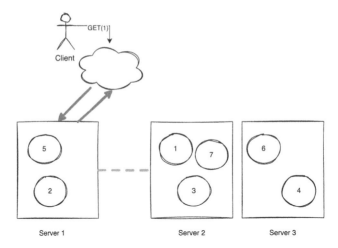

Fig. 2. A horizontally scaled actor cluster

least once and message ordering) and thus incurs more overheads than regular RPC to a cache layer.

Figure 3 illustrates at a high-level how the READ operations differ from the Thespis approach to the D-Thespis approach. Specifically:

1. D-Thespis can return a causally consistent version of an entity from the cache, an operation that executes within a context where concurrency is allowed;
2. Within the Actor logic, D-Thespis stores the latest causally consistent version of a data entity in the cache if all known events can be applied before completing a READ operation.

Figure 4 compares the WRITE operation of Thespis and D-Thespis. Here, the only difference is that the Actor logic in D-Thespis is responsible to delete any cached version of the data entity before completing the WRITE operation.

To retain correctness and scalability, the D-Thespis protocol requires the cache layer to provide:

1. **Key-based lookups**, to allow efficient loading of a cached version of a particular data entity;
2. **Key-based version storage**, to allow the middleware to save a causally consistent version of a particular data entity;
3. **Key-level Atomicity**, such that saving a version of a data entity either succeeds or fails, without any in-between states;
4. **Key-level Isolation**, such that concurrent READ and WRITE requests for a cached data entity version are serialised and ordered correctly;
5. **Horizontal scalability**, such that the storage of entity versions can scale across several machines.

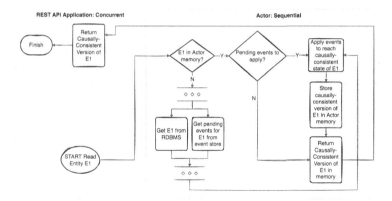

(a) Thespis READ Operation

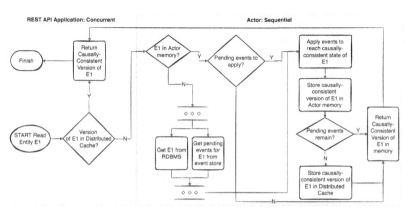

(b) D-Thespis READ Operation

Fig. 3. Thespis *vs.* D-Thespis READ operations

5.4 Choosing an Optimal Actor Framework

D-Thespis adopts an approach grounded in expressing and implementing causal consistency using the Actor model. The initial implementations of the Thespis design were based on the Akka.NET[6] toolkit. The work on D-Thespis delves deeper into two additional implementations of the Actor model, namely Akka[7] and Microsoft Orleans[8]. Microsoft Orleans, like Akka.NET, is implemented for the Microsoft .NET framework and executes in the Common Language Runtime (CLR), whilst Akka is a Java implementation and therefore executes in the Java Virtual Machine (JVM). Conversely, Akka and Akka.NET toolkits are very similar in their implementation of the Actor model, whereas Microsoft Orleans implements the abstract Virtual Actor model.

---

[6] https://getakka.net/.

[7] https://akka.io/.

[8] https://dotnet.github.io/orleans/.

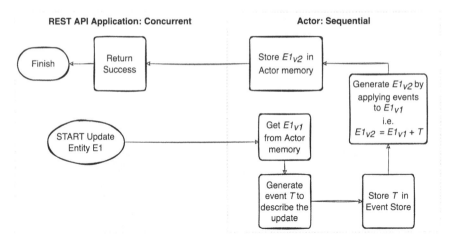

(a) Thespis WRITE Operation

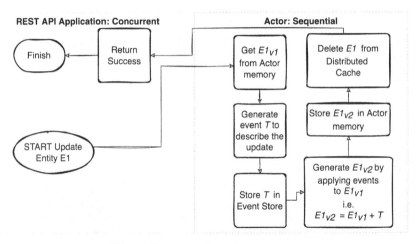

(b) D-Thespis WRITE Operation

Fig. 4. Thespis *vs.* D-Thespis WRITE operations

The Virtual Actor model, as delivered by the Orleans framework, aims to isolate the programmer from the complexities of the Actor model by providing a more familiar API to the underlying Actor model. This includes:

1. Actors, called **Grains**, expose an RPC interface i.e., Grains are coded very similar to classes in standard object-oriented programming, exposing methods that can be called to trigger a specific Grain behaviour.
2. Each Grain is a stand-alone entity;
3. From the point of view of a programmer, Grains always exist and can be called at any time. The responsibility to manage Grains existence is fully abstracted by the framework;

4. Grains live in **Silos**, and multiple Silos form an **Orleans Cluster**. When a Silo runs on a dedicated machine, the cluster is running a distributed infrastructure;
5. Grains are distributed across the available Silos using some **Placement strategy**.

The Microsoft Orleans framework still carries over all the guarantees of the traditional Actor model, including the guarantee that a Virtual Actor (i.e., *Grain*) can only process one message at a time, and that at most one instance of a Virtual Actor with a particular identifier exists within an Orleans Cluster. This framework is used in various works and is reported in the literature. For example, it has been shown that the Microsoft Orleans framework is suitable for the implementation of an Actor-Oriented database for an Internet of Things (IoT) use case [45]. Therefore, the Microsoft Orleans framework is also considered adequate to serve as the basis for a middleware that delivers causal consistency over an RDBMS.

We performed an empirical evaluation to compare the performance of Akka, Akka.NET and Microsoft Orleans, with Akka running in the JVM and Akka.NET and Microsoft Orleans running on the CLR. Details of these benchmarks are published elsewhere [15] and are therefore omitted for brevity. Out of the options tested, our results show that the CLR platform is the most apt one for an implementation of D-Thespis. This decision allows a framework-agnostic implementation to be developed, such that D-Thespis can be configured to run either in single-machine or horizontally scalable configurations.

In single-machine configuration, D-Thespis should implement the protocol on the basis of the Actor model guarantees provided by the Akka.NET toolkit. When running in a horizontally scalable configuration, the D-Thespis protocol should be based on the guarantees of the Orleans framework.

This decision is, first and foremost, driven by results of our empirical performance benchmarks. The benchmarks show that the Orleans framework achieves the best performance out of the three frameworks tested when deployed in a horizontally scalable configuration. Naturally, this is considered an advantage and helps achieves the performance requirements of an implementation of D-Thespis. The benchmark results also show that this is especially important when deploying a distributed Actor cluster, which is precisely what is required from a horizontally scalable middleware.

On the other hand, benchmarks show that when running in a single-machine configuration, the performance of the Orleans framework and that of the Akka.NET toolkit is very comparable. These results do not encourage a decision to disregard the Akka.NET toolkit. Both Orleans and Akka.NET are, at the time of writing, open source projects with very active communities, and therefore it cannot be excluded that different results are obtained as these toolkits continue to evolve.

Finally, this decision also provides an opportunity to show that the D-Thespis protocol and framework does not necessarily depend on any single Actor model implementation, but only on the guarantees given by a correct implementation of the Actor model, including the Virtual Actor model. Therefore, building a solution that generalises, through configuration, and uses both the Microsoft Orleans Virtual Actor framework and the Akka.NET Actor toolkit allows a further assertion that the ideas discussed, and designs proposed, can generalise to any implementation of the Actor model.

6   D-Thespis System Design

D-Thespis retains the conceptual model illustrated in Fig. 1, and therefore keeps to the approach of delivering CC through a middleware that:

1. Connects to an RDBMS
2. Exposes REST endpoints to client applications
3. Can be deployed across multiple DCs, with each DC having a fully autonomous replica of the RDBMS

However, several aspects in the architecture and protocol of D-Thespis differ from those of Thespis, as discussed in the next few sections. The architectural design also supports generalisation in terms of de-coupling the protocol from the technical choices.

6.1   D-Thespis Domain Model

Figure 5 illustrates the core domain model of D-Thespis. An *Entity* represents a record in a table within the RDBMS. It comprises an identifier and its data. The data for an entity is represented by the *Record* data structure, which is an array of *FieldBase*. The type *FieldBase* is an abstract key-value pair data structure that represents a field within the record, which serves as the basis for type-specific fields. For example, the *FieldInt* represents an integer field within the table of the RDBMS.

A WRITE operation on an *Entity* is represented as a *DataEntityEvent*. An instance of a *DataEntityEvent* is uniquely identifiable, and comprises an array of *EntityEventItem*. Each *EntityEventItem* in the list describes the change to a particular field of the *Entity* requested by the WRITE operation.

The time when the *DataEntityEvent* happened is represented by the *Event-Timestamp*. This includes the *OriginDataCentreId*, which defines the DC where the event happened, and an array of *EventTime* which is a vector of physical timestamps. The length of the *Times* array in *EventTimestamp* is determined by the maximum amount of DCs that a D-Thespis cluster is configured to support. Having the *Times* data structure as a vector of physical timestamps, as opposed to the scalar physical timestamp used in the Thespis protocol, carries sufficient information to infer:

1. The physical time of the origin DC where the event happened, given by the entry in *Times* where $DataCentreId = OriginDataCentreId$
2. The dependencies of the WRITE event from other remote DCs, given by the entries in *Times* where $DataCentreId \neq OriginDataCentreId$

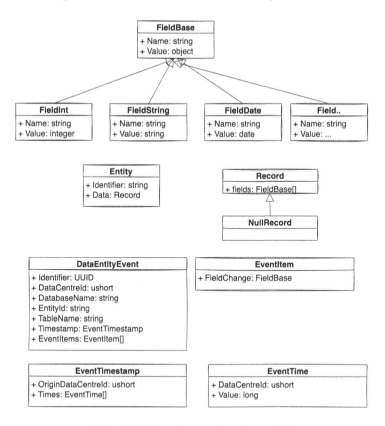

Fig. 5. D-Thespis core domain model

6.2   D-Thespis Middleware Architecture

The D-Thespis architecture is illustrated in Fig. 7, comprising several components that depend on each other through library references, network calls over the LAN (i.e., within the same DC), or network calls over the internet (i.e., across different DCs). Components that are used through library referencing expose generic interfaces, such that their implementation specifics are hidden from any dependant layers. This design choice allows multiple implementations of each library to co-exist and be used through a configuration or convention-driven setup, effectively achieving low coupling across the different layers. Furthermore, most inter-layer network communication is based upon RPC, using a binary protocol over HTTP/2 for efficiency. This design choice exploits the fact that inter-layer APIs do not need to support ubiquitous access from external clients, and therefore can use protocols which are more efficient and performant than REST calls.

The **Rest Client API** is a thin layer that exposes REST APIs through which clients can read and write data. The request information from the client HTTP

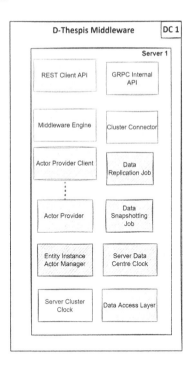

Fig. 6. D-Thespis conceptual model for a single-machine setup in a DC

calls is mapped to suitable data structures within the Rest Client API layer, and then handed off to the **Middleware Engine**.

The **GRPC Internal API** is also a thin layer that exposes a set of APIs using the GRPC[9] protocol for improved efficiency. These APIs are never exposed to clients of D-Thespis but instead are used for network communication amongst the different components of D-Thespis.

The **Middleware Engine** has access to an **Actor Provider** component. The Middleware Engine does not have any intrinsic knowledge of the Actor model implementation and serves as a thin layer that hands off requests to the Actor Provider, with one exception. If the Actor Provider supports READ operation concurrency, then the Middleware Engine attempts to serve READ requests independently by obtaining the latest causally consistent version of the requested data entity from the distributed cache. If this is not successful (i.e., there is no entry in cache for the requested data entity) then the READ operation is handed off to the Actor Provider component.

The **Actor Provider** component has intrinsic knowledge of the logic that needs to execute within the context of the Actor model. It comprises two parts, the *Actor Cluster Client* and the *Actor Cluster*. Requests received from the

---

[9] https://grpc.io/.

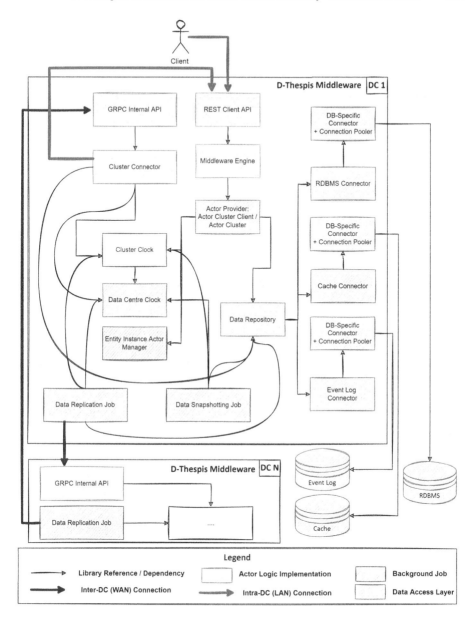

Fig. 7. D-Thespis conceptual model

Middleware Engine are packaged in suitable data structures and handed off as messages to the Actor cluster, through the Actor Cluster Client.

The Actor cluster implements the D-Thespis protocol in the specific semantics of its Actor model framework. It also accesses the **Entity Instance Actor Manager** for algorithms that are inherent to the D-Thespis but which are not influenced by the specifics of the Actor model framework. This includes, for example, logic to apply a new event to a version of a particular data entity.

The **Data Repository** is the entry point to the data access layer from all other components. It exposes an interface through which other components read data from the RDBMS, access the Event Log and access the Distributed Version Cache. Access to the different data repositories is further encapsulated within DB-specific connectors to keep the data access logic independent of the DB itself.

The **Data Centre Clock** is a component that allows other layers to obtain a physical clock timestamp. As discussed in Sect. 5, different approaches can be taken to implement the Data Centre Clock. For example, in the *Server Data Centre Clock* approach, the **Data Centre Clock** layer returns the physical timestamp from the clock of the host machine. On the other hand, with the *Middleware Data Centre Clock* approach, the **Data Centre Clock** layer becomes a thin client that calls an internal API exposed by a service on a particular machine to obtain a physical timestamp. Physical timestamps are represented as 64-bit integers that fit in the domain model discussed in Sect. 6.1.

The **Cluster Clock** is a component that provides access to read and maintain the *Stable Version Vector* (SVV). Similar to the Data Centre Clock, with the *Server Cluster Clock* approach, the **Cluster Clock** layer simply maintains an in-memory version of the SVV, whilst with the *Middleware Cluster Clock* approach, the **Cluster Clock** performs internal calls to a singleton service within one machine in the local DC to obtain or update the SVV. The SVV is represented as an array of *EventTime*, and thus re-uses a structure from the domain model discussed in Sect. 6.1.

The **Data Replication Job** periodically executes the data replication protocol to interrogate the Event Log and identify events that have been generated in the local DC but which have not yet been replicated to any of the remote DCs. Batches of events are sent to a remote peer DC through a RPC over an endpoint which every D-Thespis DC exposes to its peers.

Finally, the **Data Snapshotting Job** also executes periodically to interrogate the Event Log and identify events that represent versions of data entities for which no further dependencies are expected. These events are replayed in order onto the version of the data entity stored on the RDBMS, and the corresponding data in the Event Log is purged.

6.3   D-Thespis Middleware Deployment Configuration

Figure 8 illustrates one possible configuration of the D-Thespis model deployed in a horizontally scalable configuration over ten servers within a single DC. This illustration shows that the client-facing components, namely the REST Client API, the Middleware Engine and the Actor Cluster Client can be scaled horizontally, but independently of the Actor cluster. Client requests can be distributed across these servers through standard HTTP load balancing systems. The Actor cluster itself is scaled horizontally and relies on the specific protocol of the Actor model framework to distribute the Actors, such that only a single actor representing a data entity exists at any point in time. The Actor Cluster Clients

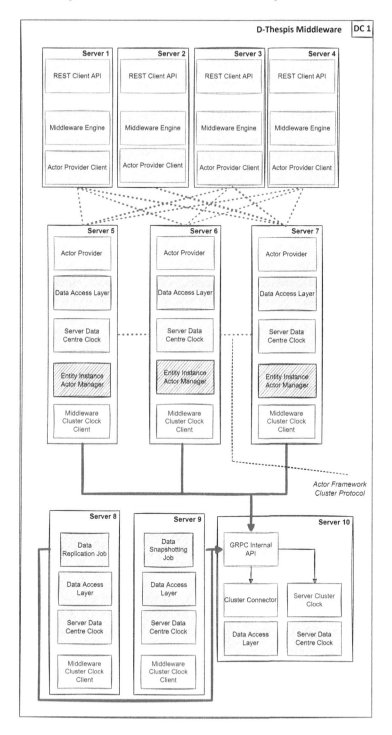

Fig. 8. D-Thespis conceptual model: horizontal scalability in a single DC

participate in the technology-specific protocol of the Actor model framework to discover servers which host Actor cluster nodes, and which can therefore accept requests to the Actor Provider component of D-Thespis.

In this configuration, it is assumed that all servers within the same DC have highly synchronised clocks, and therefore the Data Centre Clock component consists of an implementation of the *Server Data Centre Clock* which runs independently on every server. However, all servers within the same DC over which D-Thespis is horizontally scaled need to access and maintain a single instance of the SVV. Therefore, every server has access to a *Middleware Cluster Clock Client* which accesses a single instance of the *Server Cluster Clock* through internal API calls. In this configuration, *Server 10* is the authority for the SVV.

Finally, this configuration also shows that the Data Replication Job and the Data Snapshotting Job are not horizontally scalable: only one instance of each can execute at any point in time within a single DC. However, they are also largely independent of the rest of the D-Thespis modules, and therefore they can execute on dedicated hardware.

In contrast, the configuration illustrated in Fig. 6 is also valid, and shows how all D-Thespis components can run on a single machine. In this case, we can use the more efficient *server* version of both the Data Centre Clock and the Cluster Clock, as discussed in Sect. 6.2.

6.4   D-Thespis Protocol

The protocol comprises several operations, namely READ and WRITE operations, Conflict Resolution and Convergence, as well as Event Replication and Snapshotting. Algorithm 3 illustrates the READ operation in D-Thespis, as well as the main components involved. Additional details can be noted, namely:

1. In the presence of a distributed cache, the READ operation in D-Thespis only flows through the Actor model at *line 16*. The functionality before this instant executes with regular concurrency and parallelism guarantees i.e., the logic can execute concurrently and in parallel.
2. The Actor Provider and Entity Instance Actor (*lines 14–49*) are specific to the Actor model framework being used, whilst the rest of the algorithm is agnostic to the Actor model framework adopted.
3. The logic in *lines 19–49* executes in the context of an Actor, and therefore processes one call at a time in any particular instance of the *Entity Instance Actor*. Thus, the state of the Actor (*lines 19, 20*) is safeguarded from concurrency through the guarantees of the Actor model framework.

Algorithm 4 illustrates the *Entity Instance Actor Manager*, which depends on Algorithms 1 and 2. As discussed, this component primarily encapsulates functionality which is specific to the D-Thespis protocol, independent of the Actor model framework being used but is required by the framework-dependant logic. Effectively, this component serves as a thin wrapper for the data access layer and also encapsulates the logic through which events can be applied to a version of a data entity to return the freshest, causally consistent version possible at any point in time. A few things of particular note in Algorithm 4 are:

1. *Line 14* shows how the Entity Instance Actor Manager depends on the *Server Cluster Clock* to obtain the current SVV. The logic of the *Server Cluster Clock* component is given in Algorithm 1.
2. *Lines 15–21* show that not all available events may be applied to a given data entity. The rules that dictate whether an event can be applied to an entity version at any point in time are given in Algorithm 2.
3. *Line 22* shows that the logic does not depend on the Event Log to provide it with events that are in the correct order, but implements logic to define the order in which the available events should be applied to a Data Entity version. The *sort* function uses the logic given in Algorithm 5 to compare each event to every other event in the list, based on their timestamp (i.e., vector of physical timestamps), and orders the events in ascending order of the value returned by Algorithm 5.

Algorithm 1. D-Thespis Algorithm - Server Cluster Clock

Require: DataCentreClock, CurrentDataCentreId
1: $svv : Vector < ushort, EventTime >$ ▷ *A thread-safe vector of DC $\longrightarrow$ Timestamp*
2: **function** GETSVV
3:     $times \leftarrow []$
4:     $now \leftarrow$ DATACENTRECLOCK.GETNOW
    ▷ *Take timestamps from the SVV for remote DCs, and timestamp from Data Centre Clock for local DC*
5:     $times \leftarrow v \in svv.values \mid \begin{cases} v & [v.DCId \neq CurrentDataCentreId] \\ now & [v.DCId = CurrentDataCentreId] \end{cases}$
6:     **return** $times$
7: **end function**

8: **procedure** TICK($peerDC, originDCTime$)
9:     $svv[peerDC] \leftarrow originDCTime$
10: **end procedure**

Algorithm 2. D-Thespis Algorithm - Stable Version Vector

1: **function** ALLOWEVENT($originDCId, eventTimestamp$)
2:     $isSourceDCLargerInGST \leftarrow false$
3:     $areOthersSmallerOrEqualInGST \leftarrow null$
4:     **for** $eventDCTime \in eventTimestamp.times$ **do**
5:         **if** $eventDCTime.DataCentreId = originDCId$ **then**
6:             $isSourceDCLargerInGST \leftarrow this.times[originDCId] > eventDCTime$
7:         **else**
8:             **if** $eventDCTime > this.times[eventDCTime.DataCentreId]$ **then**
9:                 $areOthersSmallerOrEqualInGST \leftarrow false$
10:             **else if** $areOthersSmallerOrEqualInGST = null$ **then**
11:                 $areOthersSmallerOrEqualInGST \leftarrow true$
12:             **end if**
13:         **end if**
14:     **end for**
15:     $res \leftarrow isSourceDCLargerInGST$ AND $areOthersSmallerOrEqualInGST$
16:     **return** res
17: **end function**

Algorithm 3. D-Thespis Algorithm - READ Operation

Rest Client API
Require: MiddlewareEngine, CurrentDataCentreId
1: **function** READ(database db, table t, primary key column k, identifier id)
2:     MIDDLEWAREENGINE.READ($CurrentDataCentreId, db, t, k, id$)
3: **end function**

MiddlewareEngine
Require: ActorProvider, DataRepository
4: **function** READ(dc, db, t, k, id)
5:     **if** ActorProvider.SupportsCache **then**
6:         $res \leftarrow$ DATAREPOSITORY.GETENTITY(db, t, id)
7:         **if** $res \neq null$ **then**
8:             **return** res
9:         **end if**
10:     **end if**
11:     $res \leftarrow$ ACTORPROVIDER.READ(dc, db, t, k, id)
12:     **return** res
13: **end function**

ActorProvider
Require: ActorProvider, DataRepository
14: **function** READ(dc, db, t, k, id)
15:     $A \leftarrow$ Entity Instance Actor corresponding to record $k = id$ in table t of database db
16:     $res \leftarrow$ A.READ(dc, db, t, k, id)   ▷ *Communicate via Message Passing*
17:     **return** res
18: **end function**

Entity Instance Actor
Require: EntityInstanceActorManager EIM
19: $Entity : DataEntity \leftarrow null$ ▷ *The last-known causally consistent version of the Data Entity*
20: $Events : DataEntityEvent \leftarrow []$ ▷ *List of pending events*
21: $SupportsCache : boolean$ ▷ *true if the implementation should support a distributed cache*
22: **function** READ(dc, db, t, k, id)
23:     **if** $Entity \neq null$ **then**
24:         **if** $Events \neq \emptyset$ **then**
25:             $(fe, fev) \leftarrow$ EIMGR.APPLYEVENTS($Entity, Events, db, t, k, id, dc$)   ▷ *Alg. 4*
26:             $Entity \leftarrow fe$
27:             $Events \leftarrow fev$
28:             **if** $SupportsCache = true$ **then**
29:                 **if** $Events = \emptyset$ **then**
30:                     EIM.SAVEENTITY($db, t, id, Entity$)   ▷ *Alg. 4*
31:                 **else**
32:                     EIM.DELETEENTITY(db, t, id)   ▷ *Alg. 4*
33:                 **end if**
34:             **end if**
35:         **end if**
36:         **return** $Entity$
37:     **end if**
38:     **do in parallel**
39:         $Entity \leftarrow$ EIM.READDBRECORD(db, t, k, id)   ▷ *Alg. 4*
40:         $Events \leftarrow$ EIM.LOADEVENTS(db, t, k, id)   ▷ *Alg. 4*
41:     **end**
42:     $(fe, fev) \leftarrow$ EIM.APPLYEVENTS($Entity, Events, db, t, k, id, dc$)   ▷ *Alg. 4*
43:     $Entity \leftarrow fe$
44:     $Events \leftarrow fev$
45:     **if** $SupportsCache = true$ & $Events = \emptyset$ **then**
46:         EIM.SAVEENTITY($Entity$)
47:     **end if**
48:     **return** $Entity$
49: **end function**

Algorithm 4. D-Thespis Algorithm - Entity Instance Actor Manager

---

Require: ClusterClock, DataRepository
 1: **function** READDBRECORD(db, t, k, id)
 2:     **return** DATAREPOSITORY.READ(db, t, k, id)
 3: **end function**

 4: **function** LOADEVENTS(db, t, id)
 5:     **return** DATAREPOSITORY.LOADEVENTS(db, t, id)
 6: **end function**

 7: **function** DELETEENTITY(db, t, id)
 8:     **return** DATAREPOSITORY.DELETEENTITY(db, t, k, id)
 9: **end function**

10: **function** SAVEENTITY($db, t, id, Entity$)
11:     **return** DATAREPOSITORY.SAVEENTITY($db, t, k, id, Entity$)
12: **end function**

13: **function** APPLYEVENTS($events, entity, t, db, k, id, dc$)
14:     $svv \leftarrow$ CLUSTERCLOCK.GETSVV(dc)   ▷ *Alg. 1*
15:     $allowedEvents \leftarrow [\,]$
16:     **for** $e \in events$ **do**
17:         $isAllowed \leftarrow$ SVV.ALLOWEVENT($e.OriginDCId, e.Timestamp$)   ▷ *Alg. 2*
18:         **if** $isAllowed$ **then**
19:             APPEND($allowedEvents, e$)
20:         **end if**
21:     **end for**
22:     $orderedEvents \leftarrow$ SORT($allowedEvents$)   ▷ *Alg. 5*
23:     $resEntity \leftarrow$ MAPEVENTSTOENTITY($orderedEvents, entity$)
24:     $resEvents \leftarrow events - allowedEvents$
25:     **return** ($resEntity, resEvents$)
26: **end function**

27: **function** MAPEVENTSTOENTITY($events, entity$)
28:     **if** $events = \emptyset$ **then**
29:         **return** $entity$
30:     **end if**
31:     $v \leftarrow$ MAPEVENTTOENTITY($entity, events[0]$)
32:     $rem \leftarrow$ TAIL($events$)
33:     **return** MAPEVENTSTOENTITY(v, rem)
34: **end function**

35: **function** MAPEVENTTOENTITY($event, entity$)
36:     **if** $event.items = \emptyset$ **then**
37:         **return** $entity$
38:     **end if**
39:     **for** $i \in event.items$ **do**
40:         **for** $f \in entity.fieldNames$ **do**
41:             **if** $i.fieldName = f$ **then**
42:                 $entity[f] = i.value$
43:             **end if**
44:         **end for**
45:     **end for**
46:     **return** $entity$
47: **end function**

Algorithm 5. Ordering Events: comparing timestamp $ts1$ to timestamp $ts2$

1: **function** COMPARE(event timestamp $ts1$, event timestamp $ts2$)
2:     $hasSmaller \leftarrow false$
3:     $hasLarger \leftarrow false$
4:     **for** $t \leftarrow ts1.times$ **do**
5:         **if** $t.value < ts2.times[t.dataCentreId]$ **then**
6:             $hasSmaller \leftarrow true$
7:         **else if** $t.value > ts2.times[t.dataCentreId]$ **then**
8:             $hasLarger \leftarrow true$
9:         **end if**
10:     **end for**
                                ▷ *Vector Timestamps are equal? tie-break by Origin DC Id:*
11:     **if** $hasSmaller = false$ & $hasLarger = false$ **then**
12:         **if** $ts1.OriginDataCentreId > ts2.OriginDataCentreId$ **then**
13:             **return** 1
14:         **else**
15:             **return** -1
16:         **end if**
17:     **end if**
                                ▷ *All timestamps in ts1 are smaller or equal to those in ts2:*
18:     **if** $hasSmaller = true$ & $hasLarger = false$ **then**
19:         **return** -1
20:     **end if**
                                ▷ *All timestamps in ts1 are larger or equal to those in ts2:*
21:     **if** $hasSmaller = false$ & $hasLarger = true$ **then**
22:         **return** 1
23:     **end if**
        ▷ *ts1 and ts2 indicate that the corresponding events conflict! Perform LWW with Merge:*
24:     $max_{ts1} \leftarrow$ MAX($ts1.times$)
25:     $max_{ts2} \leftarrow$ MAX($ts2.times$)
26:     **if** $max_{ts1} > max_{ts2}$ **then**
27:         **return** 1
28:     **else**
29:         **return** -1
30:     **end if**
31: **end function**

Algorithm 6. D-Thespis Algorithm - Snapshot Operation

    Event Snapshot Service
Require: ClusterClock, DataRepository, CurrentDataCentreId
1: **procedure** DOWORK
2:     **while** $true$ **do**
3:         SNAPSHOT(CurrentDataCentreId)
4:         SLEEP($100ms$)
5:     **end while**
6: **end procedure**

7: **procedure** SNAPSHOT(dc)
8:     $svv \leftarrow$ CLUSTERCLOCK.GETSVV(dc)   ▷ *Alg. 2*
9:     $allEvents \leftarrow$ DATAREPOSITORY.GETALLEVENTS   ▷ *Get all events in the event log*

                    ▷ *For local events, consider only those replicated to all peer DCs:*
10:     $replicatedEvents \leftarrow ev \in allEvents \mid ev.OriginDCId = dc \ \wedge \ ev.isReplicated$

                    ▷ *Consider only remote events or local events replicated to all peer DCs:*
11:     $evsC \leftarrow ev \in allEvents \mid \begin{cases} ev & [ev.OriginDCId \neq dc] \\ ev & [ev.OriginDCId = dc \ \wedge \ ev \in replicatedEvents] \end{cases}$

        ▷ *Events to snapshot must have timestamp values smaller than the corresponding entry in*
        the SVV:
12:     $evsSnapshot \leftarrow ev \in evsC \mid \forall t \in ev.Timestamp.Times : t.Value < svv[t.DCId].value$

13:     $evsSnapshot \leftarrow$ SORT($evsSnapshot$)   ▷ *Alg. 5*
14:     DATAREPOSITORY.SNAPSHOT($evsSnapshot$)   ▷ *Apply to RDBMS and delete from Event Log*
15: **end procedure**

Algorithm 7. D-Thespis Algorithm - WRITE Operation

Rest Client API
Require: MiddlewareEngine, CurrentDataCentreId
1: **function** WRITE(database db, table t, primary key column k, identifier id, list of field changes fc)
2:     MIDDLEWAREENGINE.WRITE($CurrentDataCentreId, db, t, k, id, fc$)
3: **end function**

MiddlewareEngine
Require: ActorProvider, DataRepository
4: **function** WRITE(dc, db, t, k, id, fc)
5:     $res \leftarrow$ ACTORPROVIDER.WRITE(dc, db, t, k, id, fc)
6:     **return** res
7: **end function**

ActorProvider
Require: ActorProvider, DataRepository
8: **function** WRITE(dc, db, t, k, id)
9:     $a \leftarrow$ Entity Instance Actor corresponding to record $k = id$ in table t of database db
10:    $res \leftarrow$ A.WRITE(dc, db, t, k, id, fc)   ▷ *Communicate via Message Passing*
11:    **return** res
12: **end function**
13: **function** RELOAD(dc, db, t, k, id)
14:    $a \leftarrow$ Entity Instance Actor corresponding to record $k = id$ in table t of database db
15:    $res \leftarrow$ A.RELOAD(dc, db, t, k, id, fc)   ▷ *Communicate via Message Passing*
16:    **return** res
17: **end function**

Entity Instance Actor
Require: EntityInstanceActorManager EIM, ClusterClock $CClk$
18: *Entity : DataEntity* $\leftarrow$ *null*   ▷ *The last-known causally consistent version of the Data Entity*
19: *Events : DataEntityEvent* $\leftarrow$ [ ]   ▷ *List of pending events*
20: *SupportsCache : boolean*   ▷ *true if the implementation should support a distributed cache*
21: **function** WRITE(dc, db, t, k, id)
22:    $svv \leftarrow$ CCLK.GETSVV(dc)   ▷ *Alg 1*
          ▷ *Initialise a new Data Entity representing the fields to change:*
23:    $targetEntity \leftarrow$ DATAENTITY.NEW(id, fc)
          ▷ *Infer the list of events describing Entity $\longrightarrow$ targetEntity:*
24:    $deEvent \leftarrow$ DATAENTITYEVENT.NEW($dc, svv, db, id, t, Entity, fc$)
25:    **if** $SupportsCache = true$ **then**
26:        EIM.DELETEENTITY(db, t, id)   ▷ *Alg 4*
27:    **end if**
28:    APPEND($Events, deEvent$)
29:    $(fe, fev) \leftarrow$ EIM.APPLYEVENTS($Entity, Events, db, t, k, id, dc$)   ▷ *Alg 4*
30:    $Entity \leftarrow fe$
31:    $Events \leftarrow fev$
32:    EIM.SAVEEVENT($db, t, id, deEvent$)   ▷ *Alg 4*
33:    **return** $success$
34: **end function**
35: **function** RELOAD(dc, db, t, k, id)
36:    **if** $SupportsCache = true$ **then**
37:        EIM.DELETEENTITY(db, t, id)   ▷ *Alg 4*
38:    **end if**
39:    $Entity : DataEntity \leftarrow null$
40:    $Events : DataEntityEvent \leftarrow$ [ ]
41:    **return** $success$
42: **end function**

Algorithm 7 illustrates the WRITE operation in D-Thespis, as well as the main components involved. Firstly, it can be noted that a data entity event is assigned the value of the current SVV as its timestamp, which is inline with the objective of having timestamps comprising vectors of physical timestamps. Furthermore, a WRITE operation is encoded fully in Actor logic, with overarching layers (e.g., REST Client API and the Middleware Engine) marshalling the call to the Entity Instance Actor module. As illustrated in Fig. 4b, WRITE operations on the same record in the same DC are serialised, through the guarantees provided by the Actor model.

Finally, the result of WRITE operations is made immediately visible to all clients in the same DC, even in the presence of a distributed cache. By *line 21*, a WRITE operation purges any cache entries for the data entity. This is an atomic operation that executes in isolation within the distributed cache, as per the requirements given in Sect. 5.3. As soon as this operation completes, READ requests from any other clients in the same DC are forwarded to the Actor Provider layer (*line 11* in Algorithm 3). However, none of these operations start to execute before the WRITE operation completes successfully, due to the one-message-at-a-time guarantee of the Actor model. A successful completion of a WRITE operation implies that the event describing the effects of the WRITE operation is successfully persisted (*line 27*, by the guarantees of the Event Log described in Sect. 5.2). Conversely, a failed WRITE operation has no side-effects: any exception terminates the Entity Actor, and therefore any subsequent READ operation returns a version of the Data Entity according to the state of the record in the RDBMS, merged with events by successful WRITE operations in the Event Log (*lines 38–48* of Algorithm 3).

Algorithm 5 encapsulates logic used to order events that occurred both in a local DC as well as in remote DCs. It also incorporates logic to resolve any cases of conflict. Similarly to the conflict resolution strategy in Thespis, the strategy in D-Thespis borrows from the standard LWW, but augments this with a merge function such that it behaves similarly to version control systems.

Firstly, two conflicting events are sorted in ascending order of the maximum timestamp of their vector of timestamps. Then, they are applied to the entity in this order. In doing so, should both events describe a change to the same set of fields on any given entity, the event with the largest maximum physical timestamp takes priority and cancels out the effect of the other event. In this case, the strategy becomes equivalent to the standard LWW conflict resolution strategy. On the other hand, if both events conflict according to their vector of timestamps, but describe changes to different fields of a given entity, the changes of both events are merged, and no changes are lost. This case is different than the LWW strategy, which would reject the first event completely. In all cases, the conflict resolution strategy ensures convergence by ordering conflicting events in a standard way in every DC.

The logic to send and receive events between DCs is given in Algorithm 8. Of particular note, when an event is received in a recipient DC, the respective Entity Instance Actor is called (*line 23*). This ensures that any subsequent operation from clients of the recipient DC considers the changes implied by the remote operation. For example, if the remote event does not indicate (i.e., through its vector of timestamps) that it is dependent on any other event from a different remote DC that has not yet arrived at the recipient DC, then the remote update

becomes immediately visible to clients of the recipient DC: by Algorithm 3, lines
38–48 would execute after *line 23* of Algorithm 8 executes.

The logic to persist events in the RDBMS is given in Algorithm 6. This logic
ensures that the side-effects of events are only persisted in the RDBMS (and
thus, made available to other systems connecting directly to the RDBMS) when
an event has been replicated to all DCs. This can be determined by comparing
the values of the SVV to the vector timestamp of an event: if all the values in
the SVV are larger than the values in the vector timestamp, then all DCs have
necessarily received the event, which can be safely persisted to the RDBMS.

Algorithm 8. D-Thespis Algorithm - REPLICATION Operation

Event Replication Service
Require: ClusterClock, DataRepository, CurrentDataCentreId, DataCentreClock, PeerDataCentres
1: **procedure** DoWork
2:    **while** *true* **do**
3:       Replicate(CurrentDataCentreId, PeerDataCentres)
4:       Sleep($10ms$)
5:    **end while**
6: **end procedure**

7: **procedure** Replicate($dc, peerDataCentres$)
8:    $svv \leftarrow$ ClusterClock.GetSVV(dc)
9:    $now \leftarrow$ DataCentreClock.GetNow
10:   **for** $peerDC \leftarrow peerDataCentres$ **do**
                ▷ *Get all events from the Event Log which are not replicated to peerDC:*
11:      $pendingEvents \leftarrow$ DataRepository.GetPendingEvents($dc, peerDC$)
12:      $eventsToReplicate \leftarrow ev \in pendingEvents \mid ev.Timestamp[dc] \leq now$
13:      $orderedEvents \leftarrow$ Sort($eventsToReplicate$)
14:      SendEvents($peerDC, orderedEvents$)   ▷ *RPC call to the remote peerDC*
                 ▷ *Update Event Log to flag orderedEvents as replicated to peerDC:*
15:      MarkEventsReplicated($peerDC, dc, orderedEvents, now$)
16:   **end for**
17: **end procedure**

GRPC Internal API
Require: DataRepository, ClusterClock, CurrentDataCentreId dc, ActorProvider AP
18: **procedure** ReceiveEvents($originDC, orderedEvents, originDCTime$)
19:    $svv \leftarrow$ ClusterClock.GetSVV(dc)   ▷ *Alg. 1*
20:    $now \leftarrow$ DataCentreClock.GetNow
21:    **for** $ev \in orderedEvents$ **do**
22:      DataRepository.SaveEvent(ev)
23:      AP.reload($dc, ev.db, ev.tableName, ev.entityId$)   ▷ *Alg. 7*
24:    **end for**
25:    ClusterClock.Tick($originDC, originDCTime$)   ▷ *Alg. 1*
26: **end procedure**

---

7   D-Thespis Middleware Correctness Evaluation

The D-Thespis protocol follows techniques that are well-established in the literature to provide causal consistency, such as the use of event timestamping and
version vectors to track causality with lean meta-data overheads. Nonetheless,
we give a correctness evaluation of the D-Thespis protocol, following closely that
of a similar, yet distinct, protocol that also provides causal consistency for a partitioned database using the key-value data model [36]. In the rest of this section,
we adopt the following definitions and nomenclatures:

SVV_d The Stable Version Vector in a DC d

$SVV_d[x]$ The element in the Stable Version Vector of a DC d that corresponds to DC x

Visible+ A version k_y of a record with identity k is visible+ for READ operations by a client c of DC d where a conflict resolution function f is used, such that for any READ operation by c, version k_x is returned such that $k_x = k_y \vee k_x = f(k_y, k_x)$.

7.1 The Stable Version Vector

Lemma 1. When a DC DC_x has not received a version n_y of a record n written in DC DC_y at time t_{yv}, $SVV_x[y] < t_{yv}$.

Proof. WRITE events in each DC are timestamped by a version vector corresponding to the local SVV. The element in the SVV of a local DC takes a monotonically increasing value from the physical time clock of the DC. Events are also replicated in FIFO fashion to peer DCs. Therefore, data element versions are received in remote DCs in the same order that they are created in their original DCs. Therefore, when a version n_y is not received in DC DC_x, the entry in the SVV of DC DC_x that corresponds to DC DC_y is necessarily less than t_{yv}.

7.2 Monotonic Read Consistency

Theorem 1. The D-Thespis protocol guarantees *monotonic read consistency.* Monotonic read consistency can be defined as: if a client c reads the value v of record k, any subsequent read operations by c always return the same value or a newer one [42].

Proof. Assume that:

1. $O = READ(k)$ represents an operation whereby client c reads the value of record with identifier k that was created at time t in DC DC_x.
2. O happens at time t', where $t' > t$.
3. There exists set θ that represents all the versions of k observed by c up to time t.
4. There exists set ρ that represents all the versions of k that are considered stable in DC_x at time t'.
5. A version k' is considered stable if its version vector $k'.vv$ is smaller than the Stable Version Vector. $\therefore \forall x \in \rho, x_{vv} < SVV$.

If O does not satisfy monotonic-read consistency, there exists $w, w \in \theta$, where w originates in DC DC_y and $w \notin \rho$. By *Lemma 1*, $SVV_x[y] < t$. Since O happens at time t', where $t' < t$, this is a contradiction.

7.3   Read-your-Writes Guarantees

Theorem 2. The D-Thespis protocol guarantees *read-your-writes consistency.* Read-your-writes consistency can be defined as: if a client c writes the value v of record k, any subsequent read operations by c always return v or a newer version [42].

Proof. Assume that:

1. $O_w = WRITE(k, v)$ represents an operation whereby client c writes the value v of record k at time t in DC DC_x.
2. $O_r = READ(k)$ represents an operation whereby c reads the value v of record k.
3. O_r happens at time t', where $t' > t$.
4. There exists set ρ that represents all the versions of k that are considered stable in DC_x at time t'.

Firstly, O_r is guaranteed to happen in DC DC_x, since clients are sticky in D-Thespis.

If O_r does not satisfy read-your-writes consistency, $v \notin \rho$. By *Lemma 1*, $SVV_x[x] = t'$ for O_r. Since $t < t'$ this contradicts the fact that $v \notin \rho$, i.e. in fact $v \in \rho$. Therefore O_r necessarily satisfies read-your-writes consistency.

7.4   Monotonic Write Operations

Theorem 3. The D-Thespis protocol guarantees *monotonic write consistency.* Monotonic write consistency guarantees that if a client c performs a write operation w on a record k, this completes before any successive write operation w' by c [42].

Proof. Assume that:

1. $O = WRITE(k, v)$ represents an operation whereby client c writes the value v of record k at time t in DC DC_x.
2. There exists set ρ that represents all the versions of k that are considered stable in DC_x at time t', where $t' > t$.
3. There exists set Λ that represents all the versions of k that are written by c in DC_x at time t, where $t < t'$.

If O breaks monotonic write guarantees, there exists a scenario where $O \in \rho$ (i.e., O is available to clients connected to DC_x) and another client c', connected to DC_x, reads v', another version of k, where $v' \in \Lambda$ and is created by operation $w \neq O$. All D-Thespis servers in a single DC have access to a shared, monotonically increasing clock. Therefore, O has a timestamp that is larger than t. Since $O \in \rho$, v' is necessarily a dependency of v. Therefore, the D-Thespis protocol never returns v' if there exists v with a larger timestamp than v'.

Indeed, since all WRITE operations in D-Thespis are modelled using the Actor model of computation, WRITE operations on any record k by all clients in a DC DC_x are necessarily sequential.

7.5   Writes Follow Reads

Theorem 4. The D-Thespis protocol guarantees *Write-follows-reads consistency.* Write-follows-reads consistency guarantees that if a client c reads a value v of record k, and subsequently writes a value v' of k, the WRITE operation is guaranteed to be performed on v or a later version of k.

Proof. Assume that:

1. $O = WRITE(k, v)$ represents an operation whereby client c writes the value v of record k at time t' in DC DC_x.
2. There exists set θ that represents all the versions of k observed by c up to time t, where $t < t'$.
3. There exists set ρ that represents all the versions of k that are considered stable in DC_x at time t'', where $t'' > t' > t$ and $O \in \rho$.

Write-follows-reads consistency requires that no client of DC_x performs a READ operation in DC_x at time t'', and observes a value v' where $v' \in \theta$.

READ operations in the D-Thespis protocols always return versions that are either created locally, or created in a remote dDC but the local SVV has advanced beyond their version vector. In the above, if $v' \in \theta$, it will not be observed at time t'' since v is more recent.

7.6   Causal Consistency

The D-Thespis protocol guarantees *causal consistency.*

Observation 1. Let j_x and k_y be two versions of records j and k respectively. Let $j_x.vv[d]$ represent the element in the version vector of j_x corresponding to DC d, and similarly $k_y.vv[d]$ for k_y. Assume also that k_y originates in DC d. If j_x depends on k_y, then $j_x.vv[d] > k_y.vv[d]$.

Observation 2. Let j_x and k_y be two versions of records j and k respectively. If j_x depends on k_y, then $j_x.vv \geq k_y.vv$.

The D-Thespis protocol assigns a version vector for each record version. This consists of the value corresponding to the local Stable Version Vector (SVV). The value in the SVV corresponding to the local DC is always set to the physical time, and is therefore always monotonically increasing (Observation 1 and *line 5* in Algorithm 1). The values in the SVV corresponding to the remote DCs are set to the timestamp observed in versions received from the relative remote DC (*line 25* in Algorithm 8). Therefore, the D-Thespis protocol always timestamps a new record version with a version vector that is greater than the version vectors of its dependencies (Observation 2).

Observation 3. Assume that function f represents a convergence function that implements the last-writer-wins resolution strategy. $f(j, k) = j$ iff:

1. $k \longrightarrow j$
2. $\neg(k \longrightarrow j) \wedge \neg(j \longrightarrow k) \wedge (max(j.vv) > max(k.vv) \vee (max(j.vv) = max(k.vv) \wedge j.dcid > k.dcid))$

Lemma 2: Data versions written by clients of DC d are immediately visible+ for READ operations of any client in DC d

Proof: Suppose a local version k_y is not immediately visible+ for READ to a client c. That means that for a READ operation by c, another version k_x is returned such that $f(k_x, k_y) = k_y$. However, in this case and according to Observations 1 and 2, $k_y.vv > k_x.vv$. By contradiction therefore, the D-Thespis protocol does not return k_x in this case.

Lemma 3: Assume that a version k_y is written in DC d_y. If k_y is not visible+ for READ operations by a client c of d_x in the presence of conflict resolution function f then:

1. k_y has not been replicated to d_x, or
2. given SVV_{dx}, the stable version vector in DC d_x, $\exists x \in SVV_{dx}$ such that $SVV_{dx}[x] < k_y.vv[x]$.

Proof: When k_y is not visible+ for READ operations in DC d_x, it means that the READ operation returns another version k_x such that $f(k_y, k_x) = k_x$. By Observations 1 and 2, this is possible if $k_x.vv > k_y.vv$.
   Suppose that both conditions of this lemma are false i.e., k_y has been replicated in d_x and $SVV_{dx}[x] > k_y.vv[x]$. Then, by contradiction, the READ operation in the D-Thespis protocol cannot return k_x but returns k_y.

Observation 4: Given a cluster of M DCs, in every DC d, $\forall m, m >= 1 \wedge m \leq M$, $SVV_d[m]$ never decreases. This is because:

1. $SVV_d[d]$ is always assigned the physical timestamp of the data center clock. This is monotonically increasing (*line 5* of Algorithm 1)
2. $\forall m, m >= 1 \wedge m \leq M \wedge m \neq d$, $SVV_d[m]$ is updated when an event is received from a remote DC (*line 25* of Algorithm 8). Events in remote DCs are delivered in order (*line 13* of Algorithm 8), and are also timestamped via a monotonically increasing vector of physical timestamps.

Lemma 4: Once a version k_y becomes visible+ for a READ operation for a client c in DC d_x, it remains visible+ for READ operations of any client in DC d_x.

Proof: Assume that a version k_y was visible+ to a client c of DC d, but later it is not visible+. That requires a scenario where a READ operation in d returns another version k_x such that $f(k_y, k_x) = k_y$. This means that $k_y.vv > k_x.vv$. Because k_y was at some point visible+ in d, it is necessary that k_y is either produced by a local operation, or $\forall x \in SVV_d, SVV_d[x] \geq k_y.vv[x]$.

Lemma 5: The D-Thespis protocol enforces causal++ consistency for all READ operations with a conflict resolution function f

Proof: Firstly, D-Thespis provides read-your-writes guarantees, as per *Lemma 2* and the fact that clients are sticky to a single DC.

Secondly, once a client c connected to DC d_1 reads a version k_y, then k_y remains visible+ for c, as per *Lemma 4*.

Finally, in order for k_y to be visible for c, then all its dependencies are necessarily visible to c. This is proven by contradiction as follows.

Let j_x and k_y be two versions of records j and k respectively, such that $k_y \longrightarrow j_x$. Suppose a client c reads j_x but k_y is not visible+ for c. By *Lemma 3* this is possible under two cases. Either k_y has not been replicated to DC d_1, or k_y has arrived in DC d_1 but $k_y.vv > SVV_{d1}$.

In the former case, k_y is necessarily not the result of a local operation. Suppose k_y was created in remote DC d_2. Then $SVV_{d1}[d_2] < k_y.vv[d_2]$. But by *Observation 2*, because $k_y \longrightarrow j_x$ then $k_y.vv < j_x.vv$. Furthermore, also because $k_y \longrightarrow j_x$, then if c performs $READ(k)$, DC d_1 returns k_y. The D-Thespis protocol only makes a remote version k_y visible to local clients if $k_y.vv \leq SVV$. Therefore, SVV_{d1} is necessarily greater than $k_y.vv$ and therefore a contradiction exists: $SVV_{d1}[d_2]$ is necessarily greater or equal to $k_y.vv[d_2]$ and so c cannot read j_x without having k_y visible+.

In the latter case, because $k_y \longrightarrow j_x$, the client c first performs $READ(k)$, which returns k_y, and then performs an operation on record j. $SVV_{d1}[d_1]$ at the time that c accesses j is necessarily larger than $SVV_{d1}[d_1]$ at the time that c performs $READ(k)$, because in the local DC, the corresponding entry in SVV monotonically increases according to physical time. Also because $k_y \longrightarrow j_x$, by *Observation 1* and *Observation 2*, $k_y.vv < j_x.vv$. Therefore, $SVV_{d1}[d_1]$ at the time that c accesses j is greater than $k_y.vv$, contradicting the claim that k_y has arrived in DC d_1 and $k_y.vv > SVV_{d1}$. In effect therefore, under the D-Thespis protocol, given that $k_y \longrightarrow j_x$, all the dependencies of k_y are visible for c.

7.7   Event Snapshots

In D-Thespis, the effects of events are applied to the RDBMS via snapshotting. An event e_j can be snapshot in a DC DC_x if no remote peers DC_y can send an event e_k such that $e_k \longrightarrow e_j$ or $e_k \parallel e_j$ i.e., DC_x cannot receive a remote event that e_j depends upon, or that conflicts with e_j. Algorithm 6 implements these guarantees inline with similar approaches in the literature (e.g., the Garbage Collection protocol discussed by [17]).

Lemma 7: For a version r_y generated in DC_y and received in DC_x, if all values in its vector of timestamps are smaller than the corresponding timestamps in SVV, r_y is eligible for snapshotting in DC_x.

Lemma 6: For a version k_x generated in DC_x, k_x is eligible for snapshotting in DC_x by Lemma 7 but only once k_x has been replicated to all peer DCs.

Proof: Assume that snapshotting of r_y has happened at time $t1$. Assume also that r_w is received in DC_x from DC_w at time $t2$ where $t2 > t1$ such that $r_w \longrightarrow r_y$. For $r_w \longrightarrow r_y$, by *Observation* 1 and *Observation* 2, $r_w.vv < r_y.vv$ and therefore $r_w.vv[w] \leq r_y.vv[w]$. But DC_w replicates events, in order, to DC_x and thus $SVV_{DCx}[w] < r_w.vv[w]$ at time $t1$. Thus by contradiction if r_y is snapshot at $t1$, $r_w \longrightarrow r_y$ cannot be received at time $t2$.

8   Discussion

This paper presents D-Thespis, an approach that builds upon the Thespis approach [11] to deliver causal consistency over an RDBMS.

D-Thespis retains the objectives and principles of Thespis, in that it is a middleware that delivers causal consistency modelled over the Actor model of computation, whilst encapsulating the complexities of the consistency model by exposing a familiar REST interface for application developers.

However, D-Thespis tackles three important aspects which were not within the scope of Thespis. Firstly, we outline the system design and algorithms required for the middleware to scale horizontally and elastically within a single DC. Given the memory-bound characteristics of the Thespis middleware, adding horizontal scalability capabilities through D-Thespis makes the approach applicable even to data sets that are subject to specific workloads such that an in-memory representation in terms of Actors does not fit in the main memory of a single machine. The horizontal scalability characteristics of D-Thespis differs from the approaches of state-of-the-art systems, which assume a strictly-partitioned key-value data model. Instead, in D-Thespis we make no assumptions as to the number of servers available: these can vary over time and can be different in every DC. This approach is effective at ensuring that D-Thespis can be deployed in multiple DCs but allows the configuration of each DC to be optimised for the types and sizes of workloads that are expected to be handled in the specific geographic location.

Secondly, D-Thespis adopts established techniques to improve remote update visibility latency through the adoption of vectors of timestamps, rather than scalar timestamps, as meta-data for every data entity version generated. Whilst this increases the size (and thus, the overheads) of the meta-data compared to Thespis, it makes D-Thespis more resilient to slow DCs and network partitions.

In tackling these aspects, a study of the literature as well as empirical micro-benchmarks show that a "one-size-fits-all" approach is not ideal, both in terms of logical approach as well as implementation. Retaining correctness under horizontal scalability introduces several complexities when compared to single-machine installations, primarily because, in a horizontally scaled installation, the middleware comprises a number of stand-alone machines. However, modern hardware infrastructures can vary significantly in terms of capabilities available to clusters of machines. In parallel, although different implementations of the Actor model provide the same guarantees that can be built upon for the correctness of CC, their performance has been shown to differ, especially in the context of horizontal scalability. Furthermore, serving client requests from a set of servers without having intrinsic knowledge of the distribution of data entities across the Actor cluster at the load-balancing layer introduces additional overheads in terms of relatively-expensive intra-cluster messages. This shows the need that deploying D-Thespis in horizontally scaled mode requires different considerations than the same system deployed on a single server. D-Thespis is therefore designed from the ground up to de-couple the protocol that delivers CC from the specific implementations of the different layers. This design lends itself well to the implementation of a version of D-Thespis that is tuned for both single-machine and horizontally scaled setups and incorporates the protocol in both the Actor model [2] and the Virtual Actor model [7].

Finally, although D-Thespis, like Thespis, is based upon approaches that have been shown to deliver CC correctly in the literature, this paper includes a relative formalisation of the specific D-Thespis protocol that shows the correctness of the approach.

9   Conclusion

A number of novel contributions are described in this paper. Firstly, the design of D-Thespis improves upon the innovation of Thespis in delivering causal consistency over an RDBMS by introducing elastic horizontal scalability within a single DC. This differs from other works in the literature in that D-Thespis does not rely on a uniform and fixed infrastructure configuration in each DC. The approach of having a horizontally scalable middleware but without considering a strictly partitioned dataset lends itself well to information systems that connect to full replicas of a database managed by an RDBMS.

Secondly, the study of different capabilities in modern infrastructures and different implementations of the Actor model showed that an optimal approach would be able to exploit the strengths of different combinations of such capabilities. This shows that the D-Thespis protocol generalises to more than one implementation of the Actor model, and can be used to have a configurable setup that could be tuned differently for single server and horizontally scaled setups. This is a novel and different approach compared to related works, where the protocol is not strictly decoupled from the system model.

As future work, an implementation of D-Thespis following the requirements elicited in this paper is planned, enabling us to perform empirical benchmarks to study its performance and capture memory usage profiles. The implementation effort intends on making D-Thespis a native of public cloud infrastructures by exploiting cloud capabilities such as "container-as-a-service" setups.

Acknowledgements. This work is partly funded by the ENDEAVOUR Scholarship Scheme (Malta), part-financed by the European Union - European Social Fund (ESF) under Operational Programme II - Cohesion Policy 2014–2020.

References

1. Abadi, D.: Consistency tradeoffs in modern distributed database system design: CAP is only part of the story. Computer **45**(2), 37–42 (2012)
2. Agha, G.A.: Actors: A Model of Concurrent Computation in Distributed Systems, MIT AI-TR, vol. 844. MIT Press, Cambridge (1986)
3. Ahamad, M., Neiger, G., Burns, J.E., Kohli, P., Hutto, P.W.: Causal memory: definitions, implementation, and programming. Distrib. Comput. **9**(1), 37–49 (1995). https://doi.org/10.1007/BF01784241
4. Akkoorath, D.D., et al.: Cure: strong semantics meets high availability and low latency. In: 2016 IEEE 36th International Conference on Distributed Computing Systems (ICDCS), pp. 405–414. IEEE (2016)
5. Bailis, P., Ghodsi, A., Hellerstein, J.M., Stoica, I.: Bolt-on causal consistency. In: Proceedings of the 2013 ACM SIGMOD International Conference on Management of Data, pp. 761–772. ACM (2013)
6. Barbará-Millá, D., Garcia-Molina, H.: The demarcation protocol: a technique for maintaining constraints in distributed database systems. VLDB J. - Int. J. Very Large Data Bases **3**(3), 325–353 (1994). https://doi.org/10.1007/BF01232643
7. Bernstein, P., Bykov, S., Geller, A., Kliot, G., Thelin, J.: Orleans: distributed virtual actors for programmability and scalability. MSR-TR-2014-41 (2014)
8. Bernstein, P.A., Hadzilacos, V., Goodman, N.: Concurrency Control and Recovery in Database Systems, vol. 370. Addison-Wesley, Reading (1987)
9. Braun, S., Bieniusa, A., Elberzhager, F.: Advanced domain-driven design for consistency in distributed data-intensive systems. In: Proceedings of the 8th Workshop on Principles and Practice of Consistency for Distributed Data, pp. 1–12 (2021)
10. Brewer, E.A.: Towards robust distributed systems. In: PODC, vol. 7 (2000)
11. Camilleri, C., Vella, J.G., Nezval, V.: Thespis: actor-based causal consistency. In: 2017 28th International Workshop on Database and Expert Systems Applications (DEXA), pp. 42–46. IEEE, August 2017. https://doi.org/10.1109/DEXA.2017.25
12. Camilleri, C., Vella, J.G., Nezval, V.: ThespisDIIP: distributed integrity invariant preservation. In: Elloumi, M., et al. (eds.) DEXA 2018. CCIS, vol. 903, pp. 21–37. Springer, Cham (2018). https://doi.org/10.1007/978-3-319-99133-7_2
13. Camilleri, C., Vella, J.G., Nezval, V.: ThespisTRX: initial results for causally-consistent read transactions. In: Information Systems and Management Science, Valletta, Malta. Proceedings.com, February 2018. http://www.proceedings.com/38672.html
14. Camilleri, C., Vella, J.G., Nezval, V.: ThespisTRX: causally-consistent read transactions. Int. J. Inf. Technol. Web Eng. (IJITWE) **15**(1), 1–16 (2020)
15. Camilleri, C., Vella, J.G., Nezval, V.: Actor model frameworks: an empirical performance analysis. In: 5th International Conference on Information Systems and Management Science (2022)
16. Corbett, J.C., et al.: Spanner: Google's globally distributed database. ACM Trans. Comput. Syst. (TOCS) **31**(3), 8 (2013)
17. Du, J., Iorgulescu, C., Roy, A., Zwaenepoel, W.: GentleRain: cheap and scalable causal consistency with physical clocks. In: Proceedings of the ACM Symposium on Cloud Computing, pp. 1–13. ACM (2014)
18. El-Sayed, N., Sun, Z., Sun, K., Mayerhofer, R.: OLTP in real life: a large-scale study of database behavior in modern online retail. In: 2021 29th International Symposium on Modeling, Analysis, and Simulation of Computer and Telecommunication Systems (MASCOTS), pp. 1–8. IEEE (2021)

19. Elbushra, M.M., Lindström, J.: Eventual consistent databases: state of the art. Open J. Databases (OJDB) **1**(1), 26–41 (2014)
20. Fowler, M.: Event sourcing, December 2005. https://martinfowler.com/eaaDev/EventSourcing.html
21. Gilbert, S., Lynch, N.: Brewer's conjecture and the feasibility of consistent, available, partition-tolerant web services. ACM SIGACT News **33**(2), 51–59 (2002)
22. Harizopoulos, S., Abadi, D.J., Madden, S., Stonebraker, M.: OLTP through the looking glass, and what we found there. In: Making Databases Work: The Pragmatic Wisdom of Michael Stonebraker, pp. 409–439. Association for Computing Machinery and Morgan and Claypool (2018)
23. Herlihy, M.P., Wing, J.M.: Linearizability: a correctness condition for concurrent objects. ACM Trans. Program. Lang. Syst. (TOPLAS) **12**(3), 463–492 (1990)
24. Hewitt, C., Bishop, P., Steiger, R.: A universal modular actor formalism for artificial intelligence. In: Proceedings of the 3rd International Joint Conference on Artificial Intelligence, pp. 235–245. Morgan Kaufmann Publishers Inc. (1973)
25. Kulkarni, S., Demirbas, M., Madeppa, D., Bharadwaj, A., Leone, M.: Logical physical clocks and consistent snapshots in globally distributed databases (2014)
26. Lakshman, A., Malik, P.: Cassandra: a decentralized structured storage system. ACM SIGOPS Oper. Syst. Rev. **44**(2), 35–40 (2010)
27. Lamport, L.: Time, clocks, and the ordering of events in a distributed system. Commun. ACM **21**(7), 558–565 (1978)
28. Lamport, L.: The part-time parliament. ACM Trans. Comput. Syst. (TOCS) **16**(2), 133–169 (1998)
29. Lima, M.I.V., de Farias, V.A., Praciano, F.D., Machado, J.C.: Workload-aware parameter selection and performance prediction for in-memory databases. In: SBBD, pp. 169–180 (2018)
30. Lloyd, W., Freedman, M.J., Kaminsky, M., Andersen, D.G.: Don't settle for eventual: scalable causal consistency for wide-area storage with COPS. In: Proceedings of the Twenty-Third ACM Symposium on Operating Systems Principles, pp. 401–416. ACM (2011)
31. Mahajan, P., Alvisi, L., Dahlin, M.: Consistency, availability, and convergence. Technical report 11, University of Texas at Austin (2011)
32. Mathew, A., Min, C.: HydraList: a scalable in-memory index using asynchronous updates and partial replication. Proc. VLDB Endow. **13**(9), 1332–1345 (2020)
33. Mehdi, S.A., Littley, C., Crooks, N., Alvisi, L., Bronson, N., Lloyd, W.: I can't believe it's not causal! Scalable causal consistency with no slowdown cascades. In: 14th USENIX Symposium on Networked Systems Design and Implementation (NSDI 2017), pp. 453–468 (2017)
34. Meyer, B.: Eiffel: The Language. Prentice-Hall, Inc. (1992). https://doi.org/10.1016/0950-5849(92)90131-8
35. Neumann, T., Mühlbauer, T., Kemper, A.: Fast serializable multi-version concurrency control for main-memory database systems. In: Proceedings of the 2015 ACM SIGMOD International Conference on Management of Data, pp. 677–689 (2015)
36. Roohitavaf, M., Demirbas, M., Kulkarni, S.S.: CausalSpartan: causal consistency for distributed data stores using hybrid logical clocks. In: 36th IEEE Symposium on Reliable Distributed Systems, SRDS 2017, Hong Kong, 26–29 September 2017, pp. 184–193 (2017). https://doi.org/10.1109/SRDS.2017.27
37. Spirovska, K., Didona, D., Zwaenepoel, W.: Wren: nonblocking reads in a partitioned transactional causally consistent data store. In: 2018 48th Annual IEEE/IFIP International Conference on Dependable Systems and Networks (DSN), pp. 1–12. IEEE (2018)

38. Spirovska, K., Didona, D., Zwaenepoel, W.: PaRiS: causally consistent transactions with non-blocking reads and partial replication. In: 2019 IEEE 39th International Conference on Distributed Computing Systems (ICDCS), pp. 304–316. IEEE (2019)

39. Spirovska, K., Didona, D., Zwaenepoel, W.: Optimistic causal consistency for geo-replicated key-value stores. IEEE Trans. Parallel Distrib. Syst. **32**(3), 527–542 (2020)

40. Stonebraker, M.: The case for shared nothing. IEEE Database Eng. Bull. **9**(1), 4–9 (1986)

41. Taft, R., et al.: CockroachDB: the resilient geo-distributed SQL database. In: Proceedings of the 2020 ACM SIGMOD International Conference on Management of Data, pp. 1493–1509 (2020)

42. Tanenbaum, A.S., Van Steen, M.: Distributed Systems: Principles and Paradigms, 2nd edn. Pearson (2006). Paperback edn

43. Terry, D.B., Theimer, M.M., Petersen, K., Demers, A.J., Spreitzer, M.J., Hauser, C.H.: Managing update conflicts in Bayou, a weakly connected replicated storage system. ACM SIGOPS Oper. Syst. Rev. **29**(5), 172–182 (1995)

44. Vogels, W.: Eventually consistent. Commun. ACM **52**(1), 40–44 (2009)

45. Wang, Y., Dos Reis, J.C., Borggren, K.M., Salles, M.A.V., Medeiros, C.B., Zhou, Y.: Modeling and building IoT data platforms with actor-oriented databases. In: EDBT, pp. 512–523 (2019)

46. Yang, Y., Zhu, J.: Write Skew and Zipf distribution: evidence and implications. ACM Trans. Storage (TOS) **12**(4), 1–19 (2016)

47. Young, G.: CQRS Documents (2010)

Correction to: Semantic Similarity in a Taxonomy by Evaluating the Relatedness of Concept Senses with the Linked Data Semantic Distance

Anna Formica⬵ and Francesco Taglino⬵

Correction to:
Chapter "Semantic Similarity in a Taxonomy by Evaluating the Relatedness of Concept Senses with the Linked Data Semantic Distance" in: A. Hameurlain and A. M. Tjoa (Eds.): *Transactions on Large-Scale Data- and Knowledge-Centered Systems LIII,* **LNCS 13840,**
https://doi.org/10.1007/978-3-662-66863-4_3

In an older version of this paper, the online xml is fine but in the pdf the characters > and < are not recognized on page 69. This has been corrected.

The updated original version of this chapter can be found at
https://doi.org/10.1007/978-3-662-66863-4_3

Author Index

Printed in the United States
by Baker & Taylor Publisher Services